Derashot LeDorot
A Commentary for the Ages
Genesis

Norman Lamm

DERASHOT LEDOROT
GENESIS

EDITED BY

Stuart W. Halpern

FOREWORD BY

Meir Y. Soloveichik

The Michael Scharf Publication Trust
RIETS/YU Press

OU Press

Maggid Books

Derashot LeDorot
A Commentary for the Ages
Genesis

First Edition, 2012

Maggid Books
An imprint of Koren Publishers Jerusalem Ltd.

POB 8531, New Milford, CT 06776-8531, USA
& POB 4044, Jerusalem 91040, Israel
www.korenpub.com

The Michael Scharf Publication Trust
of Yeshiva University Press

OU Press
An imprint of the Orthodox Union

11 Broadway
New York, NY 10004
www.oupress.org

ISBN 978 1 59264 361 5, *hardcover*

A CIP catalogue record for this title is
available from the British Library

Printed and bound in the United States

Contents

v

Foreword

In an article in the *Weekly Standard*,[1] the essayist Joseph Epstein once wrote with annoyance of how cell phones have changed what was once a quiet commute to work:

> Everyone, I suspect, has had a moment when he wished he could grab the cell phone from a boisterous talker and smash it on the sidewalk. A friend of mine named Ann Poole told me about sitting on a commuter train from her suburb into Chicago, in front of a young woman who made no fewer than ten cell phone calls to friends, explaining in great detail why she was changing the restaurant in which she was giving a lunch party that Saturday… in a loud and irritating voice, she left elaborate instructions on voice mail about the change in plan along with the reasons for the change. "Hi, this is Amy Hemstead [I'm making up the name], and I thought I'd let you know that I've changed the location of Saturday's lunch from the Zodiac Cafe to Phil Stefani's. We're still

---

1. 11:30 (April 2006).

meeting at noon…" My friend Ann, who fervently believes that trains are for reading not phoning, seethed in a quiet but genuine rage. "Did you do anything about it?" I asked. "I said nothing," she replied, "but when I got to work, I called Stefani's and, using dear Amy's name, I cancelled her reservation for Saturday."

On *Kol Nidrei* night, 1965, Rabbi Norman Lamm delivered a sermon entitled "Divine Silence or Human Static?" His thesis was that if we do not hear the voice of God in today's day and age, it is not because God is not speaking, but because we are not listening, because, in his words,

> We are too busy talking. We are too involved in so many other things that are inconsequential and meaningless. Our society is too wordy, we are drowned in the verbosity of our mass media of communication. Words come to us not in sentences, but in veritable torrents, from mass media.

If there was too much human static and mass media in 1965, imagine how difficult it must be today for the still, small voice of the divine to penetrate. When our world has gotten so much noisier, and human listeners so spiritually insensitive, the voice of God becomes reduced to the question asked in the cell phone commercial: Can you hear me now? It is in a world of so many distractions, so much noise and *narishkeit*, that we are in such desperate need of the gifted *darshan* to hone and focus our minds to hear the voice of God. For the art of listening, in Rabbi Lamm's own words, "involves more than the use of the ear. It means opening one's heart, one's mind, one's soul, and sharpening one's sensitivity to listen to the divine voice." It is the *darshan* that helps us sharpen this sensitivity, and this book contains the words of a master communicator, or, as he has called himself, an "unrepentant *darshan*."

Since the Lamm archives were first published online, it has been my privilege to immerse myself in the PDFs of sermons painstakingly typed out on an ancient machine known as the typewriter. And in these pages I have discovered a world which existed not that long ago, and which, in certain respects, was quite different from our own age. It was a world in which Orthodoxy appeared outmoded and irrelevant, on its way out, and it was in this age that this young rabbi engaged in a passionate defense of the Torah and the relevance of its obligations to our lives.

United States Supreme Court Justice Stephen Breyer, reflecting on all the readings of briefs and all the composing of opinions that take place at the court, commented as follows: "I used to tell my son, 'You see? If you do your homework really well, you can get a job where you do homework for the rest of your life.'" In Rabbi Lamm's sermons I discovered a young rabbi, around the age I am now, who exhorted his congregants that being successful, modern, American adults was no excuse for lack of spiritual homework, that they were obligated to work every day at growing in their connection to God, knowledge of His Torah, and observance of His mitzvot. He did so through his extraordinary *derush*, in which the beauty of the Torah and its laws were made relevant and clear to congregants in a symphony of gorgeous, passionate prose.

Today, of course, thanks to the efforts of Rabbi Lamm and others, we live a proud, thriving, unabashed Orthodoxy. And yet, as Rabbi Lamm himself noted in a 1986 essay, despite the extraordinary amount of Torah study in today's day and age, the homiletical beauty, or *derush*, that produced these original defenses of Judaism can scarcely be found in synagogues today; we have experienced, in Rabbi Lamm's own words, a "loss of verbal potency." Ironically, in our noisy world, because we have so much language, so much email and texts and tweets, so many words, we no longer take the time to craft them with care.[2] And that is a shame, for, as Rabbi Lamm noted, if halakha is the science of Torah, then *derush* is its art, its song. It is the way that the beauty of the Torah can be exposed, so that not only the words, but the song of Torah can be sounded generation after generation.

One of my ancestors, Reb Yitzchak Zev Soloveichik, the father of the Beit HaLevi, was one of the few religious Jews known in his age able to speak Russian eloquently. As such, he was often asked to represent members of the Jewish community on trial before the Russian court. Punning off the name "Soloveichik," which means "little nightingale," Reb Yitzchak Zev would be asked by the Russian prosecutor, "What will the *solovei* sing now?" This is a question that I ask myself as I seek to

2. See "Under the Terebinth" in this volume.

craft *derashot* today. What will the *solovei* sing now? How can I follow in the footsteps of Rabbi Lamm, and attempt to inspire a new generation by engaging in the art of *derush*? How can I defend the truths and traditions of Orthodoxy, which today remain on trial in much of the world? It is at this moment that I have, time and again, been inspired by the insights and art of Rabbi Lamm, and I eagerly seized the opportunity to quote him and his words to a new generation, my own humble attempt at a *solovei's* song, drawing on the sheet music of a maestro. In a noisy world so desperately in need of inspiration, I am so grateful for this gift.

Rabbi Meir Y. Soloveichik is director of the Zahava and Moshael Straus Center for Torah and Western Thought at Yeshiva University and associate rabbi at Congregation Kehilath Jeshurun in Manhattan.

Editor's Preface

Stuart W. Halpern

It is an honor to present to the reader this selection of Rabbi Norman Lamm's sermons on the book of Genesis. Selected from among the numerous *derashot* given by Rabbi Lamm between the years 1952 and 1976 in both Congregation Kodimoh in Springfield, Massachusetts, and the Jewish Center in New York, New York, these *divrei Torah* are no less powerful or pertinent today. The luminance of the exegesis, the sharpness of the observations, and the care and concern for *Am Yisrael*, *Torat Yisrael*, and *Medinat Yisrael* that they convey can best be described by the words in Deuteronomy 34:7 describing Moses' skin: "*Lo nas leḥo*," their "natural force" has not abated. As examples of passionate pulpit pedagogy, brilliant biblical insight, and steadfast communal commitment, these essays stand in testimony to a master rabbi and teacher, whose words spoke to his congregants – when they faced war, political upheaval, social unrest, and rapidly developing technology – and continue to speak to us today.

These sermons are presented as they were first articulated, with only minor editorial tweaks. The "current events" referenced in many of the *derashot* are an integral part of the power and relevance of the pieces, and thus those parts that describe them in detail have been retained so that the reader can best appreciate the historical and communal situation to which Rabbi Lamm was responding at the time. On occasion, the reader will note certain sensitivities of language that have developed since these words first were spoken.

Much gratitude is owed to the many individuals who assisted in the production of this volume. As these sermons were gleaned from the selection on the Lamm Heritage website at Yeshiva University, many thanks go to the Dean of Libraries of Yeshiva University, Mrs. Pearl Berger, whose idea it was to create such a wonderful online collection of *derashot*. Rabbi Mark Dratch's helpful guidance throughout the entire process of creating this volume, as well as his assistance in locating many of the sources cited within, was truly invaluable. Mr. Shalom Lamm's ongoing support is also tremendously appreciated, as is the enthusiastic encouragement from my wife, Ahuva Warburg Halpern, and the entire Lamm, Dratch, Halpern, and Warburg families. I would also like to thank Rabbi Meir Y. Soloveichik for his heartfelt and eloquent foreword. The publication of this book was made possible by the OU Press as well as the support of the Michael Scharf Publication Trust of RIETS/ Yeshiva University Press, which, for many decades, has played a vital role in the production of Torah scholarship under the auspices of Yeshiva University. Many thanks are also due to the entire Maggid Books team, Mrs. Deena Nataf, and Mrs. Nechama Unterman for ensuring the high quality of this volume.

From the moment they were first spoken, the words in this volume cried out, "Write me for generations" (*Megilla* 7a). May they echo for generations to come.

Bereshit

Reflections on the Divine Image[1]

Parashat Bereshit teaches us one of the most fundamental concepts of our faith. It is something we speak of often, and that is perhaps why we frequently fail to appreciate its depth and the magnitude of its influence. The concept of man's creation *betzelem Elohim*, in the image of God, is one of the most sublime ideas that man possesses, and is decisive in the Jewish concept of man.

What does it mean when we say that man was created in the image of God? Varying interpretations have been offered, each reflecting the general ideological orientation of the interpreter.

The philosophers of Judaism, the fathers of our rationalist tradition, maintain that the image of God is expressed, in man, by his intellect. Thus, Sa'adia Gaon and Maimonides maintain that *sekhel*, reason, which separates man from animal, is the element of uniqueness that is in essence a divine quality. The intellectual function is thus what characterizes man as *tzelem Elohim*.

However, the ethical tradition of Judaism does not agree with that interpretation. Thus, Rabbi Moshe Chaim Luzzatto, in his *Mesilat*

---

1. October 15, 1960.

Yesharim, does not accept reason as the essence of the divine image. A man can, by exercise of his intellect, know what is good – but fail to act upon it. Also, the restriction of *tzelem Elohim* to reason means that only geniuses can truly qualify as being created in the image of God. Hence, Luzzatto offers an alternative and perhaps more profound definition. The *tzelem Elohim* in which man was created is that of *ratzon* – the freedom of will. The fact that man has a choice – between good and evil, between right and wrong, between obedience and disobedience of God – is what expresses the image of God in which he was born. An animal has no freedom to act; a man does. That ethical freedom makes man unique in the creation.

But how does the freedom of the human will express itself? A man does not assert his freedom by merely saying "yes" to all that is presented to him. Each of us finds himself born into a society which is far from perfect. We are all born with a set of animal drives, instincts, and intuitions. If we merely nod our heads in assent to all those forces which seem more powerful than us, then we are merely being passive, plastic, and devoid of personality. We are then not being free, and we are not executing our divine right of choice. Freedom, the image of God, is expressed in the word "no." When we negate that which is indecent, evil, ungodly; when we have the courage, the power, and the might to rise and announce with resolve that we shall *not* submit to the pressures to conform to that which is cheap, that which is evil, that which is indecent and immoral – then we are being free men and responding to the inner divine image in which we are created.

The late Rabbi Aaron Levine, the renowned Reszher Rav, interpreted, in this manner, the famous verse from Ecclesiastes (3:19) which we recite every morning as part of our preliminary prayers. Solomon tells us, "*Umotar ha'adam min habehema ayin*," which is usually translated as, "And the preeminence of man over beast is naught." Rabbi Levine, however, prefers to give the verse an interpretation other than the pessimistic, gloomy apparent meaning. He says: "And the preeminence of man over beast is – *ayin*, 'no.'" What is it that gives man his distinction? What is it that makes man different from the rest of creation, superior to the rest of the natural world? It is his capacity to say *ayin*, his capacity to face the world and announce that he will *not* submit to it, that he

4

will accept the challenge and respond "no". An animal has no choice – no freedom – and therefore must say "yes" to his drives, to the world in which he lives. But a human being *can* say "no" to that which is unseemly and beneath his dignity. And when he says "no" to all that is ungodly, he is being Godly. He is showing that he was created in the image of God.

Adam and Eve had to learn this lesson, and their descendants forever after must learn from their failure. We are nowhere told in the Torah that the fruit of the Tree of Knowledge was in any way different from the fruit of the other trees in the Garden of Eden. Yet when she was tempted by the serpent, Eve looked at the fruit, and in her mind's eye its attractiveness grew out of all proportion to reality. It looked more luscious, it looked more juicy, it looked more appetizing. She even imagined that this was some kind of "intelligence food." Her instinct bade her to do that which was in violation of the divine command. But counter to this she had the capacity, as a free agent created in God's image, to say *ayin*, to say "no" to her instinct and her temptation. But she forfeited her opportunity. The first human couple did not know how to say "no." This was the beginning of their downfall.

Abraham was a great Jew – the first Jew. Yet in our tradition he is not famous so much for saying "yes" as he is for saying "no." Abraham was the great iconoclast. It was he who said "no" to the idolatries of his day, who said "no" to his father's paganism, who was the one man pitted against the entire world, shouting "no!" to all the obscenities of his contemporary civilization.

Moses was a great teacher. He gave us 613 commandments. When you investigate the commandments, you find that only 248 are positive – commanding us what to do. But 365 of them are negative – they say "no" to our wills and our wishes. For when we learn to say "no," we are being free men and women under God. The famous Ten Commandments have only three positive laws; the other seven are negative. Indeed, it is only through these negatives that we can live and survive and thrive at all. Without "You shall *not* murder," there can be no society. Without "You shall *not* steal," there can be no normal conduct of commerce and business. Without "You shall *not* commit adultery," there can be no normal family life. Without "You shall *not* covet," the human personality must degenerate and man becomes nothing more than an animal, a beast.

"And the preeminence of man over beast is *ayin*" – it is this which gives man greater dignity and superiority over the animal – his power to say "no." It is this freedom of the human personality taught by our Jewish tradition that we Jews must reassert once again in our own day.

The author Herman Wouk told me some time ago that a number of years earlier he was boarding a ship to go on a trip overseas. Several hours after he boarded, a cabin boy brought him a note from the apostate Jewish author Shalom Asch, asking Wouk to come to his cabin. There Asch complained to him and said, "I don't understand you, Mr. Wouk. You are a young man – yet you are observant and Orthodox. When my generation of writers was young, we were rebels, we were dissenters. We rejected tradition, we rejected authority, we rejected the opinions of the past. What happened to you? Why do you conform so blandly?"

Wouk gave the older man an answer that I believe is very important for all of us to know. He answered, "You are making a terrible mistake, Mr. Asch. You seem to forget that the world we live in is not a paradise of Jewishness. You seem to forget that the world we occupy has become corrupted, assimilated, emptied of all Jewish content. In a world of this sort, one does not have to be a rebel at all in order to ignore the high standards of Judaism. If you violate the Sabbath, if you eat like a pagan, if you submit to the cheap standards of morality of the society in which we live, then you are being a conformist; you are merely allowing your own animal instincts to get the better of you. Today, if I and some of my contemporaries are observing the Jewish tradition, then it is because we are the dissenters, the *nein-sagers*. For we are the ones who say 'no' to the desecration of the Sabbath, 'no' to the creeping assimilation that ridicules all of Judaism and threatens its very life, 'no' to all the forces that seek to degrade our people and diminish the uniqueness of Israel that is its dignity and its preeminence. You are the conformist."

This is the kind of force, the kind of courage, the kind of conviction that has sustained us throughout the ages. It is that which has given us the power to say "no" to the threats of Haman, the cruelties of Chmielnicki, the genocide of Hitler, as well as the sugarcoated missionizing of more enlightened enemies of Judaism. We demonstrated the image of God when we exercised our freedom and said "no" to all this.

I am not suggesting that we ought to be destructively negative. It is, rather, that when we fully exercise our critical functions and faculties, then the good will come to the fore of itself. It is because I have confidence in the innate powers of the good that I suggest we concentrate on denying evil. "Depart from evil and do good" (Psalms 34:15). If you pit all your energies into negating evil, then good will be done of its own accord.

It is this power to say "no" that we must exercise in our relations with our fellow Jews in the State of Israel. For, in addition to all our constructive efforts on behalf of the upbuilding of the land, we must also be able to call a halt to the creeping paganism that plagues it.

When we find that in our own Orthodox community in Israel certain things are done which serve only to desecrate the name of God, we must not be shy. We must rise and as one say "no" to all those forces which would compromise the sanctity of the Torah and the sanctity of the Holy Land.

In our own American Jewish community, we must, here too, be the critics. And when, to mention just a seemingly trivial matter, certain artists and entertainers who are Jewish, and who rely upon the community as such for acceptance of what they have to offer, elect to entertain on Yom Kippur, the holiest day of the year, we must say "no." We must realize that it is no longer the domain of one's own conscience, when the matter is a public demonstration of contempt for American Jewry. "And the preeminence of man over beast is *ayin*" – we must not sheepishly go along with everything that "famous people" are willing to tell us. We must be men, we must be human beings, we must use the freedom that God gave us when He created us in His image, and learn when to say "no."

I conclude with the statement by one of the greatest teachers of Judaism, a man who indeed showed, in his life, that he knew the value of "no." It was Rabbi Akiba, the man who was able to stand up to the wrath and the might of the whole Roman Empire and say "no" to tyranny and to despotism, who taught us, "Beloved is man that he was created in the image of God" (*Avot* 3:18). Beloved indeed, and precious and unique and irreplaceable is man when he has the freedom of will that is granted to him by his Creator. And furthermore, "Ḥiba yeteira noda'at lo shenivra *betzelem"* – a special love was given to man by God, it is a special gift when man not only *has* that freedom but when he *knows* that he has that freedom – and therefore uses it to combat evil and to allow the great, constructive forces of good, innate in himself, to come to the fore so as to make this a better world for all mankind.

Looking at the World with New Eyes[1]

At the beginning of his immortal *Guide for the Perplexed* (1:2), Maimonides records a question that was posed to him concerning the story of Adam and Eve. These first two humans were given a single commandment by God: not to eat of the fruit of a certain tree. They violated that commandment. One might imagine that as a consequence they would suffer some severe punishment. Yet the major result of their transgression is that *"vatipakaḥna einei sheneihem,"* "the eyes of both of them were opened" (Genesis 3:7). Is this not an amazing story, an astounding turn of events? Does this mean that sin is to be rewarded with knowledge? Does crime pay?

The answer Maimonides gives is a profound one, and crucial to his whole philosophy. It is not easy to understand; the commentators on the *Guide* are not of one mind concerning its precise meaning. I wish to propose another answer, one suggested by a legendary and intriguing personality in the history of Hasidism, Rabbi Yitzchak Isaac of Komarno. It is an important explanation, and one to which I think Maimonides would have given his consent.

---

1. October 3, 1964.

The Rabbi of Komarno tells us that man was initially endowed with two sets of eyes, i.e. two ways of viewing life, two kinds of vision. He was given the *einei basar*, eyes of flesh, and *einei ruah*, eyes of the spirit. The *einei basar* represent man's physical and material outlook. They offer a direct channel to the senses; they are mere sight. The *einei ruah* are the eyes of the soul, man's spiritual vision; they represent insight rather than just sight. They are what Yehuda Halevi in his *Kuzari* has called *ha'ayin hanisteret*, the hidden eye – man's deeper, inner vision.

Before they committed their sin, Adam and Eve looked at the world and at each other only with *einei ruah*, with their spiritual eyes. They did not measure everything in terms of their own wants, needs, and desires. They saw the best in others. They perceived nothing untoward, unseemly, ungodly. After their transgression, their *einei ruah* were blinded – that was their main punishment – and, instead, "*vatipakahna einei sheneihem*," their physical eyes, their *einei basar*, were opened. They exchanged their higher vision for a base and lowly view of the universe. Henceforth they were sensitive to all that is ugly and degrading. What they now saw, which previously had no effect upon them, led them to thoughts of passion, temptation, and uncontrollable appetites. For instance, before the sin, they beheld the human body as something noble and decent, as natural and therefore worthy, as the creation of God's hands. Such is the view with *einei ruah*. Afterwards, however, when their *einei basar* were opened, the nakedness they beheld became for them a frightening phenomenon, something repulsive precisely because it was so immorally attractive, something dangerous and fraught with baseness – and hence it was something to be ashamed of.

Interestingly, the *haftara* of this Torah portion seems to support this interpretation of the two sets of eyes. The selection from the book of Isaiah contains no less than eight references to eyes, blindness, and seeing again.

And what a difference between these two ways of looking at the world! Where you behold a man with your *einei basar*, you see not a man but a mere animal who just happens to be a step or two ahead in the evolutionary scale. And if man is but an animal, then he can be used, manipulated, and exploited; for then he is an object, a "thing," an "it." But if you regard him with your *einei ruah*, then man is, as King David put it, "but little lower than the angels" (Psalms 8:6). Then he is a person, endowed with his own unimpeachable value. Then he is, as Kant taught, an end in himself.

Look at the world with *einei basar,* and a home appears as but a house populated by related individuals. Look at it with *einei ruah,* and they are a family; and even a mere table becomes a *mizbe'ah,* an altar!

There is an important philosophic difference between these two types of "eyes." The *einei basar* see in the world only diversity, differentness, atomization, and fragmentization. They behold powerful forces pitted against each other in relentless struggle and ceaseless strife, a society caught up in calamitous conflict, where ultimately only the law of the jungle prevails. It is man-eat-man, and every man for himself. With *einei ruah,* however, one has a completely different *weltanschauung,* an utterly different view. One sees the world's rich diversity kept together by an underlying unity – the oneness of its Creator; a world where cooperation and symbiosis accomplish more than collision and war; where peace makes sense; where man can unite about the oneness of God. The view of *einei basar* is that of *dis*integration, and is characteristic of idolatry, both ancient and contemporary. That of *einei ruah* is the vision of *in*tegration, and is of the essence of Judaism, which aspires to the time that "God will be King over all the earth and He and His Name will be One" (Zechariah 14:9).

If one's *einei ruah* are blinded and he uses only *einei basar,* then he will build his city in a way that is haphazard and neglectful and harsh – just like ours! Then, any building that does not prove itself completely functional and practical and efficient and thoroughly economical must be torn down mercilessly and replaced by those cavernous, impersonal, aluminum-and-steel monsters that swallow their armies of willing victims who troop in every day exactly at 9:00 AM and are disgorged precisely at 5:00 PM. Such a limited, foolish view has no use for elegance or beauty or esthetics or sentiment or tradition or the past or graciousness or memory. A city built – or, better, unbuilt – in this manner is impersonal, cold, and gray; it lacks charm and intimacy. It is not a place to live in. To live, one needs at least a little of the *einei ruah*!

Or take a synagogue. The practical man who possesses only *einei basar* looks at the synagogue and his questions reveal the sad narrowness of his view: How big is it? What is the size and wealth of its membership? What about the budget, the deficit, and the dues? Approach it, however, with the vision of *einei ruaḥ* and you ask: How many of its members truly *"daven"* in it? What is the level of their observance? Do they study Torah and partake of the adult education opportunities made available for them? How warm and authentic is their prayer? Such is the difference between the two sets of eyes!

Look at the State of Israel only with *einei basar* and you see nothing essentially different from any other small, struggling Middle East country. Torah has no special place in it. But view it with *einei ruaḥ* and you have not the State of Israel, the modern version of Palestine, but also the Holy Land, the land of prophecy, concerning which we so fervently pray, *"Veteḥezena eineinu beshuvekha leTziyon beraḥamim"*: May our eyes – our inner, spiritual eyes as well as our physical eyes – behold the return of the *Shekhina* to Zion!

Of course, a modern state must be highly concerned over such questions as technology, economy, and security, as must a modern man be involved in business and making a living. I do not mean to suggest that we can or should completely close our *einei basar*. Once those eyes have been opened, they can no longer be closed. We cannot expect to return to the paradise from which Adam and Eve were exiled. But at least we can attempt to recapture some of the vision and wider horizons of what the Torah tells us of primitive man. At least we can try to open those eyes which are usually shut tight. At the very minimum, we must add the *einei ruaḥ* to the *einei basar*; or, if you will, we must learn to look at life with bifocals, through a double set of spectacles of both self-interest and higher, deeper spiritual insight.

This matter of general outlook, of regarding the world with new eyes, those of *einei ruaḥ*, is crucial to being a religious Jew. To return to Torah requires more than accepting a number of new observances heretofore neglected. These observances or mitzvot must necessarily initiate an inner transformation, so that one gains a new *hashkafa*, a new outlook. If we become more observant but continue to see the worst in people, read the same inane literature, watch the same insipid and vulgar entertainment, approach our fellow-men with suspicion and contempt and vindictiveness, imagine that the world of the spirit is a convenient

BERESHIT: Looking at the World with New Eyes

fiction – we are not yet really religious Jews. We must still experience shame for the spiritual blindness that afflicts us.

A highly relevant and charming (though perhaps trivial in its immediate implications) example of the opening of the *einei ruah* as part of becoming a religious Jew is found in a modern *teshuva*, or responsum. The responsa literature, that of *she'elot uteshuvot*, the legal answers written by great rabbis to those who sent them questions in halakha, has long been considered an excellent source of the inner history of our people. That holds true for our modern times as well. I would like to mention, therefore, a contemporary responsum which sheds light on the return to Judaism in our days, if not quantitatively then at least in quality. The *teshuva* appears in the most recent volume of responsa, *Iggerot Moshe*, by an outstanding rabbinic scholar, Rabbi Moshe Feinstein. A teenager who evidently came from a nonobservant home, and who had but recently become a *ben Torah* and a student in a yeshiva, addressed an intriguing question to the rabbi. He harbored guilty feelings over his lack of observance prior to his accepting a life of Torah, and wanted to know how to repent. What was it that so disturbed him? Was it his neglect of *kashrut* or Shabbat? No, it was not; there was nothing that could be done about that retroactively. But this young man, having become a true and authentic Torah Jew, had gotten himself a new set of eyes, *einei ruah*. His new approach, his new attitude, his new vision included the Torah principle that injuring a fellow-man to the extent of one penny was as bad as that of a hundred dollars. He felt contrite over the child-ish pranks of his youth: for taking money his parents had given him for food and misappropriating it for entertainment; for ducking under the turnstile when entering the subway; for pocketing money from the telephone coin-box which did not belong to him. As a *ben Torah* he had acquired a new vision, a new outlook, and his previous misdemeanors bothered him. Therefore he wrote this question, and received a serious and solemn answer from his *rebbe*! This is only a small indication of the difference made by opening the right eyes!

When our first ancestors sinned, they lost their spiritual vision and instead were confined to their material views. If we are to live lives that are decent and blameless and genuinely Jewish, then we must reverse the process.

The rabbis of the Mishna had some excellent advice on how to do that. They taught us (*Avot* 2:1), "Consider three things and you will avoid sin." One of those three things is, "*Da ma lemala mimkha: ayin ro'a,*" "Know what is above you: a seeing eye." Perhaps what they were referring to is not, as is the usual interpretation, a heavenly, angelic, or divine eye, but – a higher human eye! They perhaps meant to tell us that there is something *lemala*, something higher and loftier and nobler *mimkha*, which issues from the deepest recesses of our selfhood, and that is an *ayin ro'a*, a spiritual vision, a new way of looking at the world! Every man and woman has such an eye or set of eyes, which too often remain closed all through life. If you are to avoid a life of sin and moral blemish, however, open them up, reassert them. Develop a new perception, a new vision.

As we begin a new cycle of Torah reading with *Parashat Bereshit*, the answer given by the Rabbi of Komarno to the question recorded by Maimonides is of utmost relevance to all of us. Let us get ourselves a healthier, broader, more sublime outlook, one filled with true Torah insights, and we shall then discover that our lives can indeed be transformed. We will experience *Da ma lemala mimkha*, we will find within our own selves new resources for self-transcendence, moral growth, and spiritual greatness.

"*Ve'eineinu tirena malkhutekha,*" "May our eyes behold Your kingdom." If we make use of our *einei ruaḥ*, then the Almighty will grant that even our *einei basar* will have the privilege of beholding the Kingdom of God: a world of peace and plenty, of joy and serenity, of splendor – and spirit.

The Three Faces of Adam[1]

The Torah's story of Adam was never meant to be simply the biography of the first human being, a biblical attempt to satisfy our idle curiosity about our origins. Rather, it is a source of what might be called biblical anthropology, God's view of man. It is therefore the stuff of profound interpretation as to the nature of man, from the earliest, brief insights of the Midrash to the latest philosophical dissertations.

I will suggest three insights, all drawing on the name Adam. For the Torah hints, but never openly states, that the origin of the name is *adama*, earth or ground, and therefore leaves open the question of the derivation of the name Adam and its significations.

Some distinguished Orientalists and lexicographers assert that the Hebrew *Adam* is related to the Assyrian *adamu*, to make or produce.[2] From this derivation, we learn that man's superiority, his charismatic endowment, his spiritual dignity, lies in his technological genius. He is, like his Creator, creative. He was placed in the Garden of Eden

---

1. October 11, 1969.
2. Gesenius, Brown, Driver, and Briggs, *A Hebrew and English Lexicon of the Old Testament* (Oxford: Oxford University Press, 1952).

"to work it and to guard it" (Genesis 2:15), to develop it and improve it. Rabbi Leibele Eger, a great scholar who became a Hasid of the Rabbi of Kotzk, once returned from a visit to his master and said that one of the three things he learned in Kotzk was: *"Bereshit bara Elohim."* When asked what he meant thereby, he said: "I learned that God created only *bereshit,* only the beginning – man must do all the rest." Man, *Adam,* must be *adamu,* a maker, producer, and creator.

In a remarkable interpretation, the sages (Proverbs Rabba 19:1) revealed to us the same insight in yet another fashion. We read that when Abraham met the king of Salem after defeating the captors of Lot, the king, Melchizedek, said to him, *"Barukh Avram leEl Elyon, Koneh shamayim va'aretz"* (Genesis 14:19), usually translated as: "Blessed be Abram to God the Most High, Possessor (or: Creator, since 'koneh' actually means 'the one who makes') of heaven and earth." The rabbis, however, maintain that the last phrase, *"Koneh shamayim va'aretz,"* refers not to God but back to Abraham! Melchizedek blessed Abraham who was creator of heaven and earth, to God the Most High. What the rabbis meant, of course, was that Abraham was the creator of the world in a spiritualized fashion; that is, by virtue of his merit and his righteousness he sustained the world. Today, however, we can give that rabbinic statement a quite literal turn: man has become the master of earth, and heaven as well! With our thrusts into space, we, the successors of Abraham, have extended our hegemony over the heavenly bodies as well as our own globe. Indeed, Rabbi Menachem M. Kasher, in an article which appeared in *Hapardes,*[3] maintains that the landing on the moon was a fulfillment of a prophecy of Isaiah that has to do with the end of days. Isaiah says that in the time of the Messiah, the moon will be embarrassed or ashamed (24:23). Mankind once worshiped the moon, then sang about her and admired her – and now men have landed on the moon, violating her integrity, humiliating her. We have established our mastery of our nearest neighbor.

Hence, by exercising our *adamu* function, we enhance science, engineering, and medicine; we build cities, tame nature, and enjoy the benefits of modern life.

---

3. October 1969.

However, this is not the totality of man. Were it so, man would be nothing more than a machine with a computer on top. Unlike machines or animals, man has the capacity for personal relations. Man is involved not only with *things*, but with *beings*; he has not only a brain, but a heart, and this quality derives from the divine "breath of life" that God blew into the nostrils of man (Genesis 2:7).

In blatant disregard of the principles of scientific linguistics, a famous talmudic scholar offers a penetrating insight into the nature of man that is no less valid because of its faulty etymology. Rabbi Ezekiel Landau, the Rabbi of Prague, and known as the author of *Noda biYehuda*, avers that the Hebrew *Adam* comes from *adameh*, which means, "I shall be like unto." Adam fulfills himself when he achieves *adameh*, when he compares himself to and imitates God, who is *ḥanun veraḥum ve'erekh apayim*, merciful and gracious and patient. *Adameh* therefore spells the dimension of warmth and relatedness.

So man is more than a functionary, more than a producer or consumer. He is more than a grocer or mechanic or lawyer or industrialist. He is a human! His net worth may be measured in dollars, but his ultimate and real worth can be judged only in terms of friendships and loves, of influence and good deeds.

There is a common maxim: "You can't take it with you." The Psalmist, however, put it slightly differently: "For at his death a man shall not take everything with him" (49:18). We do not say that you can't take it with you absolutely; just that you can't take "everything" with you. But there are certain things that you can take along as your portion for the world-to-come: cherished memories, a good reputation, love, good deeds, mitzvot performed. The *adamu* function of man ceases with his last breath; the *adameh* function continues beyond that.

The conflict between the generations – and it is not really between the generations as such as much as between two lifestyles and philosophies: one established and defensive, the other emerging and militant – can be expressed as the attitude to the balance between *adamu* and *adameh*. The pragmatic philosophy which made America great – which ideologically founded Western civilization, spurred on science, and gave the impetus to technology – viewed Adam as *adamu*. Man's greatness lies in his creativity, his productivity, his mastery.

The new thinking, however, rejects this role as the major definition of man. It emphasizes Adam not as *adamu* but as *adameh*: man's existential plight, his freedom, his love, and his self-expression, his relations with his family, his neighbors, his community – and his integrity. It desires not to build the mute world all around but the living self within; not to produce but to experience; not to create but to relate.

The lines are being drawn in our times. The established generation takes a hard line against the revolutionaries, condemns all critics of society and the status quo as "hippies." And there are times that the established segment of society invites excesses of criticism – as, for instance, when the government announces with a flourish that last week we lost only sixty-four men in Vietnam – meaning to say, that we are pleased it was so low, but revealing meanwhile its basic orientation: for the purpose of the smooth functioning of the military machine, sixty-four men are indeed expendable. In the same week, the financial leaders of the government inform us that by a stroke of good fortune and great wisdom, we have achieved a 4 percent degree of unemployment. Here again, the government indicates that in its attempt to relieve the pressure of inflation for the total population, a certain amount of "inconvenience" is inevitable. But the younger critics do not want to accept this excuse. Perhaps in the system of economics under which we live, a certain amount of unemployment is unavoidable and even necessary. But then, if we look at the problem from the point of view of these downtrodden, miserable, humiliated individuals who are thrown out of jobs, perhaps the whole system of economics should be overthrown! Perhaps all of society is rotten and corrupt if this is all it can do. Perhaps our form of government that allows an involvement in Vietnam which can revel in a death rate of sixty-four per week should be disbanded.

And the rebels, on their part, are indiscriminate in their rejection of society and its values. They fail to select the enduring values while they reject those that are damaging. They disdain work and productivity, science and technology. They take its advantages for granted, and uncritically condemn the whole philosophy that made these benefits possible.

Obviously, both are right and both are wrong, for both are necessary. *Adamu* alone leads to a hard, depersonalized view, and reduces humans to cogs in a wheel. But *adameh* alone results in a society where there are no wheels in which we ought not to be cogs! It means that insofar as civilization is concerned, we stagnate, and we must ultimately be defeated by Nature, by illness and storm and all else against which technology is a shield.

So both definitions or faces of Adam are needed, *adamu* and *adameh*. However, these two are still insufficient. Even with material progress and viable personal relations, man must remain dissatisfied, unhappy, possessed of an inner vacuum. With all this, he still lacks something transcendent, something holy, something beyond nature and beyond man – something supernatural. With all his achievements, Adam today is haunted by the same question that confronted the first Adam: *"Ayeka?"* "Where are you?" Where are you going, what is the meaning of your life, what is the purpose of it all?

Adamu and *adameh* do not exhaust the meaning of Adam, for Judaism requires a third dimension, yielding three faces of Adam. It demands yet another facet to the totality of man's existence.

In a typical, characteristic flight of romantic, speculative philology, which often has little bearing on scientific facts, Rabbi Samson Raphael Hirsch maintains that the name Adam derives from the Hebrew word *hadom*, which means "footstool." Thus, Isaiah says in the name of God, *"hashamayim kisi veha'aretz hadom raglai,"* "the heavens are My throne and the earth My footstool" (66:1). And David says, *"vehishtaḥavu lahadom raglav kadosh Hu,"* "Bow down to His footstool, for He is holy" (Psalms 99:5).

What does this mean? Man always wants to feel significant and needed, that what he does has meaning and purpose. Therefore, Judaism tells us that every man must be a *shaliaḥ*, a messenger or an ambassador. Each of us must feel that we are the *hadom raglav*, the footstool of God, that we carry out His mission, that what we do or are all lead to a higher, divine end. This is not a separate explanation, but an interpretation of the other two suggestions: Whether *adamu* or *adameh*, whether at office or at home, whether at factory or with family, I must seek to advance God's causes by acting as His *hadom*. Whether as a technical creator or as a human in relation with others, I must see myself as a footstool of the Lord. Only then can I be sure of avoiding the extremes of becoming too hard – a mere producer; or too soft – one who revels in ethereal relationships that have no objective worth or enduring value.

Perhaps that is what the rabbis of the Kabbala meant when they said that the patriarchs became a *merkava*, a chariot or vehicle for the Lord. The righteous man is one who puts his life at God's disposal and carries out His causes. Not always do we know in advance what function has been assigned to us, but the discovery and execution of that purpose – that is all of life.

No wonder that Dr. Viktor Frankl, in his great book, *Man's Search for Meaning*, maintains that psychologically and existentially man needs purpose and meaning in life as much as nourishment and sex and power. It is a fundamental dimension of his being. Man as *hadom*, as a mission-bearer, is God's ambassador, and it makes *adamu* bearable and *adameh* enduring.

When man explores the *hadom* aspects of his nature, he aspires to be more than human. But without it, he must perforce remain less than human. Man can be commercially, scientifically, domestically, and socially successful if he pursues only the *adamu* quality of his life and enhances the *adameh* dimension, but remains woefully inadequate if he is ultimately meaningless in all his actions.

So as a people and as individuals, we must recapitulate the story of the first Adam. Like Adam, we must strive for *adamu*, to transform life into a Garden of Eden. Like Adam, we must attempt to be successful in *adameh*, in our personal relations, in fulfilling our humanity. But again like Adam, that little but powerful voice that unnerved him still pursues us: "*Ayeka?*" Where are you, what meaning does your life have?

And the answer must be forthcoming without hesitation: I, an *adam*, am ready to become a *hadom*, a footstool of God, and place my life at His service.

Noaḥ

If You Need Help – Call![1]

The high point of the story of Noah and the Flood comes when Noah and his family enter the ark. The Torah describes it in the following words: "And Noah and his sons and his wife and the wives of his sons came into the ark with him from before the waters of the flood" (Genesis 7:7).

The rabbis were somewhat taken aback by the last phrase. Did Noah enter the ark only because of the waters of the flood? Was he not "a righteous man" who should have been motivated to enter the ark by the divine command, rather than by the threat of the actual flood waters?

Rabbi Yochanan replies that the Torah means what it says quite literally. "Noah was lacking in faith (*mehusar emuna*). Were it not for the fact that the flood waters reached his ankles, he would not have entered the ark!" (Genesis Rabba 32:9).

Rashi gives us the same message, but uses a slightly different expression: "*Noah ma'amin ve'eino ma'amin*," "Noah believed and did not believe" – in other words, Noah was a man of shaky faith. He wavered

---

1. October 19, 1974.

in his belief in God's prediction that the flood would come, and that is why he entered the ark only when forced to by the raging waters.

However, this interpretation too is quite troublesome. It does not take into consideration the fact that Noah had believed in God all along, that he had already proved his faith under far more difficult circumstances when he built an ark – according to tradition, this took him 120 years – risking the ridicule of his peers. Is it reasonable to assume that a man who had invested all this time in establishing his principles and his faith would fail at the last moment?

I therefore suggest that the object of the *emuna* (faith) in this context is not God but oneself. The problem is not a religious one, whether or to what extent Noah believed in God, but a psychological one: did he believe in *himself*? And I take Rashi's idiom quite literally: *"ma'amin ve'eino ma'amin,"* "Noah believed and did not believe." The rabbis, according to this interpretation, fault Noah for two things: for believing in himself, and for not believing in himself!

Let me explain. All of us, by virtue of our mortality and finitude, must rely upon each other. Especially in more advanced civilizations, we are not fully independent and autonomous. We all know that we need God, and God knows that we need each other. It is impossible to survive without interdependence. And yet, we so often fail to seek help on time and frequently wait until it is too late, until the flood waters reach not only our ankles, but our very noses! Why?

There are two reasons, each the opposite of the other. One of them is too much self-confidence, an excess of security, egoism, and arrogance. A man is a *ma'amin* (believer) in his own powers and image, and he is afraid that asking for help will put him in a position of dependency, inferiority, and subservience.

The second reason is an utter lack of faith in oneself. A man is an *eino ma'amin* (nonbeliever), who lacks a sense of security, who experiences lowliness and diffidence and unworthiness, and sinks in despair.

Remarkably, both of these can be and usually are present at once. It is the phenomenon of ambivalence, where two opposite tendencies conspire to paralyze us without reason.

After 120 years of building the ark, Noah still had to be driven into it by the waters reaching his ankles, because of both reasons: he was a *ma'amin* who thought to himself, "I have been spared for so long; I will be spared longer. If I really am such a righteous man, such a *'tzaddik tamim,'* then nothing will happen to me now." But Noah was also an *eino ma'amin*; he lacked faith in himself. He probably thought, "I am doomed with the rest of the world. There is nothing in me that is worthy of being saved while the rest of the world drowns. I am helpless and hopeless."

When one is so beset by these extremes of over-confidence and under-confidence, of both an excess and a want of faith in himself, it is a sign of serious spiritual defect. It shows that he is *mehusar emuna*, that he lacks faith – in the Almighty.

I mention this not only as a way of explaining a text, but more important, as a way of bringing to your attention a disturbing problem, namely, that many people come for help when it is too late, or don't come at all, because they are either too sensitive to their own egos or too considerate of those whom they consult; because they have too much confidence – they think they can handle every problem by themselves; and too little confidence that anyone in the world can help them.

I speak to you from a background of counseling experience. I am constantly worried by people who hesitate too long before calling out for help. Parents who have a problem with a child sometimes wait until the problem is unmanageable. Religious problems are sometimes allowed to fester beyond the possibility of successful solution. Domestic tensions should lead a couple to ask for help before an eruption is irrevocable. Yet too often, people believe that to ask for help is a blow at the ego, a sign of weakness – or, the opposite, that they are so far superior that no one else can help.

The same holds true for medical assistance. This week, by startling coincidence, the wife of the vice president-designate was operated on for the same disease as was the wife of the president. All this helped in calling attention to the importance of seeking medical help – on time! It is amazing how many people defer examinations because of these two opposite reasons: because of *ma'amin*, the feeling that "it can't happen to me," and *eino ma'amin*, the feeling that "it's too late; I'm afraid to find out because if I have it then I'm finished." Both reactions are dangerous, both false, both to be shunned in every way.

But even more than these, there is something else that comes

25

up most frequently in my experience. In mentioning it to you, I should like to make it clear that I do not refer to anyone individually – but I refer to everyone individually. I refer to situations where there are emotional or family problems, and where psychological or psychiatric help is clearly indicated.

Now, I do not believe that every psychologist is a modern version of a witch doctor who can, by certain incantations and the payment of appropriate fees, cure everything and anything. I am not sufficiently affluent to indulge in such fantasies. I do not think that psychological help is the right of the poor and the duty of the rich. But I never fail to be startled by intelligent and sophisticated people who shrink from consulting psychologists, when to do so is the only rational recourse. I am amazed at how often I have to speak to intellectual and sensitive and *au courant* people, and explain to them as simple as teaching the A-B-C, "If you take a broken knee to the orthopedist, and an injured eye to the ophthalmologist, why not take your bruised emotions to a psychologist?"

The answer is that these people are *"ma'amin ve'eino ma'amin,"* they suffer from both extremes. On the one hand, they cannot admit to their supposed inferiority by asking someone else to help, and on the other hand, they inwardly feel that their problems are too enormous, that they are beyond salvation. But this is a perfect formula for perishing in the flood of personal anguish.

Of course, as with any other profession, one must seek out a competent person. Moreover, in the case of religious Jews, we must also make sure that the therapist in question is, if not personally observant, at least sympathetic; if not sympathetic, at least understanding. At the very least, he or she should be an ethical professional, who understands and abides by the canons of his or her own discipline, according to which the therapist must fully respect the values and principles of the patient and not seek to dissuade him from them.

I urge all of you: seek help on time! If you need help – call!

Recent events of the past week or two impel me to add one more point to what I have said. I mention it not because there is anything any of us can do about it, but perhaps to help express in some small way the frustration and anger all of us feel.

It is easy enough to get individuals to seek help. That is a comparatively simple thing. The big problem is not what does one person do when he needs help but does not ask for it, but what of a *whole world* which desperately needs help but does not realize it?

This past week the United Nations, by an overwhelming majority vote, invited – in a precedent-breaking act – the Palestine Liberation Organization to have the right to appear before it as observers. Arafat or one of his deputies will soon come to New York to address the UN. The world organization is extending its hospitality to the chief international gangster. And by the perverted power of radical rhetoric, this butcher is presented to us as a genuine revolutionary and guerilla!

The ghosts of the slain children of Maalot will testify that such a world is sick, very sick, and desperately needs help!

Sometimes I think back to those naïve and romantic days when, in the euphoria of expectations following World War II, we hypnotized ourselves with those progressivistic incantations about the UN being the "family of man," and we spoke about it as the "concert of nations," attributing to it some supernal moral authority. We overlooked the simple and obvious fact that a collection of nations with self-interest, some of it malicious, means that it has more malice than does one nation individually, not less!

We used to tell ourselves: if only we had a UN in the days when Hitler came to power we might have escaped the terrible experience of World War II. That was what we thought. But now we know the truth. This week we have begun to realize: if there had been a UN then, they would have overwhelmingly invited Hitler to address them as their honored guest! And who knows but that a vote to condemn the "final solution" would have been defeated by a lopsided majority?

Where shall we find a psychiatrist wise enough to deal with a whole UN that not only acts in brazen cynicism – and according to some theories of diplomacy, such amoral conduct may be necessary – but whose outrageous and shameless acts are greeted with applause and murmurs of consent in the corridors, without contrition or remorse?

Where, oh where, can we find a couch big enough for nine-tenths of mankind?

If I were the analyst or the chaplain of the UN, I would diagnose the illness as a critical case of ambivalence, of *ma'amin* and *eino ma'amin*!

The UN is *ma'amin*: it arrogantly expects to get away with it, it is willing to vent its hostility in a kind of diplomatic gang-mugging, and then honor the bully.

And it is *eino ma'amin*: the Western nations and the "developing nations" do not have enough confidence, nor enough will, to organize and unite against the common threat. They do not understand that if they do not confront the Arabs now in the case of Israel, they will have to do so later under far worse circumstances.

If I were to make that diagnosis, I would add that both attitudes lead to a *mabul*, a deluge – not a flood of oil, but a flood of blood and tears.

So the Noah syndrome is upon us again. From Hitler's election in Munich, to Maalot and the invitation to the PLO, is some thirty-five years – what a short memory the intellectual community has! What are we when we do not understand that God will not long let the world get away with it?

For ourselves, in addition to bearing in mind what I said urging each of you to seek help on time, I also would like to add two things we can do, one large and one small. The big thing is to stand by Israel and support her in every way in the days ahead. The small thing is that before that day of infamy comes at the UN, let us assemble, two weeks from this coming Monday, in peace and in dignity, but vigorously, to goad the UN into the awareness of the enormity of its infamy. Of course, no one will listen. But so what? We must do it as an act of conscience to ourselves, and as human beings, to protect and maintain the dignity of mankind despite what has occurred.

We recognize that the extremes of *ma'amin* and *eino ma'amin*, both of which lead to the flood, stem from lack of faith in the Almighty. We must therefore respond with more faith – faith in God, faith in ourselves, faith in our holy Torah – and also faith that this faith will redeem an unworthy world.

Noah and Jonah[1]

I t is instructive to compare the story of Noah with another biblical tale, that of Jonah. The two stories have a number of elements in common. The scene of each is set, largely, in water; each of them is a moral drama of sin and punishment; the hero of each is a reluctant prophet: Noah, who builds an ark for himself but fails to arouse his contemporaries to repentance, and Jonah, who would rather flee from God than undertake the mission of preaching to Nineveh; and, in each case, the major sin of the generation is described by the Hebrew word "*ḥamas*," which is usually translated as "violence," and which generally means any outrageous overreaching, and more specifically, robbery. Yet there the comparison ends. For the Jonah story has a happy ending, one of repentance by the king and the people of Nineveh, whereby the city is saved. Whereas the Noah story ends in tragedy – the cataclysm of the great deluge which destroyed all life save that of Noah and the inhabitants of the ark.

Why this difference? I suggest that the solution turns on the word "*ḥamas*." Note the idiomatic distinction in the two different contexts

---

1. October 11, 1975.

in which the word appears. In *Parashat Noaḥ*, we read that *"vatimalei ha'aretz ḥamas"* (Genesis 6:11) – the entire earth was filled with violence: *ḥamas* seeped into the soil, it polluted the water, it was present in the very atmosphere, the air that people breathed. It was ubiquitous. It was simply a given, an accepted part of life. Whereas in the book of Jonah, we read, *"Umin haḥamas asher bekapeihem,"* "The violence that was in their hands" (3:8).

The hand or palm is the symbol of grasping, of taking for oneself. The "violence of the hand," hence, is individual; it speaks of the satisfaction of personal wants, the gratification of desires, of natural or material or political appetites. Such *ḥamas* is culpable, it is wrong – but it is understandable for it is natural. When man practices this kind of *ḥamas*, he is like an animal. Few animals die of old age or sickness. Most die violently – they are devoured by other animals. No wonder that the king of Nineveh, in his act of repentance, commands that his entire people fast, and that the animals too shall fast during this period. For the sin that was committed was that his people had become animals, that they had ignored the norms of justice and fairness, and had grasped and devoured for their personal satisfaction. It was a crime, but it was forgivable.

With Noah, however, the generation was guilty of something far worse. Their violence filled all the world. It was injustice for its own sake, as a way of life, not for the satisfaction of personal desires. The world was filled with the senseless violence of vandalism, not the violence of the venal, selfish kind. When man indulges this species of *ḥamas*, he descends to a level lower than that of the animals.

Perhaps this is what the rabbis really meant when they said that the stealing of the generation of the flood was "less than a penny's worth." Remarkable: people commit such minor, trivial versions of petty thievery, stealing only half a penny at a time, and for this God ordains that the entire world will be destroyed in a swirling flood! Where is the sense of fairness?

What the rabbis meant, I believe, was to indicate that the *ḥamas* was not for profit. It was not in order to benefit the people, but rather just for the joy of stealing as such. Violence became its own justification, stealing almost casual. Various psychological explanations are often offered for this kind of violence. Whether they are valid or not, they are irrelevant to this discussion. For there is no excuse for a crime committed for its own sake, without benefit to the criminal.

Indeed, on Yom Kippur day we confess, among others in that long list of sins, for the sin we committed by the evil inclination (*yetzer hara*). But are not all sins committed because of the evil inclination? No, they are not. Those sins that are committed because of the *yetzer hara*, because of sensuousness or the desire for profit or self-aggrandizement, are sins and we must confess them and thereby attain forgiveness. But we are doomed if the sins we have committed cannot be justified on the basis of selfishness or graspingness, the sins that are committed without even the excuse of the *yetzer hara*.

Hence, too, at the Ne'ila service on Yom Kippur – the climax of the whole year – in the two major passages of the service, we emphasize *oshek* (a synonym of *hamas*) and twice we say, "*Lema'an neḥdal me'oshek yadeinu*": we ask forgiveness and hope that henceforth our *hands* will desist from violence, from robbery. It is possible to pray for forgiveness for "the violence of the hands." But the other, unselfish, blind, unmotivated meanness, whether *oshek* or *hamas*, violence for its own sake – for that there is never any forgiveness. Thus we may answer a question that the rabbis ask: Why does the Torah specify that the punishment of the generation of the flood came because of the *hamas* (which, as indicated, is narrowly interpreted as robbery), when the people of that generation also committed idolatry and immorality? Are not the latter two far more serious crimes than mere robbery?

The answer, according to the theory we have been presenting, is that indeed *hamas* is worse than all, precisely because it was not a response to an inner, personal need. At least immorality has the excuse of a hyperactive libido, and idolatry can be justified as the primitive stirrings of fear, apprehension, and awe within the human soul. But the violence that has become second nature, that fills the earth and the world, and in which one has no personal stake – this can be rectified only by drowning in the flood.

This difference between senseless violence and self-serving violence was illustrated to us amply during our own lifetime, in the history of the Second World War. Nazism represented hatred for its own sake, not merely for well-defined reasons. After the war all of us wondered:

How could this have happened? How shall we explain this diabolical outburst? And because we had all along accepted that there are rational explanations for history, we sought them here too. We told ourselves that it was revenge for the Treaty of Versailles; that a scapegoat was needed; that there were political reasons or economic explanations.

Professor Lucy Dawidowicz, in her book *The War against the Jews*, has presented a different thesis, and one which is shared by a number of other historians. German anti-Semitism was virulent even when it hurt the German war effort militarily and economically. The destruction of European Jewry robbed the Germans of a work force of tremendous proportions when the Germans needed it most, in the most desperate phase of the war. There was no selfish excuse for the murder of six million Jews. It was simply that *"vatimalei ha'aretz hamas,"* their entire world was filled with this kind of hatred for its own sake. Raoul Hilberg, one of the most distinguished historians of the Holocaust, has calculated that from the point of view of the economics of the German war effort, the "final solution" cost so much that it reduced to zero all the spoils of war that the Nazis took from their victims!

It is because of this type of hatred without reason that the time is overdue for getting rid of – and helping others get rid of – the image of the Third World countries as either political innocents who must be excused on romantic grounds; or symbols of our own guilt for being a wealthy country which we must expiate by catering to their every whim; or as people whose poverty entitles them to uncivilized conduct without suffering the consequences of such conduct. And while most of the Third World nations are very poor, others are much too rich.

Our own residual naïveté was shattered as irremediably as Humpty Dumpty when, this past week or so, the Third World delegates to the United Nations gave an enthusiastic standing ovation to that crude, illiterate, national butcher of Uganda, Idi Amin. To have elected this international mugger as head of the Organization of African States was bad enough; perhaps someone with an incredibly elastic sense of tolerance can find some excuse for it. But for the delegates to give such glowing testimony of their personal respect and affection for this walking obscenity is nothing less than a sign that in our generation, too, *"vatimalei ha'aretz ḥamas"* – the atmosphere itself, the entire world, is poisoned by hatred and violence.

I am still not recovered from an encounter some two or three years ago in Geneva. It was at an international conference, attended by all kinds of people. One young man from Cameroon, a diplomat and a professor and a Christian theologian, turned to me and said, "You Jews are all racists because of your support of Israel and your theory of the Chosen People." I was aghast at the crudeness and stupidity of his remarks. I asked him publicly, "Have you ever seen a Jew before?" Of course, he had not. Out of respect for my colleagues at the conference, I refrained from pursuing the issue and asking the next question: Do you have any idea where Israel or Palestine is? I am sure that he would not have known, as he knew so very little of anything else.

Ambassador Chaim Herzog was right when he branded the document that issued recently from the Lima Conference of Third World Nations as anti-Semitic. One does not have to have a touch of Jewish paranoia to see in it all the classical signs of the Noah variety of *ḥamas*.

Perhaps I may be guilty of a little paranoia – but paranoiacs sometimes see the truth – when I detect a link between the young barbarians who taunted Lubavitcher Hasidim attending the funeral of one of their number who was killed this past holiday and called out, "Heil Hitler," and the older barbarians who gave that enthusiastic applause for Idi Amin, whose avowed idol is Adolf Hitler.

And consider how the Third World representatives tried to justify this obscene display. I wondered, when I read the remarks of the ambassador of Dahomey: What does he know about Israel or Zionism, except that his country and neighboring African countries have shown that they are ingrates to Israel, the country which first gave them the best help they ever got? I wonder more: What kind of self-defeating hatred is it that throws Africans into the Arab corner – when Africans, above all others, were the chief victims for centuries of the Arab slave trade which exploited and pillaged and raped their population?

It is a task not only of American diplomacy, press, and government, but of the public as well, to expose malice and violence and injustice and political vandalism and *ḥamas* of any kind when it is practiced by rich or poor, by former colonialists or by former colonies, by advanced or developing nations, by black or white.

Hence, we must give our unreserved praise and congratulations to the American ambassador to the United Nations, Dr. Daniel Moynihan, for his courageous telling of the truth in public about the Third World countries. It is not enough for us to send telegrams and letters to the president, congressmen, or senators when we are in opposition to any stand taken by the government. It is equally important that we notify our leadership when we are pleased with a stand that they have taken, such as that so ably articulated by Ambassador Moynihan.

Israel is today threatened from many quarters. Among them are the Arabs and the Third World countries. The Arabs represent the Jonah type of enmity, *ḥamas bekapeihem*, the "violence of the hand." The Third World nations embody the Noah type of enmity, *"vatimalei ha'aretz ḥamas,"* violence for its own sake.

I can foresee, in my more hopeful moments, that Arabs and Jews will someday achieve peace. The hatred of the Arabs for Israelis, though unjustified, is understandable on the grounds of a narrowly conceived self-interest. I can understand them in the way I can understand a criminal who wants things for himself. But I wonder how long, how very long, it will take for Jews or Israelis or any morally sensitive non-Jew to take up real friendship again with the Third World. Of course, in international affairs, friendships and loyalties come and go. But I refer specifically to those people who did the applauding – to those moral misfits, those malice-mongers of third-rate autocracies which constitute so much of the Third World, after the shameful demonstrations of this past week and month and year.

Sadly, this has proved to be a Noah kind of world, not a Jonah kind of world. According to the strictest canons of justice – the *middat hadin* – they are deserving of a cataclysmic, watery end, the flood all over again. Yet I remain hopeful. The Torah, after all, promised us that no more would such floods decimate the population of the world; that even if we deserved it, divine compassion would prevail.

But more than that, I am hopeful because of the words of David in the Psalms (29:10): "The Lord sat enthroned at the *mabul*, the flood, and the Lord will remain enthroned as King *le'olam*" – which means both "forever" and "for the world"; for the world will survive.

But its survival cannot remain forever that of the human jungle, which is worse than that of the animals – the jungle of *ḥamas* for its own sake. For the next verse must inevitably follow: "The Lord will give strength to His people, the Lord will bless His people – and all the world – with peace."

The Generation of the Tower and a Towering Generation[1]

In this *sidra* we read of the generation of Noah and the evil lives they led. Their punishment, as it is recorded in the Torah, was complete destruction – except for Noah and his family – in the great flood. Following that episode, we read of another generation following in the footsteps of the first. This is *Dor haHaflaga* – the Generation of the Tower. The people of this generation had evidently failed to learn from the tragic lesson that its predecessors had been taught. They were a people marked by arrogance and haughtiness.

The Torah does not describe merely poetic myths. We have substantial corroboration of that episode from the science of archeology. We know that the Mesopotamians of about 3,600–3,800 years ago began to dwell in big cities, and to build tremendous pagan temples in them. These temples were constructed as high towers as a sign of the equality of the builders with the pagan gods they worshiped. In their writings, some of which we still have, they boast of building into the

---

1. October 22, 1955.

heavens, even as is recorded in the *sidra*.[2] At the turn of the present century, the very tower of which the Bible speaks was discovered, in ruins, by a German archeological expedition. It was clearly an impressive and imposing structure. These tremendous towers expressed the desire of the Babylonians to imagine themselves a superior race, a *"herrenvolk."* Ultimately, the cities and the towers were destroyed, and all further construction was frustrated.

If you will reread the story of the tower, you will observe the terrific sarcasm with which the Torah describes the entire episode. Just one example: the name *Bavel* (or Babel or Babylon) given to that place by God. This is a sarcastic pun, as the Mesopotamians themselves called their city Babel because in their language the name was derived from the words *bab-ili*, meaning the Gate of the God – or in the plural, *bab-ilani*, the Gate of the Gods (hence: Babylon). However, in Hebrew the name *bavel* is similar to the root *b-l-l* which means: confusion. So the Torah tells us that what these mortals thought was the gate to their own divinity was nothing more than the confusion of their poor minds.

And yet, despite the sarcasm, bitterness, and ridicule which the Torah heaps upon the generation of the tower, the indictment of this generation is not complete. Just compare these two generations, that of the flood and that of the tower: the generation of the flood was, with the exception of Noah and his family, completely and utterly destroyed; the generation of the tower was not destroyed at all – it was merely punished by internal dissension and great exile and dispersion. Why is it that the generation of the tower was treated with such comparative leniency despite their sins of arrogance?

Our rabbis (Genesis Rabba 38:6) gave us the answer, based upon a clue in the Bible itself. Our Torah mentions that the whole world spoke one language, meaning of course that there was unity, cooperation, friendship. And therefore, "The generation of the flood, since they were steeped in theft, *lo nishtayra mehem peleita* – none of them remained. But the generation of the tower, since they loved each other, there remained from them a remnant."

---

2. See Umberto Cassuto, *MiNoaḥ ad Avraham* (Jerusalem: Magnes Press, 1953), for more information.

There is something that can be salvaged from the generation of the tower, something of lasting and permanent value, and that is: love, friendship. What our rabbis got from this episode of the generation of the tower was that every generation can become a towering generation if it learns to love; that even if people are arrogant and Godless and criminal, they can escape heavenly wrath if they will learn to love God's creatures. The only way of *nishtayra mehem peleita*, of surviving a world of coldness and treachery and mass-production and bold projects which obscure the individual, is through love.

It is told[3] that a Jew once asked his rabbi, "Why do we say *"lehayyim"* to our friends before reciting the blessing over wine or schnapps? Isn't it disrespectful to bless our neighbor before we bless God? The rabbi answered that the practice is valid since the Torah commands us to accept the mitzva of "Love your neighbor as yourself" (Leviticus 19:18) before it tells us, "Love the Lord your God" (Deuteronomy 6:5).

We frequently speak of the mitzva of neighborly love, and yet we usually fail to understand it – and therefore to practice it. The difficulty is a simple one: some people are simply unlovable. You ask me to have real affection for so-and-so? How can I, when I think he is repulsive? Or, how can I when I simply don't approve of him and what he thinks and what he does? I am critical of so many things about him, and I refuse to surrender the right to be critical of him; it is part of a man's rational makeup to be critical. And if I don't approve of him and have no emotional ties to him, how can I possibly observe the commandment to love him?

That is a good question, which you have no doubt thought of, and which we must be able to answer if we will ever succeed in making of ourselves, who have so many of the faults and evil traits of the generation of the tower, a towering generation – if we are to manage to survive as decent human beings and good Jews.

A most profound and adequate answer is the one suggested by that great German Jew, Rabbi Samson Raphael Hirsch. Hirsch makes the observation that regarding the verse, "Love your neighbor as *yourself*,"

---

3. See Louis I. Newman, *Hasidic Anthology* (Prague: Schocken Books, 1934), 223.

the Torah does *not* say "*Ve'ahavta et reiakha*," but "*lereiakha*," which is difficult to translate. But what does that actually mean? "*Et reiakha*" implies an emotional tie, a complete and uncritical love of your neighbor, which may be very good but is not usually possible. But "*lereiakha*" carries with it the meaning that you don't have to approve of him or anything he says or wants, but what is required is *empathy*, meaning: put yourself in his place, so that you will participate in his feelings, in whatever happens to him – that is *lereiakha*; share in what happens to him. If great good fortune happens to him – be happy for him, as if it happened to you. Don't begrudge it and don't be indifferent. If tragedy occurs to him – share his sorrow and feel it as if it happened to you – "*kamokha*." And when you can establish that identification and deeply participate in both his joys and his sorrows, then you will certainly be moved to increase the joys and alleviate the sorrows. You need agree to nothing he says and may even consider his personality faulty – but he is a human being with feelings and sensitivities, and the mitzva of neighborly love requires you to consider those feelings *as if they were your own.* The Torah asks nothing of us that is beyond our capabilities. It does not ask of us to be uncritical in accepting confidants or friends. It does not ask of us that we gush in sweetness over someone we loathe. It does say that no matter what our opinion of a person, we must have enough love in our souls that we feel not only *for* him – not only *sympathy*; but as if we *were* him – *empathy*.

This demand of the Torah that we practice neighborly love is not a demand to be an angel. It is a challenge to be human. Few of us find it possible to approve of any one person completely and uncriticaly. Few of us can form deep emotional attachments with everyone we know. But all of us were created in the image of God. And that means that we can practice neighborly love "*lereiakha*"; we can learn empathy, we can consider another's feelings as if they were our very own. For that is the meaning of the Torah's commandment – it is practicable, manly, and supremely human.

It is that and that alone which can make us the *peleita*, the survivors in this generation, which like the one mentioned in this *sidra*, is feverishly busy in building all kinds of structures and weapons and industries, and deriving therefrom the collective arrogance that makes us think we are supermen. The generation of the tower was a wicked one and therefore doomed to failure. But their one redeeming feature, love, is that which is able to make of us and every other generation a towering generation. May that be God's will.

Lekh Lekha

Barter, Contract, or Covenant?[1]

T he dominant theme of this *sidra*, treated in two separate episodes, is expressed in one word: *brit*. It is one of the most important words in the whole of the Jewish religious vocabulary.

Brit, in essence, means: religion. For *brit* implies a relationship between God and man, a state of mutuality, a dialogue. For those for whom God is nothing but an ideal, a principle, or some abstraction, not a living reality, it is absurd even to speak about *brit*. You can discuss *brit* only in the context of the Jewish tradition in which God is taken in the theistic sense as *Elohim hayyim* – a *living* God, One who engages the heart and mind of men. Similarly, the word "religion" derives from the old French and the Latin *relegare* – which means to bind fast, to hold tight. Thus, both words, *brit* and religion, imply the forging of a close bond between God and man. How an individual reacts to *brit*, how he conceives of it and approaches it, tells us all we need to know about the quality of his religious experience.

How then should we approach *brit*? In other words, how should we be religious? First, let us briefly say what *brit* should *not* come to mean

---

1. October 29, 1960.

45

to us. *Brit* should not mean merely, as it has come to mean for some people, a form of barter, a kind of religious bargain that one strikes with God. In this sense *brit* is merely a form of religious haggling or spiritual commerce, in which a man approaches God on a *quid-pro-quo* basis: I will give charity, You take care of my portfolio; I will fast on Yom Kippur, You provide me with health; I will recite the *Yizkor*, You take care of my family until the next such occasion. This is akin to paganism. Such a person acts as if Judaism and *brit* mean that in isolated moments and on rare occasions man comes close to God and makes a "fast deal" with Him. This is a distortion of the concept of *brit*, a vulgarization of religion – no matter how popular it is.

For others, *brit* means not barter but contract. The contract interpretation of *brit* does not limit the meeting with God to rare occasions. It understands that the dialogue between God and man must be an ongoing one – but it is only an ongoing contract. It shares the same misunderstandings, the same basic fallacies, as does the barter or bargain interpretation of *brit*. Its underlying mood is a religious commercialism, a kind of trade. Its unspoken presupposition is that man acts in certain decent ways only because in this manner he will receive certain rewards from God. Now, while it is true that we believe in reward for virtue and ultimate punishment for vice, still we have never based our religious experience squarely upon this concept. Our rabbis taught us that we should "not be like servants who serve the Master only on condition that they receive reward" (*Avot* 1:3). The contract interpretation is more advanced than the barter interpretation, but it is not good enough.

The true, the highest interpretation of *brit* is that of covenant. The covenant in the sense that I mean it here does not deny reward and punishment. There are terms and conditions in a covenant – but they are not its essence. The clauses are affirmed, but they are irrelevant to the major meaning of *brit*.

Exactly what is the nature of covenant-*brit*? What should be the ideal Jewish religious experience? Let us turn to our *sidra* and investigate, first, the two situations in which the Torah speaks of *brit*.

The first is the "*brit bein habetarim*," "the covenant between the pieces." As God was about to seal the covenant with Abram, Abram took three animals, a goat, a heifer, and a ram, split them each in half, and separated the halves from each other. Then, in a prophetic vision, he beheld a flame passing between the pieces. At this occasion, God gave Abram *havtahat ha'aretz*, the promise that He would give him or his descendants a special land – the land of Israel – which would be his.

The second occasion in which our *sidra* speaks of *brit* is *brit mila*, the covenant of circumcision. God commands Abram to circumcise himself and all his male children to be born thereafter on the eight day of their life. At this occasion, God gives Abram *havtahat hazera*, the promise that he will be survived by children and children's children who will become a great people.

These two episodes tell us a world about the whole Jewish conception of religion.

First, the covenant between the pieces. One of the most profound interpretations of this mysterious rite was provided by one of the last of the great Jewish medieval philosophers, Rabbi Joseph Albo, in his *Sefer haIkkarim*. The cleaving of the animals' bodies, says Albo, was a profound symbol that just as one-half of a body cannot live without the other, so are the two parties to the covenant inextricably bound up with each other in an indissoluble bond, saying that henceforth, one will find existence impossible and unthinkable without the other. Man cannot exist without God, and while God can certainly exist without man, He *needs* man to fulfill the purpose of creation. Without man, the whole drama of God's creation is, in the words of Shakespeare, "full of sound and fury signifying nothing." So the covenant between the pieces taught man, and especially Israel, that the relationship with God must be intensely personal, intimate, one of deep communion; so bound together as to be indivisible.

It is appropriate that at the sealing of this covenant, God should have given Abram the the promise of the land. For God chose the land and willed to have His spirit dwell therein and when Israel chooses to pioneer in it, to settle it and live in it and hope for it and dream for it, then the land is a bridge uniting God and Israel. The first episode, then, teaches us that the dialogue between God and man, though it is one between subordinate and superior, must be one of deep, indissoluble intimacy.

Only with this kind of covenant, with this kind of understanding of *brit* or religion, can man survive in this lonely universe. Only thus will man not shrivel up in utter, terrifying solitude. When the metaphysician or philosopher speaks of the "First Cause," or the "Prime Mover," that is not the God of Abram, the God of the covenant between the pieces. When we intone "Father in heaven" at an invocation, we are still far from the God of the *brit*. When, however, we recognize that God is not only in heaven, but that He is here and now, that our destinies are linked and our fates intertwined, then we are coming close to the God of the covenant of Abram. Rabbi Samson Raphael Hirsch correctly pointed out that one of the differences between the Greek and the Hebrew conceptions of God is that, while the Greeks had a sophisticated view of God, only Israel was able to use such expressions as *Eloheinu* or *Eli* – "our God," "my God." The possessive case reflects the intimacy, the indivisibility of God and man. Perhaps even more expressive than the Hebrew is the Yiddish word "*Gottenyu*," that deeply affectionate yet reverent expression of the Jew's closeness to his God.

Allow me to present a brief prayer that I recently found, a prayer both simple and beautiful, naïve and elegant, recited by the busy and harried mother of a great Jewish scholar – Rabbi Abraham Abele Gumbiner, the seventeenth-century author of the famous commentary on the Jewish Code of Law called the *Magen Avraham*. Every morning his mother would recite the following words: "*Gut morgen, Gottenyu! Ich hab nisht kein tzeit lang tzu balamutchen, ich darf aheim gein geben essen mein Avrehme'ele, er zal haben koyach tzu lernen Dein heilige Torah. Aguten tag, Gottenyu!*" Translated loosely from the Yiddish, this means "Good morning, my God! I have no time for long discussions, I must go home to feed my little Abraham so that he should have enough strength to study Your Holy Torah. Good day, my God!"

Here you have that profoundly human intimacy with the Deity – that is the God of the covenant between the pieces.

The second quality is revealed in *brit mila*. The covenant must not only be one of closeness, of oneness of God and man, but it must also be eternally binding. Thus, circumcision became the *ot brit* – the sign of the covenant. Just as the *ot*, the sign, is cut into the human flesh and is permanent, indelible, and irrevocable, so the *brit* itself, the covenant, is eternally binding. Abraham's descendants are forever committed to God and Torah – permanent, indelible, and irrevocable. *Brit mila* tells us that God and Israel are forever pledged to each other, that there can be no commutation of the terms of the covenant and no change in the relationship of the parties to each other. That is why at this time God gave Abraham the promise that he would be survived through the ages by children and children's children. For if the covenant is eternal, there must be a Jewish people to continue as one of the parties of that covenant.

That is why a father on the eight day of his son's life, at the circumcision, makes the blessing, "Blessed are You who has commanded us *lehakhniso*, to enter this child into the covenant of our father Abraham." "*Lehakhniso*" – "to enter him," and not to seal a new covenant; for it is the old and ancient covenant of Abraham with God that preexists. We are only continuing the covenant with this child, as a sign of its permanent and irrevocable character.

It is this that separates Torah Judaism from all other varieties. We cannot agree that every age is free to choose from the covenant what it wishes. We cannot agree that in every generation people may accept what they wish and reject what they do not like. We cannot agree that man can at his own discretion and by his own whim deny what he wishes to deny of the covenant. The *brit* is indelible and unchangeable.

It is this that makes us gasp with astonishment when parents of a child will move heaven and earth to provide their child with a proper circumcision, and yet six or seven or eight years later, they will refuse to provide a proper Jewish education for that child, maintaining, "Let him choose for himself!" Here they affirmed the unchanging and irrevocable character of the covenant, and only a few years later they will let the precocious youngster choose for himself!

It is this that provides an analysis of the problem that plagues the new generation of Israelis – as it does the new generation of American Jews. Only this past week, the prime minister of Israel, in opening the new session of the Knesset, complained of the lack of idealism that prevails among the new generation. They lack, he said, true patriotism for the Holy Land. They lack a sense of historical continuity with their people.

Mr. Ben-Gurion spoke well. But he has done nothing more than describe the symptoms. What is the cause? What is the pathogenesis of this disease?

Perhaps someday Mr. Ben-Gurion will appreciate our diagnosis. And it is this: A generation or two ago, many Jews rebelled, they denied the *brit*. And so the oneness of Israel with God began to fall apart. When we have denied the oneness of the covenant, the element of *brit bein habetarim*, then we must expect that there should be a weakening of *havtahat ha'aretz* – the loyalty of both God and Israel to *Eretz*, the land of Israel. When we renege on our pledge, God reneges on His.

And secondly, when that generation rebelled against the *brit*, they denied the eternally binding character of Torah, they rejected the principle of the continuation of the relationship of God and people. Therefore, they must expect that God is not bound to His *havtahat hazera*, to His commitment that our people will continue as a historical unit throughout the ages.

If the founders of modern Israel, including the prime minister, want to know why they have failed in matters of *eretz* and *zera*, it is because of their own attitude to the *brit*, to the Jewish religion.

There is one last aspect that I wish to discuss: as partners to the covenant we are bound not as individuals, but as a people. In this *sidra*, God tells Abraham, "I will make of you a great nation." We are bound to each other as the seed of Abraham, our father. Therefore, one Jew is to another a brother or sister. We must remember not only the first two aspects, but also the third: our bond to our fellow Jews. We are the people of the covenant. With our God we are linked indivisibly; our covenant with Him continues eternally; with our fellow Jews, let us always act fraternally.

"And as for Me, this is My covenant with them, says the Lord. My spirit that is upon you and My words that I have placed in your mouth, they shall not depart from your mouth and from the mouths of your children, and from the mouths of your children's children, says the Lord, from now and forevermore" (Isaiah 59:21).

Down the Up Staircase[1]

For over a thousand years, the weekly Torah portions have been known by their present names with only minor changes. According to the Lubavitcher Rebbe,[2] these titles are "Torah names," headings to which the Torah gives special significance, for they somehow reveal the inner essence of the whole of the *sidra*.

This Torah portion is called *Lekh Lekha*, which means, "Get thee out," be active and move. Literally, the idiom means, "Go to yourself," return to your spiritual identity, climb up the ladder to spiritual heights, reach your own soul in your ascent. A Jew must never be static. He must be dynamic and progressive in his service of the Lord, in moving himself and history in the direction of God. This, then, is the essence of all that is related in this *sidra*. Thus, we read of how Abram goes to the land of Israel. He is not traveling as a sightseeing tourist with first-class accommodations. His journey is a symbolic conquest. As Nachmanides points out, Abram's journeys in Canaan prefigured the Jewish possession of the

---

1. October 30, 1971.
2. Discourse on *Lekh Lekha*, 5731 (1970).

51

land by actual possession when he staked out the territory. All of this is part of Abram's "going," his *lekh lekha*.

However, there are several important incidents which spell not progress but decline. The foremost failure or setback is the verse: "And there was famine in the land and Abram went down to Egypt" (Genesis 12:10). This is not merely an incidental decision to change residence. Psychologically, it was a major crisis for Abram. He had left Canaan with the divine promise, "I shall make you into a great nation and I shall bless you." Some blessing! He had just come to Canaan, and instead of bringing with him prosperity, he had become the harbinger of hunger, and he was already fleeing the land.

What a disappointment – history's first *oleh* had become history's first *yored*.

Religiously, too, Abram's descent to Egypt was frustrating, almost abortive of his whole mission. His journey to Canaan was meant to be a *kiddush Hashem*, an act of sanctifying the divine Name by making the one God available and accessible to humans. The Midrash compares the situation to an open box of incense. If it stands in a corner, no one can smell it and it is of no use. But if you take it and move it about in the middle of the room, then your motion causes the odor to be wafted and to benefit all who are present. So God said to Abram: "Move yourself from place to place in Canaan, and thus will your name be made great in the world" – and through your reputation will the divine Name be sanctified and the divine message be known. The journey to Canaan was to be the launching of Abram's religious career. However, if Abram "went down" to Egypt, that canceled out his mission and vitiated his message.

Domestically, this descent to Egypt was the cause of many troubles for Abram. For in Egypt there took place the abduction of Sara – she was kidnapped and taken into the harem of Pharaoh. So our *sidra* relates troubles as well as triumphs.

And, spiritually and historically as well, we are faced with problems in this *sidra*. We know the principle that our rabbis laid down, *"Ma'aseh avot siman levanim"* – the deeds of the fathers are the symbol of the recurring patterns in the lives of their children. But some Jewish teachers, especially Hasidim, taught that this does not mean only that the lives of the patriarchs were symbolic of the historic patterns of their descendants, but that the patriarchs actually participated in the history that came after them, that their actions were the commencement of Jewish history. Therefore, "And Abram went down to Egypt" means not only that Abram's descent to Egypt was a historic symbol of the later Egyptian exile, but that it was in some way itself the beginning of that terrible and bitter exile.

If that is the case, and such were the blows suffered by Abram and Sara, how can we account for the name *Lekh Lekha*, which indicates progress, growth, and advancement?

The answer provided for us by the Lubavitcher Rebbe is, in essence, this: Sometimes descent is for the purpose of ascent; often you must go down in order to go up to an even higher level than that at which you began. Some failures are merely temporary; they are the future successes in disguise. Sometimes the setback is instrumental to later success. Often you must retreat in order to move on, in which case the retreat is preparatory and part of progress and advance.

Therefore, "*Vayered Avram Mitzrayma*," Abram's going down to Egypt, led to and was part of "*Vaya'al Avram miMitzrayim*," Abram's going up again from Egypt. His going down was part and for the purpose of his later going up.

Even Sara's abduction to the harem of Pharaoh served such a function. One of the great Hasidic teachers has taught us that Sara's chaste conduct in the court of Pharaoh was so exemplary that it became the model for Jewish conduct through the centuries of exile in foreign lands. The descendants of Sara, inspired by her model, refused to assimilate. They did not permit the purity of their faith be defiled, they protected the honor of their *emuna* in God.

And so it is with the redemption from Egypt. Bad as the exile was, the positive values of the redemption were even greater. The Torah tells us that when the Israelites left Egypt, they took with them "*rekhush gadol*," great wealth. Our kabbalistic tradition maintains that this wealth was not only or even primarily material, but that it was spiritual: they took out from Egypt the "*nitzotzot hakedusha*," "the lost sparks of sanctity" embedded in Egyptian culture. By this they meant to say that despite the corruption of Egypt, there were some aspects which one might consider divine or of enduring value, and that these "sparks" were not condemned to destruction with Egypt. They were redeemed by Israel who learned them from the Egyptians and, by taking them along with them, preserved them forever.

So *"vayered"* is part of *"vaya'al,"* the descent leading to the ascent is all part of *lekh lekha*, of general progress. Or, to use a metaphor more familiar to us from the popular literature of recent years, sometimes you go down, but it is only going "down the up staircase"; your decline is merely a part of the procedure of ultimate ascent. So it is with our national life. Joseph was sold by his brothers into slavery. At the time Joseph, and later all the brothers, thought that this event was an unmitigated disaster. But, as Joseph later told them when he revealed his identity to them, "The agony of my slavery was part of the divine plan to save the entire family now." He went down – but it was on the up staircase, which led even higher.

Or, to take a more recent case: In 1947, British Foreign Secretary Bevin refused to issue 100,000 visas to Jewish refugees languishing in camps in Europe and Cyprus. How grief-stricken we all were! We were facing a blank wall. Yet we now appreciate that had he issued these visas, the pressure for independence would have been severely reduced, and perhaps a million or two million other Jewish immigrants would never be living today in the State of Israel. It was descent for the purpose of ascent.

The same is true with the State of Israel today. Often we are plunged into a gray mood when we consider our international and even internal situation. The constant attrition, the state of no-war-no-peace, the ever-impending threat of greater warfare involving the great powers, the increasing isolation of Israel from neutrals and friends – all this is not calculated to encourage great cheer on behalf of those who love Israel. Nevertheless, we must never permit ourselves to lose our sense of balance. We are only humans, and therefore our perspectives are limited. Even we, in our present situation, can begin to appreciate that quite possibly our present situation is the best of all, that the alternatives may be far worse, that what is happening at the present may be propaedeutic to something much greater, much nobler, much happier. Our present descent may well be part of an ultimate ascent. May God grant that!

And the same holds true for personal life. Life is full of crises. No human being can be spared trauma in his existence. If we lose heart and are discouraged and become crushed, then our pessimism is a self-fulfilling prophecy. We lose sight of opportunities, and we almost wish ourselves into a plunging descent. But if we look at our situation as descent for the sake of ascent, if we adopt a more sanguine attitude, then our optimism becomes self-fulfilling as it sensitizes us to the creative possibilities in descent. So let us leave the pessimistic views to the anti-Semites. Recall what Zeresh, wife of Haman, told him when his star began to dim: "If Mordecai, before whom you have begun to fall, is one of the children of the Jews, then you shall not prevail over him but you will fall completely" (Esther 6:13). There was a descent which was permanent. Jews must take a different attitude. For ourselves we must learn to endure the descent as integral to the ascent, as but a temporary setback, preparation for a greater rise.

How often has a middle-aged man, suffering a heart attack, been told by his physician: How lucky you are! This is a warning which may well save your life and prolong it. The same is true for business or professional or academic setbacks. It may be a warning, it may save us from more disastrous adventures, it may teach us something whereby we will better be able to attain our ultimate goal.

This message is not simplistic, unrealistic, or happy-go-lucky. On the contrary, I am pleading for a more sophisticated and higher realism: the confidence and rational understanding that, caught in crisis, man is often prone to depression because he takes an overly dim view, because he is limited emotionally and his vision is therefore curbed; the knowledge that life is never all up or all down, but a series of zigzags – and he never knows when he is zigging or zagging; the faith that while our own personal perspective is limited, that we can only begin to discern events and their true proportions in retrospect but never in prospect, that from the perspective of God what seems to us like descent is really for the purpose of ascent. Because we are so affected personally by our own situation, we tend to exaggerate, and we do not know that we are doing so or in what measure. In the depths, it is hard to realize that you have gone down in order to go up. But it is an act of faith – and intelligence as well.

So, *Lekh Lekha*, both by content and by name, leaves us with this encouraging message: If we suffer, whether it be illness, financial

55

reverses, or any form of domestic misery or loneliness or frustration, remember "descent for the purpose of ascent." I do not mean that things will *always* get better, but they often do, little as we expect it. Let us then not despair. Let each of us, in his or her own situation, bear this in mind – not as a palliative or peace-of-mind preachment, but as part of *emuna*, part of Jewish faith.

Then it will be true of us, as it was said of Abram in this *sidra*: "And he (Abram) believed in the Lord, and He accounted to him as *tzedaka*, as righteousness" (Genesis 15:6). By this is meant that God considered Abram's faith as a special act of righteousness. But the word "*tzedaka*" derives from the word meaning "justice." We might therefore translate the verse as: "And Abram believed in the Lord, and God accredited it to him and justified his faith."

When we will have faith that the downturn is part of an up-going, that the descent is for the ascent, and that faith will prove *tzedaka*, our confidence will be vindicated and justified, and indeed *aloh na'aleh*.

The call of *Lekh Lekha*, of climbing ever higher, will be ours to achieve.

The Shield of Abraham[1]

In the very first revelation to Abraham, God promises the patriarch: "And I will make of you a great nation, and I will bless you, and make your name great; and be a [source of] blessing" (Genesis 12:2).

The Talmud (*Pesaḥim* 117b) identified the four elements in this verse in a most unusual yet familiar way. The benediction, they said, refers to the *Shemoneh Esreh* prayer, and the promise was that henceforth and for all time the name of God was to be linked with Abraham, with his son, and with his grandson. So the rabbis said, "'And I will make of you a great nation' refers to the expression [in the *Shemoneh Esreh*], 'God of Abraham'; 'And I will bless you' refers to the expression, 'God of Isaac'; and 'I will make your name great' refers to the expression, 'God of Jacob.'" Thus it is that in the very beginning of our *Shemoneh Esreh* we bless God who is "God of Abraham, God of Isaac, and God of Jacob."

However, there is yet a fourth element in that promise, the final one, namely, "And be a [source of] blessing." What does this mean? To this the Talmud gave the following answer: "One might think that because the name of God is linked to all three patriarchs, therefore the

---

1. November 11, 1967.

57

conclusion of the blessing would similarly include all three patriarchs. Therefore God says to Abraham, 'Be a [source of] blessing,' to indicate that the conclusion of the blessing would mention only the name of Abraham and not the name of his son Isaac or his grandson Jacob. Thus it is that the 'seal' of the first blessing of the nineteen of the *Shemoneh Esreh* is, *'Magen Avraham,'* 'Blessed are You, God, Shield of Abraham.'"

What a strange remark! We can understand Abraham's joy at knowing that his child and grandchild would, like him, be bound up with the divine Name. Who of us would not give all he has if he could be assured that his children and grandchildren would follow in his footsteps of loyalty to God? But what is astonishing is the implication that Abraham does not want to share the limelight with his own progeny, that he wishes to reserve the choicest part of the blessing exclusively for himself. Does this mean that Abraham was a spiritual egotist? Did not our rabbis teach us that a father is not jealous of the achievements of his son and a teacher does not envy the attainments of his students (*Sanhedrin* 105b)?

An answer to this question is offered by the great Rabbi of Kotzk, who reinterprets the entire talmudic passage. He maintains that it does not at all refer to the living personalities of Abraham, Isaac, and Jacob, but rather to the values which they symbolize in the Jewish tradition. Abraham has always been the symbol of *ḥesed*, of charity or love. It is he who prays even for the wicked men of Sodom; it is he who demonstrates noble generosity toward Lot; it is he who extends himself for Hagar. Isaac symbolizes *avoda*, service. This term encompasses both sacrifices and prayer – Isaac was the sacrifice in the great *Akeida*, and it was he whom his bride Rebecca first met while he was praying. Finally, Jacob is representative of the quality of Torah, for he is described as "one who dwells in the tents" – and our tradition has identified these tents as the tents of Torah, the schools.

Therefore, when we say in our *Shemoneh Esreh* that we praise God who is the God of Abraham and of Isaac and of Jacob, we are offering a symbolic affirmation of the mishna (*Avot* 1:2) that the world rests on three great principles: on the study of Torah, on service (prayer), and on the doing of good deeds. These represent, in reverse order, Abraham, Isaac, and Jacob.

Yet – and this is the climax of the blessing according to the interpretation of the Kotzker Rebbe – the greatest of all these qualities, the most preeminent of these three sublime Jewish principles, the one which alone can lead us out of exile into redemption and is therefore the most redemptive of all, is *gemilut ḥasadim*, the doing of good deeds, symbolized by Abraham. Thus, when the rabbis quote God as saying to Abraham that only he, Abraham, would be present in the seal of the blessing, they meant that deeds of kindness are superior to study and to prayer as Jewish qualities. Hence, when we bless God who is "the Shield of Abraham," we affirm in the form of prayer that *gemilut ḥasadim* is greater than the other two.

Now, this is a beautiful and satisfying explanation – but not satisfying enough. For to assert that the doing of good deeds is accorded greater value in the Jewish tradition than either Torah or prayer is to violate the spirit of the mishna which tells us clearly that the world rests on three principles – a statement which implies the equality of all three values. A world, like a tripod table, is unstable and wobbly if one leg is longer than the other two.

I would therefore venture the following modification of the Kotzker's interpretation of the talmudic passage. All three values are equal in essence, in content. However – and this is the whole point of the *aggada* – each of these three must be expressed and effectuated in a manner of *gemilut ḥasadim*. It is possible to practice Torah and service and good deeds in a way that is crude and ungracious; and it is possible to endow the same three acts with the seal of *ḥesed*, with love and with warmth. When, therefore, we mention only the name of Abraham in the seal of the blessing, as "the Shield of Abraham," what we are saying is that all three qualities, represented by the three patriarchs, must find their final form or expression, their seal, in the manner symbolized by Abraham: *ḥesed*. Take service, for instance. It is possible to offer up our service, or prayer, in a very ordinary manner: dry, dessicated, formal, and deadly boring. But it is also possible to express service in the form of *ḥesed*, to seal our prayer with love and with charm, by offering up our inner participation, our warmth, our passion.

An English poet once wrote that prayer must be –

The motion of a hidden fire
That trembles in the breast.
Prayer is the burden of a sigh,
The falling of a tear,
The upward glancing of an eye
When none but God is near.

I think this helps us define what is meant by prayer expressed as *gemilut hasadim*. I do not believe that this kind of loving service, this kind of prayer with charm, can possibly survive in an atmosphere of spiritual discourtesy where neighborly conversation takes precedence over the dialogue with God, where prayer is punctuated by the exchange of information about fashions, about the stock market, or about real estate deals.

I know very well that there are those who are irritated with such admonitions from the pulpit. They maintain that a dose of whispering and conversation is important in order to preserve the quality they refer to as *heimishkeit*. But let us make it clear: there are two kinds of *heimishkeit* – one, when you bring your home into the synagogue, when you introduce into the sanctuary the spirit of the dining room and the living room and the office; and the second, when you take the spirit of the House of God and bring it into your own apartment and residence and place of business. The first kind we can certainly do without. It develops into rudeness and crudeness. It is the second which is truly *heimishkeit*, and which brings with it the possibilities of prayer in the form or seal of *gemilut hasadim*. To practice the first kind of *heimishkeit* is to strip the service of any kind of *hesed*, and in effect to break to smithereens the Shield of Abraham.

Torah, too, can be expressed with or without the quality of *gemilut hasadim*. How unfortunate when the principles of Torah, its halakhot, are dispensed as if they were programmed in a computer within the cranium and can be effected merely by pushing a mental button without regard for those to whom they are directed. Torah taught in such a manner, decisions of halakha offered in such a spirit, is a violation of the principle of *hesed*. The Torah itself is described in the Torah as "*Befikha uvelevavekha la'asoto*," "It is in your mouth and in your heart to do it." If we of the Torah community want Torah to be practiced in real life, *la'asoto*, then we must make sure that we know how to articulate it graciously, *befikha*, and that we know how to apply it charitably, taking into consideration the fears and the aspirations and the hopes and the sensitivities of *uvelevavekha*, the heart of each and every one of those to whom we speak. A teaching of Torah is often rejected if it is presented in an authoritarian manner, with negativism and obvious unconcern for people. Yet the same principle when enunciated with *ḥesed*, with warmth and humility and compassion, will not only be accepted but even admired.

And this is true not only of a proclamation of Torah, but also of the response to it by people of Torah. If sometimes we are unhappy with a decision, and we have good reason to oppose it, let us do so – but always charitably, graciously, with *ḥesed*. One of our problems is that in our Orthodox communal controversies – and there is nothing wrong with controversy as such – the level of our debate has not been high enough. We must get rid of the strident accents of our public discourse. We must do away with the bellicose posturing and the ubiquitous belligerence that have tended to corrupt serious dialogue within the Orthodox community. Our expression of our opinions of Torah must be done with a healthy dose of *ḥesed*.

Thus, in commenting on the verse in Proverbs, "The Torah of *ḥesed* is upon her tongue" (31:26), the rabbis ask (*Sukka* 49b), Is there, then, a Torah of *ḥesed* and a Torah without *ḥesed*? And they answer, Yes, a Torah without *ḥesed* is the Torah one studies but does not teach, whereas a Torah of *ḥesed* is when one is successful both in learning and in teaching. What they meant is that one can become a great scholar even without *ḥesed*, but without this "seal" he never can be successful in transmitting what he knows to others, for they will never accept it: *lo hakapdan melamed* – a man who is stingy and strict and ungenerous can never be a teacher. It is only when one has the quality of *ḥesed* that he can be successful in imparting his knowledge and in persuading others to accept the point of view and the whole spirit of Torah.

This holds true not only for Torah in its formal religious sense, but for any principle to which we are deeply committed. In our times, for instance, our country is split down the middle in very serious dissent on questions of life and death, questions of war and peace, questions of poverty and wealth, questions of civil rights and their absence. The entire population is polarized as it has rarely been before in the living memory of most of us. Now, dissent is not bad for a democracy; it may even be very good. Only a short while ago we were complaining that the college population seemed to be asleep and insensitive to the great issues of the day. But dissent, too, must be performed in an atmosphere of *ḥesed*. When dissent becomes unruly and crude, then it reflects unworthily on the principle of dissent itself. When college students wish to make their opinions known in opposition to the government, that is a healthy sign of a vigorous democracy. But when their dissent is expressed in discourtesy to a secretary of state or a secretary of defense, if there is no *ḥesed* in their souls, no respect for the right of the so-called Establishment to have its own opinions, then that dissent becomes dangerous and reprehensible.

Finally, the most interesting aspect of this interpretation is the conclusion that *gemilut ḥasadim* itself must be expressed in the form of *ḥesed*! Even kindness must be conveyed in a kind manner. One can give alms to the poor in such a manner that he sustains the body yet destroys the soul of the poor man by humiliation. It is possible to lend a man money without taking any interest, seemingly an example of *gemilut ḥasadim* – but if in doing so you embarrass him and take a part of his heart away from him, there is no *ḥesed* in such good deeds.

In our own society it is not usual for the donor to give his contribution directly to the recipient. It is usually done through an agency or an institution for which other individuals solicit gifts. No wonder the rabbis say that the solicitor performs a greater mitzva than the contributor – for all too often, alas, the solicitor is met with an attitude which is most discouraging. If I give, whether I give much or little, even if I do not give at all, at least I must do so in a manner of *ḥesed*, with grace and with charm. The solicitor is here to help me perform a mitzva; he should not be the butt of my resentment. If I only give, that reveals an intellectual decision. But if I give with *ḥesed*, it reveals my character and personality. Merely to give, but to do so gruffly, means that I am more of a *gomel* than one who practices *ḥasadim*. Both components are necessary – at all times.

Let us therefore learn how to express all three great values, those of Torah and service and *gemilut ḥasadim*, in the way that Abraham would have wished: in the way of *ḥesed*, as taught to him by Almighty God, the Shield of Abraham.

Having learned this, we shall then be able to turn to the Almighty Himself and ask of Him not only that He deal with us kindly, but that this kindness itself be expressed in a form of graciousness; not only that He be a *gomel ḥasadim* to His people Israel, but that He be a *gomel ḥasadim tovim le'amo Yisrael* – that He perform *good* acts of kindness toward His people Israel.

Vayera

Putting a Bad Conscience to Good Use[1]

Thﬁe story of the *Akeida* is, together with the revelation at Sinai, the central event in Jewish history and religion. One of the most remarkable aspects of this episode is the one word by which Abraham accepts upon himself this historic trial and its mental agonies and spiritual sufferings. God called to him, "Abraham!" and, in magnificent simplicity, the response is forthcoming: "*Hineini*," "Behold, here I am," or, "I am ready" (Genesis 22:1).

One of the commentators, Rabbi Abraham ben haRambam – the only son of Maimonides – emphasizes the quality of this response by contrasting it to that of Adam. He writes, "How great the difference between Abraham who answered the divine call with the word '*hineini*,' and Adam who, when God called out to him, 'Where are you?' answered, 'I saw that I was naked and so I hid.'"

Now this comparison is somewhat disturbing. The answer of Adam is, after all, the response of a human being pursued by God who demands an explanation for a terrible failure, whereas Abraham's response is to a divine call not necessarily connected with any human

---

1. October 29, 1966.

offense. Is this not an invidious comparison? Is not Abraham great enough in his own right without seeking to enhance his reputation at the expense of his grandfather Adam?

I believe the answer I wish to offer not only justifies the comment of Rabbi Abraham ben haRambam, but has the widest ramifications both for a proper understanding of the Bible and for our own lives. This answer is that both men – Adam and Abraham – were, in a sense, being reprimanded!

The story of the *Akeida* begins with the words, "And it came to pass after these things." What things? asked the rabbis (Genesis Rabba 55:4). In their answer they indicate that the words of the Bible imply some severe introspection. The *Akeida* took place, they say, after *hirhurei devarim*, deep meditation and self-analysis by Abraham. Abraham, according to the rabbis, was troubled. He had a bad conscience which caused these *hirhurei devarim*, these introspective sessions. The *Akeida* was a kind of punishment, and it was brought on by Abraham's errors.

What is it that troubled Abraham? There are several interpretations (see Genesis Rabba 55). One of them (a midrash cited in *Kav haYashar*) refers to the special celebration arranged by Abraham in honor of the weaning of his son Isaac. The Bible refers to that party as "*mishteh gadol*," a great feast. Our tradition maintains that the greatness of this banquet was due to the guests who attended: "*Gedolim hayu sham*" – a party which was attended by all the giants of the time. Shem attended, Eber was there, Og was one of the guests – all the crowned heads of the ancient Near East were at the great party that Abraham prepared. But this is precisely where the trouble lay: only the *gedolim*, the great ones, were there; but there was no mention of *ketanim*, small people, ordinary human beings, the poor, and the marginal and the unwanted. Certainly Abraham, who was renowned for his hospitality over all else, should have known enough that at his personal *simḥa* he ought to have as major participants also the poor and the rejected. Abraham's conscience troubled him; had he not contributed to a subtle transformation and dangerous degradation from hospitality to mere entertainment? For this should be an occasion for the uplifting of downtrodden spirits, not the name-dropping of high and exalted personages.

But whatever occasioned Abraham's troubled conscience, it was responsible for the *Akeida* episode. So that the divine call to Abraham was a conscience-call. What Rabbi Abraham ben haRambam meant, then, was that both Adam and Abraham responded to the call of a bad conscience – Adam for the eating of the forbidden fruit, and Abraham for his omissions at the feast – but that is where the comparison ends. When it comes to the responses of these two individuals: "How great the difference!"

When Adam sinned and heard God calling him, he said, "I heard Your voice in the garden"; in the underbrush of his mind there takes place the rustling of a primitive conscience. "I saw that I was naked"; there is a sudden awareness of his nakedness, of shame and disgrace. And so what does he do? "And so I hid"; he withdraws, hides himself, denies that he did anything wrong. He runs away and, when confronted by God, blames his wife or the serpent...

How different is Abraham! God calls him and his response is: "*Hineini*," "Here I am!" I am willing to harness my bad conscience to a good use. I am ready to go through an *akeida*, to overcome the past by creative achievement in the future, teaching the world the real meaning of faith and the lengths to which one must go in order to uphold it. Rashi tells us that the word *hineini* implies both *anava*, and *zimun* – it is the language of both meekness and preparedness. Indeed, it is the language of meekness because it reveals a bad conscience, and it is the language of preparedness because Abraham is ready to do something about it. He is ready to take the bad conscience and make good use of it.

So the difference between Adam and Abraham is in what to do with a bad conscience: whether to hide or to use it. And what a difference there is between them! A bad conscience irritates the mind and the heart, until that bad conscience is either repressed or converted into something creative and constructive. It is much like the grain of sand that is either expelled by the oyster from under its shell, or transformed into a shiny and precious pearl.

This example of Abraham has been repeated at chosen moments throughout history. The Nobel prizes which were awarded recently offer such an example. Alfred Nobel is a man who gave a fortune for awards to those who contribute to the advancement of peace in the world. Why did he do this? It was an effort to overcome his bad conscience for having created dynamite and made war more destructive. Many of the greatest Torah scholars in our history were people who brought to their spiritual and intellectual endeavors a special passion that arose from the knowledge of having strayed in their youth.

The same holds true for philanthropy. I knew a man who was very generous in his endowments of various communal institutions. As so often happens, others begrudged him this mitzva. They pointed to certain incidents in his past which were not luminous examples of all the great virtues. What should be the Jewish reaction? It should be: marvelous! God bless that man! The greatest communal institutions were built by people who knew how to use a bad conscience and convert it to good use. Hospitals, schools, synagogues, welfare institutions of all kinds, are the products of people who have learned from Abraham to take their *hirhurei devarim* and use it to say *"hineini"* to the call of God. And who, after all, is there who is so saintly that he never has an occasion for a bad or troubled conscience? On the contrary, any man or woman who honestly feels that he or she has no bad conscience at all should have a bad conscience for being so insensitive as not to have a bad conscience! Would we rather a man have no conscience at all, that he be a moral idiot? Would we rather he be like Adam who responds only with "and so I hid" – that he deny his past, that he evade his responsibility? Certainly the transformation of guilt into philanthropy has a respectable precedent in the *hineini* of Abraham.

The State of Israel was built by Western democracies reacting to a bad conscience of cosmic dimensions: insensitivity to Jewish suffering under Hitler and the turning away of Jewish refugees from the shores of Palestine. But finally the democracies learned, in however small a measure, to put their bad conscience to good use and not to oppose the founding of the state. Of course, the good use that ultimately resulted can in no way equal the enormity of the crime which the nations witnessed in silence; but at least it was better than the kind of reaction of which Adam is the stereotype.

The history of Christianity toward the Jews is a historic disgrace. Any sensitive human being who happens to be Christian ought to go through life with a bad conscience because of his religion. So that when the Catholic Ecumenical Council offers a declaration concerning the

Jews which puts us in a somewhat better light than has been true in the past, or when Billy Graham and his Evangelists announce, as they did this past week, that they apologize to the Jews – this is an attempt, which although only partially successful and inadequate, and disregarding for a moment some of the subtle implications of which we must be aware, is at least an attempt to make good use of a bad conscience.

To some extent, though not completely, even American Jewry's support of the State of Israel – whether the UJA, or the yeshivot, or other institutions – is a form of expression of a bad conscience. Many American Jews feel that we were safe during World War II while our fellow Jews suffered. After 1948 there was a State of Israel ready to receive us, yet we have not gone nor have many of us sent our children to settle there. If we feel a troubled conscience, that is a good and healthy sign, for it ought to be troubled! But we have learned how to put that bad conscience to good use – and that is in our unfailing support of the State of Israel and its great institutions.

All this brings me to a painful point: painful not because it is controversial, but that it should be at all necessary. I refer to the attitude of some Jews to certain minorities in this country.

I would like to state at the outset that I prefer to see the problem in its true perspective without any extremist appeal. We Jews, as Jews, are not responsible for the conditions of Negroes in the United States. Our grandfathers were not slaveholders who devised this cruel and inhuman system. When the Negroes were being emancipated in the 1860s, we too were being emancipated in the ghettos of Europe. Indeed, on this very day of October 29th, in 1833 in Austria, we experienced our very first instance of legal political emancipation.

Nevertheless, we have participated in a growing economy which has to a large extent thrived on the exploitation of minorities, and we have shared deeply held prejudices about them. One need not masochistically excuse bigots like Leroy Jones and embrace other fanatics of the Black Power movement in order to appreciate that all whites suffer, or should suffer, some degree of a bad conscience.

The question is, what shall we do about it? Not to feel any guilt, any troubling of the conscience, is a sign of our own moral failure. We *must* experience some *hirhurei devarim*. Yet, to go overboard and dedicate our whole life to civil rights, to make of it an ersatz religion to replace Judaism, to concentrate only on the rights of others while ignoring the preservation of our own community here and overseas – is to lose perspective and to reveal an inner moral weakness while we try to strengthen ourselves morally in some other direction.

But in between these two extremes there are two ways, one which is right and one which is wrong. The pattern of Adam is to hide and shift the blame – to Black Power bigots, to the hoodlums who riot in Watts, to Negro anti-Semitism. We conveniently ignore the fact that in whole sections of our country there are whites who hold power and yet we have tolerated it; that hoodlums come in all colors; and that while Negro anti-Semitism is terribly troubling, we have had some degree of experience with white anti-Semitism: six million killed in our own times alone! And thus, like Adam, we suppress our bad conscience and we become part of that insidious "backlash" movement.

But the pattern of Abraham is not that at all. The people of Israel do not participate in backlash or frontlash or sidelash. The descendants of Abraham do not lash – at all! Rather, they attempt to respond constructively and creatively and sympathetically. Within this framework of putting the bad conscience to good use there may be several techniques about which well-intentioned people may disagree. But they will not allow side issues to becloud their main goal of finding a clear and moral way out of our country's painful racial dilemma.

Whether in our response to Torah, to *tzedaka*, or to great national issues like civil rights and peace, we must learn to make constructive use of a troubled conscience.

Adam's reaction justifies the cynical definition of conscience by H.L. Mencken as "an inner voice that warns us that somebody is looking." Abraham's response – that of readiness to experience God's trials and teach the world how great must be the dedication of the man of faith – this response cares only for God's call and answers with the "*hineini*" of a creative conscience.

In *Pirkei Avot*, before enumerating the ten trials to which Abraham was subject, the Mishna (5:2) tells us that there were ten generations from Adam to Noah, and ten again from Noah to Abraham, during which time the world became successively worse. In other words, it took twenty generations for mankind to learn what to do with a bad conscience. In our own time, with our accelerated pace of living, we cannot afford the luxury of waiting quite that long before learning – in our lives, as Jews, as Americans, as human beings – the difference between Adam and Abraham in what to do with a bad conscience.

In the words of Rabbi Abraham ben haRambam – "What a difference between them!"

The Lot of Lot[1]

In this *sidra*, which records some of the greatest events in the history of mankind such as the *Akeida*, and through whose holy passages there move such spiritual giants as Abraham, Isaac, and Sara, we find one character more distinguished by the shadow in which he is hidden than by the light which is cast upon him. He flits through the previous two Torah portions in an incidental sort of way, a bit mysterious, never fully capturing our attention, seemingly a character accidentally and fortuitously rescued from total oblivion of history only because he had a great uncle. He is a man who intrudes upon sacred history, but never really becomes a part of it.

This man is Lot, the nephew of Abraham. And perhaps his very importance lies in the fact that he is not a major character, a chief actor in the historical drama, but rather a secondary, stagehand type. Why is that important? Because we can identify with him more easily than with Abraham. Most of us are not great, not giants, not Abrahams, but ordinary mortals with ordinary foibles and weaknesses, ordinary virtues and ordinary goals. Lot is the average man, and from him and his

---

1. November 9, 1957.

life, the average Jew can learn more in a negative way than perhaps even from Abraham in a positive way. In the life of this man we can see the pitfalls before all of us, the dangers in the life of every man, so that he can teach us how not to live and what not to do.

Lot cuts a tragic figure indeed. He was given a number of real advantages early in life. For one thing, he had a rich uncle – Abraham – who set him up in business. This same uncle provided him with a Jewish home, a decent life, and education. Lot proved loyal to Abraham even after he left him to settle in Sodom, the city of wealth and corruption. Even there he still keeps many of the things he learned from Abraham, such as hospitality. He leads an "underground" Jewish life. He is the nephew of Abraham inside, a judge of Sodom outside. He becomes a respected member of their society. He is one of their elders. He has seemingly made the best of both worlds – a Jew at home and adjusted to his society nonetheless. This is the balance struck by the average, well-meaning, good-natured, but not overly idealistic man.

But listen to what happens at this point. The angels come to destroy Sodom because of its cruelty. And here three things happen which spell tragedy after tragedy for poor Lot. A merciful God spares him from death in the destruction of Sodom, but his life has been seriously impaired.

1. He finds, after a long stay in Sodom, that he has *inverted values*; he has lost his spiritual perspective. He still retains something of the teachings of Abraham, but not in the proper proportion. Thus, when the mob asks for the three strangers who are his guests to be victims of their degenerate passions, Lot offers to protect the strangers – a virtue of no mean order. But how? By committing a far more degenerate offense: he offers his daughters in their stead. He has values, but they are lopsided.

2. He finds himself *alone in his own home*. When the angels plead with him to leave, he turns to his sons in-law. The Torah calls them "*ḥatanav, lok'ḥei venotav*" – in other words, they are not really sons-in-law, they have no relation with him, they merely married his daughters. And what is their reaction? "*Vayehi*

khimtzaḥek be'einei ḥatanav" – it was all a joke to them (Genesis 19:14). And his wife? She cannot resist a last look at the hotbed of corruption. It still lures her, and as she parts from her husband, she looks back and becomes calcified. Thus, Lot's terrible loneliness: his own family no longer understands him or sympathizes with him. He is a stranger in his own home.

3. And his greatest tragedy: when he and his two daughters are left alone as survivors, they think that the whole world has been destroyed and they are the only survivors. They become enmeshed in a deadly gloom and think that the human race will die with them. And so, out of the depths of their despair, in order to realize their destiny as humans and practice their good intentions of settling God's world, they commit the most serious of all immoralities – incest – while Lot is in a drunken stupor.

Quite a miserable end for a man who never had serious pretensions to great evil. Why is this? Why such terrible punishment? There is only one reason: *because he left Abraham*. All along, he was quite willing to follow his great uncle, willing to learn from him and lead his kind of life, but when it hit his pocketbook, when it came to money – "And there was strife between the herdsmen of Abram's livestock and the herdsmen of Lot's livestock" (Genesis 13:7) – then he leaves Abraham, and is willing to settle in Sodom, the byword of all that is evil. Now don't think that Lot completely relished this idea; after all, he was a pupil of Abraham. But business required it, he told himself, financial necessity had forced him to leave both Abraham and his ways. And besides, corrupt though Sodom was, it was a beautiful city, as the Torah describes: "It was like the garden of God, like the land of Egypt, as you come to Zoar" (ibid., verse 10). Hence we read, "And Lot traveled from *kedem*, east" – upon which our rabbis, quoted by Rashi, comment in a play on words – "He caused himself to travel away from *Kidmono shel olam*, the Eternal One of the world." Maybe Lot will carry over some small habits that he had learned in the house of Abraham. Maybe there will be some souvenirs or mementoes. But essentially he had torn himself away from Abraham, and along with that, from the God of Abraham.

77

And this is indeed the crucial event in the life of Lot, in the life of every average man: "And Lot traveled from *kedem*" – "from *Kidmono shel olam*." His departure from Abraham and all that he stood for: this was the cause of his grief and the seedling of his tragedy. And if you analyze the whole episode of Lot carefully, you will see that he was rewarded measure for measure. The resulting tragedies follow the pattern of Lot's sin.

1. Lot sinks to the most degenerate immorality because of inverted values. But did he not bring it upon himself? Was it not he himself who made the decision to leave Abraham because of "economic pressures"? Was it not he who first consciously inverted his own values?

2. He was lonely in his own home, and an alien to wife, children, and children-in-law. But he brought it on himself. By leaving Abraham, he isolated himself from Abraham's God – and now found himself isolated by others.

3. He was led to his ultimate degradation, the depths of immorality and disruption of his family – the act of incest – because of the doom and pessimism which made him think that he and his daughters were the only survivors, that the world was destroyed. But did he not bring upon himself this feeling of no choice, of absolute necessity? Did he not begin this life of pessimism when he decided to settle in Sodom, to leave Abraham – because business required it, because otherwise he could never survive in the competitive market? He began by considering that there was only one way out – Sodom; and ended by having his daughters consider only one way out – his deepest and most lasting humiliation.

So then, in the one act of leaving Abraham, or as our rabbis said it, causing himself to travel away from God, Lot suffered a corresponding series of tragic consequences of inversion of values, loneliness, and a deadly and sickening pessimism. His is the story of a man who seems well established, successful, and at the peak of his career, but whose early, serious errors bring his life crashing into a conclusion of shame and disgrace.

It does not take too much to see why and how this story of Lot is a parable for Jews of all eras, especially for the "average Jew" of today. Just look at what has happened to so many of our fellow Jews:

1. We have suffered an inversion of values, just as Lot did. Thus, we place Ḥanukka, with all its colorfulness and festivity, on a much higher rung than the Sabbath. Many a person who would never dream of forgetting to celebrate Ḥanukka in the grand manner will not think twice of violating the sanctity of the Sabbath. Similarly, there are many other inversions of values. In many a home where *kashrut* has long been abandoned, the unveiling of a tombstone is regarded as one of the fundamentals of our faith. How horrified some people are when they hear their rabbi minimizing the importance of the unveiling. And how irritated they are when they hear that same rabbi emphasizing the significance of *kashrut*.

2. All modern man, and especially Jews, suffers from intense feelings of alienation, from both philosophical and emotional loneliness. We feel that we do not really belong in this world. We know that we are not *completely* accepted by our beloved country – not with the pact with Saudi Arabia, not with the constant emphasis of this being a Christian country, not with the plague of the Sunday Blue Laws which discriminate against Saturday Sabbath observance. Our relations with Israel are only philanthropic and sentimental, not sufficiently strong to diminish our sense of estrangement and loneliness. So much of what goes by the name of "American Judaism" has absolutely nothing to do with God, so that we are estranged from Him too. And in our loneliness, in our estrangement and solitude, we nervously look about for more and more entertainment, we obsessively seek our luxuries; even our laughter becomes anxious instead of relaxed. No wonder so many moderns find that they must, out of their solitude, turn to the couch of the psychiatrist to seek solace and a sense of being wanted.

3. Jews of certain kinds come to conclusions which are bleakly pessimistic. They become prophets of complete assimilation, prognosticators of doom. You recall the two prophets, one a

79

professor and one a historian, who recently wrote in the *B'nai Brith Monthly*, that we Jews have no religious future in this country.

So that like Lot of old, the value-inversion, the loneliness, and the pessimism are our heritage.

And were we to trace these consequences to their original source, we would find this too identical with the source of Lot's woes. The "original sin" of American Jewry is: "And Lot traveled from *kedem*." We have used all kinds of excuses, especially that of financial necessity, as the reason and justification for leaving *Kidmono shel olam*, Almighty God. Like Lot, we do keep up certain practices that come from the house of Abraham in order to assuage our consciences: we hang Jewish paintings on the walls, we display a big Ḥanukka menora, our living rooms are amply stocked with Israeli ashtrays... but Judaism and Jewishness are otherwise not noticeable in our lives. Like Lot, we have begun to live an underground existence insofar as our Jewishness is concerned; for, like the nephew of Abraham, we have learned to adjust to every conceivable kind of Sodomite practice in the world around us. "He caused himself to travel away from *Kidmono shel olam*."

By running out on the God of Abraham, we have brought on ourselves all these undesirable and unfortunate consequences.

But of course things need not necessarily be thus. We are not – yet – too far gone. There can still be a realignment in Jewish life in this country. But in order to accomplish that, the process has to be reversed: instead of going away from Abraham and all he stands for, we must go back. We must not leave *kedem*, but go back to *kedem*. "Return" is, indeed, the original meaning of *teshuva*. We must return to *Kidmono shel olam*. The only way to achieve the proper spiritual orientation and perspective, to keep our sense of values; the only way to achieve a sense of being wanted, warm, closest to God, a sense of rootedness; the only way to arrive at an optimistic, healthful, sanguine attitude to Jewish life, and life in general – is to return to *Kidmono shel olam*, to reverse the process of "And Lot traveled from *kedem*."

And to facilitate that great return is one of the chief functions of our synagogue, and of any other genuine Orthodox synagogue. One of the three meanings of *"kadima"* is "back to *kedem*," back to *Kidmono shel olam*, back to God.

If we are to escape the lot of Lot, we must heed the call of *"kadima*," the return to God, to Torah, to tradition, to the origins of our life and the spiritual resources through which it can thrive and through which it will survive.

Tradition and Innovation[1]

I find myself returning again and again to the theme of tradition and innovation in Judaism. We are incessantly bombarded by shrill cries for change from the religious Left, as if a truncated tradition is equivalent to progress, as if "adaptation" is a magic word that will solve all our problems. At the same time, I am perplexed and even vexed by the doctrinaire inertia and resistance in some circles to the least change, as if the fact that something never has been done is sufficient reason never to do it.

I am proud and happy to be part of an unbroken tradition of law and teaching and worship and philosophy that overarches the generations, that links me through my parents and grandparents with the *rishonim* and *tanna'im* on to Moses and Abraham. But I am distressed when "tradition" becomes an excuse for insensitivity to new needs, for refusing to confront new issues.

The whole subject of change is, of course, too large to discuss within the confines of a sermon. So let us set down certain axioms: we are not talking about the halakha. In halakha, change is generally not the accepted rule. The few places where it can take place require a high

---

1. November 2, 1974.

degree of technical competence, and cannot be decided by plebiscite. But I am concerned by the tendency of some people, especially religious folk, to act as if the world never changes, who evince symptoms of the hardening of cultural and social arteries, and who fear that any deviation in procedure – which they themselves may have set down some years earlier – will wreak havoc in the Upper Worlds. What ought to be said about these other, non-halakhic aspects of our problem?

First, it is important to stress that while there is little likelihood of significant change in the halakha, it demands of us that *we* change! When you stop changing you stop growing, and when you stop growing you in effect stop living. Of course, tradition – *the* tradition – encourages innovation and change within us, and calls it *teshuva,* repentance. Spiritually, the Jew must always be in a state of flux, in movement, in dynamic progress.

Furthermore, not only individuals spiritually, but institutions organizationally should always be open to change. I am often aghast at the institutional inertia of Jewish organizations in the United States. Why, for instance, should an organization that was successful twenty, thirty, and forty years ago in absorbing Jewish immigrants in this country insist that the same techniques and the same approaches must be used for Russian Jews today – ignoring the profound changes in the nature of immigration?

In my travels I have come across many synagogues. Sometimes, I chance upon a synagogue which openly flouts sacred Jewish law, which treats with studied neglect the cumulative wisdom of the most profound minds of the jurists and philosophers and saints and sages of the centuries. Halakha is ignored casually, Jewish law is dismissed cavalierly. Yet the slightest deviation from the accepted procedure that the board of directors or some synagogue committee or some rabbi set down a number of years ago, as to how the cantor marches or the rabbi dresses or the president sits or the chairman of the board conducts meetings – such a deviation is considered dangerously radical and psychologically unnerving, and is often the cause for major crisis and trauma, frequently resulting in part of the membership breaking off and forming a new synagogue.

I see the signs of such senseless fixations, although in the extreme, in our *sidra.* When the angels hurried Lot and his family out of Sodom, prior to its being ravaged by fire and brimstone, Lot and his family were warned not to look backward upon Sodom while it was being destroyed. The wife of Lot was unable to suppress her curiosity and she violated the command of the angels, whereupon "She became a pillar of salt" (Genesis 19:26). The rabbis of the Midrash, quoted by Rashi, wonder why this specific punishment, that of salt, was chosen. They answer: "Lot, when the angels came to him disguised as human guests, asked his wife to serve the guests a bit of salt. She responded, 'Since when do you want to establish this new, evil custom in this place?' And so, since she sinned with salt, she was punished by being turned into salt."

I see in this more than a just criticism of inhospitality. Lot's wife was conservative to the point of being reactionary. She was so fixated upon old and conventional patterns of conduct that she became mindless and heartless, insisting upon them even when they violated the most elementary rules of human conduct and ethical living. Sodom had an old custom of turning away strangers, and she resented the effort of Lot to change the "sacrosanct" ways of her community. Not only was salt a sin and punishment, it was also the symbol of her psychological attitude. Salt is a crystalline chemical, which is very difficult to change. Whether you heat salt or freeze it, dissolve it or mix it, it is unchanging and inflexible and immutable. Salt it was, and salt it remains. Salt symbolizes the lifeless rigidity of Lot's wife. No wonder the Torah describes the event with the words, "His wife looked behind him." She was always looking backward, consulting the unchanging past as a guide to an equally unchanging, hidebound future.

But while it is fairly simple to agree that, spiritually and institutionally, innovation and change and renewal are important, the real problem of tradition versus innovation in Judaism takes place in the realm of *minhag,* sacred custom.

Consult yourself, your own attitudes and experience, and you will appreciate that most of us are ambivalent about revered custom. In Jewish literature too, you find elaborated two general opinions or attitudes. Thus, we frequently hear such words as *"minhag, halakha hee"* (custom becomes halakha); *"minhag avoteinu Torah"* (the custom of our ancestors becomes Torah); or, the words of the Jerusalem Talmud, *"minhag mevatel halakha"* (custom can nullify a halakha). And yet, on the other side, we often hear great rabbis refer to particular customs as *"minhag shtut,"* silly or stupid or foolish customs. Rabbeinu Tam, the famous Tosafist, in reply (*Responsa Ba'alei haTosafot* 11) to another French rabbi who tried to prove his point by appealing to local custom, pointed out that when you rearrange the four Hebrew letters that make up the word *"minhag,"* you emerge with the word *"gehinom,"* Hell!

Judaism, all religion, all tradition – whether law or custom – is necessarily conservative. That is the way religion has to be, and that is the way it ought to be – for at least two good reasons. First, psychologically it gives us a sense of continuity amidst all the flux and vicissitudes of life. Second, there is an innate wisdom in this conservatism of the tradition. It understands, and teaches us, that not all changes in custom, lifestyle, manners, thinking, and mores are worthy or even permanent. Do an experiment: look through the last fifteen or eighteen years of *Time* magazine, and you will notice the extremely rapid succession of ideas, fashions, and fads. The closer you come to today, the shorter the lifespan of each fashion in any field whatsoever. And then look in their Religion section, and you will become convinced of the pitiful and almost comic attempts of religious leaders to "keep up" and become the most "trendy" segment of society! The result is what has been called "mood theology," and there is hardly anything that is more ludicrous.

Yet, there are areas where perceptions do change, where style and not principle is involved, where the issues are neither halakha nor sacred *minhag*-that-is-Torah – but simply old usage that was lucky enough to survive without much to commend it. In such cases, to be immovable is to be unthinking, and to be unbending is to risk repelling new faces and new ideas, and losing Jews.

I, for one, do not aspire to be "with it." But neither do I regard it as a virtue to be without it, or outside it...

An example of an area where we must decide between tradition and innovation is the institution of bat mitzva. I am speaking, of course, within the realms of halakhic permissibility. Thus, I refer to a bat mitzva ceremony which is not performed in the synagogue proper, and in which an appropriate Torah spirit prevails. But what of the idea itself; what of the celebration as such?

One of the great decisors of our generation, Rabbi Moshe

Feinstein, is unhappy about the bat mitzva ceremony. If he permits it, it is only with the greatest reluctance. The late, eminent halakhic scholar, Rabbi Yechiel Yaakov Weinberg, writes that some people are opposed to it simply because it is an innovation: "Because it is against the custom of earlier generations which did not establish this tradition." But he himself adds the following:

> But in truth this is no argument, because in the generations that preceded us there was no need to worry about the education of girls, for they absorbed Judaism with their mother's milk. But times have changed. Straight reasoning and pedagogical understanding almost obligate us to celebrate the occasion when a girl becomes bat mitzva.

My own feeling is that I would once have discouraged it, even though it is halakhically unobjectionable. Today I accept it cheerfully – provided the young lady recites *divrei Torah* so as to distinguish it from an ordinary birthday party – but I neither encourage nor discourage it. Some day in the near future, I suspect, I may actively encourage young ladies to celebrate the bat mitzva.

Thus, I feel that this is an innovation which is becoming more meaningful, and will have to be accepted.

Yet I would also confess this publicly: I would prefer to undo the whole thing! And not only this, but I would like to discourage, actively and resolutely, both the bat mitzva and the bar mitzva! Both of them entail too much Sabbath desecration, too much exhibitionism, too much expense, too much vicarious spending and conspicuous consumption – and too little Torah, too little piety, too little seriousness, too little continuity.

Finally, with regard to local customs and usages that we find in any institution, my rule is this: if it has value, keep it. If it no longer has much value – keep it anyway. But if it is counterproductive, remove it without giving it a second thought. A *minhag shtut* is an unnecessary burden, and it is foolish to retain it.

For instance, to take a rather trivial subject, but one that externally distinguishes services at the Jewish Center: the formal clothing we wear, as part of our western European heritage. If these Sabbath clothes have any meaning, let us continue them. I believe they have such value. This particular outfit lends distinction to our perception of the holiness of the Sabbath, and it esthetically enhances our reverence for it, which, according to the rabbis, is expressed in special clothing. Were it to lose such meaning, I would keep it anyway, because continuity even in externals has a certain psychological value that we ought not to ignore. But were it somehow – because of changing circumstances and differing styles and insights – to work against the idea of Torah and Shabbat, to injure the image of Judaism, I would have no hesitation in abandoning it in favor of some other form of dress that is more functional in expressing our true and genuine religious sentiment.

So the parameters are fairly well set. In halakha, we almost always prefer tradition over innovation. Spiritually, we must always be changing and progressing. Institutionally, we should prefer innovation over tradition as a way to endless renewal. In the area of *minhag*, we must make responsible and informed choices at all times. I am biased toward the general preservation of traditional forms, but not toward *minhag shtut*, foolish customs. I am in favor of the beauty and sometimes the sanctity of ancient usage, but I am aware too that simple repetition of any act over a period of time can mortally weaken our reactions and sensitivities, and can cause the dead hand of the past to strangle any initiative of the present. I do not look with favor upon the kind of *minhag* which Rabbeinu Tam reminded us can become the word *gehinom*. So, I want the past to be alive, not dead, and the new to be religiously significant – not just change for novelty's sake.

All of this can be summed up in the famous words of the sainted Rav Kook: "The sacred shall be renewed, and the new shall be sanctified."

Ḥayyei Sara

On Remaining Unperturbed[1]

Of all the names that have been given to the period of history through which we are currently living, the most appropriate and descriptive is the "age of anxiety." Indeed, it is anxiety that most accurately describes the inner life of man in our era, his unceasing tension, and the whole range of psychosomatic ills which symbolize that tense inner life. Anxiety has even been incorporated into philosophy by some thinkers of the French Existentialist school. It is the mood which dominates all of modern man and is his most characteristic emotion.

What, if anything, does Judaism have to say about this phenomenon? It is true, of course, that Judaism should not be understood as an elaborate prescription for "peace of mind." We, of course, do not conceive of religion as a "need" to be fulfilled. And yet, I do not doubt for a moment that Judaism has a definite judgment upon this, our problem. First, because Judaism is good for people, even though that is not the reason we ought to accept it. And second, it can be shown that ultimately a good part of the emotional life of man is based upon his ethics, his spiritual character, and his religious conception.

---

1. November 27, 1959.

The teaching of Judaism that is most relevant to the problem of modern man's anxiety is expressed in two words, *hishtavut hanefesh* – equanimity, stability, keeping on an even psychological and spiritual keel. This attitude of *hishtavut hanefesh*, of the constancy of personality, is eventually based upon a religious conception – that of faith. If a man has faith, he will not be upset either by very good news or by very bad news, he will yield neither to the temptations of affluence nor to the threat of adversity – for the same God is the source of both opposites. If he is a success in his endeavors and receives compliments, he will remain largely unimpressed with his own triumph. And if he is criticized until it hurts, he will remain largely unperturbed and unshaken in his faith.

This Jewish teaching was brilliantly expounded in the comments on our *sidra* by the Reszher Rav, Rabbi Aaron Levine of blessed memory, who was a great scholar, a great preacher, and a senator in the Polish parliament. The Torah tells us at the very beginning of our portion (Genesis 23:1) that Sara lived 127 years, and then repeats, in the same verse, "These are the years of the life of Sara." Our rabbis wondered at this repetition and Rashi, quoting our sages, remarked: "All these years were equally for the good." What Rashi meant is explained by the Reszher Rav as *hishtavut hanefesh* – the lesson of stability both of mind and of soul. Sara's life had its ups and its downs, she reached very high points and very low points, there were sharp changes of fortune. In her early youth she found herself uprooted from her home, wandering from town to town and city to city following her husband. When she came to Egypt she was separated from her beloved husband, abducted by an immoral Egyptian potentate. Later, she rejoiced as she and her husband attained great wealth, and finally, at the climax of her good fortune, when God awarded her with a son in her old age, fully realizing the ambition of a lifetime. And yet, despite these vicissitudes, "All these years were equally for the good" – her basic character of goodness remained unchanged throughout. Her character was unaffected. She became neither arrogant as a result of her success and triumph, nor despairing and crushed by her failure. She knew and practiced the Jewish quality of *hishtavut hanefesh*.

Is this not a message that we moderns ought to seek out and observe in our own lives? Far too many people in our day and age have lost this capacity for psycho-spiritual stability. In conditions of adversity they have become demoralized, confused, and perplexed. They lose faith and blame their defeat upon God. And in times of prosperity, they turn arrogant, lose perspective, regard themselves as "self-made," and decide that they no longer need faith. Perhaps that is why religion suffers most during times of great stress, when circumstances are either very good or very bad. Both war and famine, and conversely, economic prosperity and well-being, cause attrition in the ranks of religious people. How right, then, was Rabbeinu Tam, the grandson of Rashi, who wrote in his *Sefer haYashar* that true character comes to the fore only in times of crisis and violent change, whether the change is to the good or to the bad. For crisis is the litmus paper of character, and change in fortune the barometer of a man's soul.

The rabbis of the Talmud saw this quality of *hishtavut hanefesh* as based upon and as a symbol of the final and greatest of the three requirements of man by God as enumerated in the famous verse by the prophet Micah: "It has been told to you, O Man, what is good and what the Lord requires of you – but to do justice and to love mercy, and to walk humbly with your God" (6:8). And commenting upon that last requirement, the Talmud (*Makkot* 24a) tells us that "to walk humbly" refers to the two opposite occasions of accompanying the bride to the bridal canopy and accompanying the deceased on his last trip – at the funeral. What our sages meant to tell us is that if you want to know if a man is indeed devout, if he is indeed a religious personality, if he "walks humbly with his God" – then test his reaction, his attitude, and his strength of character at these crucial times of either great happiness or great grief, of great joy or great tragedy. To walk humbly with God means to achieve, on the basis of a religious outlook and profound faith, the quality of *hishtavut hanefesh*. This refers to the inner stability that is retained even when life moves us back and forth across the spectrum of experience from the deep blue of misery and depression to the bright red of cheery optimism, joy, and happiness. That is why at the occasion of a death, our tradition teaches us that we must mourn and weep, for otherwise, in the words of Maimonides (*Hilkhot Avel* 13:12), we are merciless and hardened. But at the same time, tradition teaches us that we must not overdo our mourning, we must not prolong it more than is necessary, for otherwise, again in the words of Maimonides, it is a sign of spiritual foolishness, a symbol and symptom of the lack of faith in God and a lack of hope in the future. That is why, too, at the occasion of a wedding, we break the glass in memory of the destruction of the Temple. At sad occasions we introduce a note of optimism, and at happy occasions a sobering note reminiscent of life's harshness. In this manner we attempt to attain *hishtavut hanefesh* – of not being over-impressed by triumph and not being perturbed by defeat. And therefore, for the same reason, on Passover, the great holiday of liberation, we eat the *maror* – the symbol of bitterness, while on Tisha beAv, the day of great tragedy, we do not recite the *Taḥanun* prayer, for the halakha regards even this great day of tragedy as a *mo'ed* – a sort of holiday.

No wonder a great Hasidic teacher taught that every man must have two pockets; in one he must carry a note upon which are written the words of Abraham, "Behold I am only dust and ashes" (Genesis 18:27), and in the other must be the statement of the rabbis in the Mishna (*Sanhedrin* 4:5), "For my sake was the world created."

So if there is anyone who has had fortune smile upon him, who has achieved a degree of satisfaction and success – let him not forget that ultimately man is only dust and ashes; let him remember to walk *humbly* with his God. And conversely, if there is anyone who somehow suffers silently, whose heart is wounded with grief, and whose soul bears some painful sores, who perhaps has received criticism that hurts, let him not yield to self-pity or despair, let him not lose faith and submit to moodiness and especially not to the feeling of his own worthlessness. Let him remember that although he may walk "humbly," nevertheless every man and woman still walks "with his God" – and what greater consolation is there for any human being than to know that he has the dignity of having been created in the image of God, and the hope that there is a God above who listens to the heartbeat of every human being as a father listens to the pleading voice of a child.

And as this is true of us generally as individuals, certainly ought this to be true of us as Jews. How beautifully our rabbis (Genesis Rabba 58:3) describe an incident which, in its inner meaning, refers to this quality of *hishtavut hanefesh*. Rabbi Akiba was preaching and found himself beset by an audience which was falling asleep – an occurrence not unknown in the life of a speaker, and an occupational risk generally anticipated by any preacher. And so he tried to awaken them by telling them: How comes it that Queen Esther ruled over 127 countries? The answer is that she was the great-granddaughter of Sara, who lived 127 years.

I believe our rabbis had a special message in this relation and in this narrative. Rabbi Akiba lived at a time when his people were in danger of "falling asleep." This was the era of Hadrianic persecutions, when the Roman Empire forbade the study of Torah and the practice of Jewish observances. The people had only recently suffered the national catastrophe of the Temple's destruction and the loss of independence. And so, our ancestors at that time were about to fall asleep, to yield to despair and to hopelessness and to a feeling of their own worthlessness. At a time of this sort, the great Rabbi Akiba tried to wake them up, he tried to stir them into activity, he tried to get them out of the sullen mood in which they found themselves. It was he, Rabbi Akiba, who was the patron and the organizer of the Bar Kokhba rebellion against the might of imperial Rome. So he tried to urge them into a happier frame of mind and a more activist approach by reminding them that they were the descendants of Esther, and that it was Esther who herself went through a great number of vicissitudes in her life. When she was young, very young, she was already an orphan – reared by an uncle much older in years, lacking the warmth of maternal love and paternal concern. Then suddenly she found herself with the crown of Persia upon her head, the absolute monarch of 127 lands. Shortly thereafter she was faced with the catastrophic possibility of her own and her people's destruction by Haman, only to be saved at the last moment by an opposite edict by the king and the great triumph of Israel which resulted in the celebration of Purim. And yet, during all these extreme changes of fortune, our rabbis told us, "*Hee Ester,*' 'She is Esther' (Esther 2:7); she remained the same Esther both when she was queen and when she wasn't" – the same sweet, gentle, modest young woman who was only an orphan in her uncle's home, retained her good character when she was the queen of Persia, of 127 lands. She did not change. She had acquired the quality of *hishtavut hanefesh*, of psychological, spiritual, and emotional stability. And where did she get this quality from? From Sara, of course, who was the model of such behavior.

Would that we, descendants of those strong personalities, would learn this marvelous faith. Like Sara, like Esther, like Rabbi Akiba – we must learn to take life in stride without at any time upsetting the apple-cart of character. We must never be insensitive, but we must be strong and powerful of faith. We must neither yield to wild abandon or relaxation of effort when we behold the victory and triumph of the State of Israel, nor submit to defeatism and pessimism as we ponder the bitter fate of Russian Jewry. We must not turn giddy with delight when some gentile scholar or politician praises us, nor ever submit to chagrin and turn apologetic when some gentile criticizes either our people or our faith.

"*Ashreinu ma tov ḥelkeinu, uma na'im goraleinu, uma yafa yerushateinu.*" Happy are we not only that our lot is *tov* – good, ethical, true; but that in addition, our destiny is *na'im*, pleasant – it is satisfying and makes for a healthy mind and a healthy soul; and above all – happy are we that *yerushateinu*, our heritage, the great Jewish tradition, is so beautiful.

Words – Scarce and Sacred[1]

What is the value of a word?

This is a most appropriate question on the first Sabbath after our national elections took place. Elections to the presidency are a wondrous thing to behold and a glory and tribute to a free people. Yet when the elections were done our countrymen across the land heaved a blessed sigh of relief, for many of us believed that the campaigns for the election did not do much to enhance the glory. Many of us suspected that they were largely an exercise in futility. The real issues, such as they were, could have been discussed much more quickly and conclusively. Most of the words that followed were not meant for clarification as much as for tools in the projection of "images." There has been talk recently of the possible devaluation of the dollar. Much more thought should have been given to a more serious danger: the devaluation of the word. I believe the nation could have survived the election of either candidate. But we may properly doubt whether the nation could have survived another month of the endless, repetitive, meaningless torrents of words without seriously compromising its sanity.

---

1. November 12, 1960.

What then is the Jewish attitude to words? First let us understand that Israel's greatness can benefit the world only through words. We have never been a numerous people. We have never, except in the most restricted sense, been militarily significant. We have usually been diplomatically weak. Therefore, our message to the world has been transmitted only through the power of the word. Ever since our father Isaac said, "The voice is the voice of Jacob and the hands are the hands of Esau" (Genesis 27:22), our tradition has maintained that "*Yaakov koho bafeh*" – that the strength and the might of Israel lies in its mouth, in its words. The message of Torah is referred to as "the words of the covenant" (Exodus 34:28). What the Western world calls the Ten Commandments our tradition refers to as "*aseret hadibrot*" – the "ten words." And when Jews speak of a spiritual gem, they say in Hebrew, a "*devar Torah,*" "a word of Torah," or, in Yiddish, "*a gut vort*" – "a good word." The word is the medium of spiritual enlightenment, the medium for Israel's message.

But words, in our conception, have an even more universal function. Words are the mortar that binds man with his fellow-men. Without the extensive use of words, human beings would never group themselves in a society. Without words there can be no communication, no study or schools, no society or social life, no civilization or business or commerce. Neither can there be any family life. When husband and wife are "not on speaking terms," that is a real danger sign for domestic health.

Onkelos, the great Aramaic translator of the Bible, had that in mind when he offered an unusual translation of a familiar verse. When the Bible relates that God breathed the breath of life into Adam, it says, "*Vayehi ha'adam lenefesh haya,*" which we usually translate as, "And the man became a living soul" (Genesis 2:7). Onkelos, however, translates it, "And it (the breath of God) became in man a speaking spirit." The living soul of man is his speaking spirit. The uniqueness of man, his intellect, would be muted and silent were it not for his ability to use words and thus articulate his rational ideas and the feelings of his heart. A word has a life and biography and character and soul of its own. And the word can give life to or take life from the human being. A word can restore and a word can kill. One word can give a man the reputation for wisdom, one word can mark him in the eyes of his peers as a fool. The speaking spirit has a profound effect upon the living soul.

Because of this, Judaism regards words as more than mere verbal units, as more than just another form of communication. In Judaism words are – or should be – holy! When the Torah commands a man that he not break his word, it says, "*Lo yaḥel devaro*" (Numbers 30:3). Our rabbis noted (Jerusalem Talmud, *Nedarim* 2:1) that *yaḥel* is an unusual word and so they explained it as "*Lo ya'aseh devarav ḥullin*" – he shall not profane his word, not desecrate it. Only that which is holy can be made unholy. Only that which is sacred can be desecrated. Man's words therefore must be holy.

If our word is to be holy, we must keep it, honor it, and revere it. Indeed, the sanctity of a man's word is a measure of the confidence he deserves, whether in business or within the family. If he keeps his word holy, people will confide in him and trust him. If he desecrates his word, if he makes it *ḥullin*, then he does not deserve the confidence of his wife, his partners, and his fellow-men. Many, many years after *Ḥazal*, Oliver Wendell Holmes was to put it this way: "Life and language are alike sacred…homicide and verbicide are alike forbidden."

It follows therefrom that we must be careful and discriminating, not casual, in whatever we say. When the Israelites conquered the pagan Midianites and destroyed them, the Torah bade the Israelites not to use the Midianites' vessels until they had been purified and cleansed, so that even the atmosphere or memory of paganism and idolatry would be banished from Israel's midst. The Torah puts it this way: "*Kol davar* – any vessel – that is normally used over an open flame must be purified by passing it through fire" (Numbers 31:23). Our rabbis of the Talmud (*Shabbat* 58b) asked this interesting question: What of a metal megaphone, an instrument devised for magnifying the voice? Can that contract impurities, and if so how can it be purified? Yes, answer our rabbis, it can become impure, and must also be purified by passing through fire. They played cleverly on the phrase "*kol davar.*" Not only, they said, "*kol davar,*" but "*kol dibbur*" – not only every "object," but every "word" must be passed through fire. Therefore, a megaphone, used to magnify words, is included in the laws of the impurities of Midianite vessels.

Our rabbis meant, I believe, to refer more than just to a megaphone. They meant "*kol dibbur*" – every word spoken by human lips must be passed through the fire of the soul before it is spoken to the world at large. Every word must be passed through the flame of integrity, of sincerity, of consideration for others, and for the effect that the word may have on them. A word untempered in the furnace of integrity and wisdom is like a table unplaned and unfiled: its splinters and rough edges can injure far more than the table can serve. A word not passed through the fire of consciousness is the master and not the servant of him who speaks it.

Furthermore, we must be not only discriminating in our words, but sparse as well. Our words must be few and scarce. In all of Judaism, the principle of *kedusha* is protected from the danger of over-familiarity. When man has too much free access to an object or a place, he gradually loses his respect and awe for it. That is why the Torah reader uses a silver pointer. It is not used for decorative purposes. It is employed because of the halakha that "Sacred texts make the hands impure" (*Yadayim* 3:2) – that we are forbidden to touch the inner part of the Torah scroll. The reason for this is a profound insight of the Torah into human nature: if we are permitted to touch it freely and often, we will lose our reverence for it. The less we are permitted to contact it, the greater our respect for it. Similarly, the Holy of Holies in the Temple in Jerusalem was preserved in its sanctity by our tradition when it forbade any man other than the high priest to enter its sacred precincts; and even he might not do so except for one time during the year – on Yom Kippur, the Day of Atonement.

And so it is with words. The more we use them, the less they mean. When our rabbis investigated the first portion of Genesis, they discovered that the world was created by God "with ten 'words'" (*Avot* 5:1). Only ten words to create an entire universe! And yet our rabbis were not satisfied. And so they asked, "Could not the world have been created with only one word?" Why waste nine precious words? Indeed, for with regard to words, quantity is in inverse relationship to quality. If there are so many words that you cannot count them, then no individual word counts for very much.

In our *sidra* we read, "And Abraham came to mourn for Sara and *livkota*, to weep for her (Genesis 23:2). If you read the portion carefully, you will notice something strange about the word *livkota*. The letter *kaf* is smaller than normal. It is a *kaf ketana*, a miniature *kaf*. Why is that?

The commentator known as the Ba'al haTurim explains that

Abraham did not weep or speak too much. Of course Abraham said something. There had to be some weeping and mourning and eulogizing. He had to give some articulate expression to the grief that welled up in his breast. For a man who cannot speak out his grief is like a man who cannot sweat – the poison remains within. It can be psychologically dangerous not to mourn. But it must not be overdone. Abraham realized that too many words are an escape from the confrontation with reality. He realized that by using too many words he would dissipate the real feelings he contained within himself. He wanted something to remain, something deliciously private, painfully mysterious, some residue of memory and love and affection for his beloved Sara that he did not want to share with the rest of the world. And so the *kaf ketana* – indicating that he knew how to limit the outpouring of his words.

Oh how we moderns need this lesson of making our words sacred by making them scarce! How we need that lesson of the *kaf ketana*. How we must learn to pass our words through the flame of wisdom. Modern life seems centered so much about words. We are dominated by a communications industry. We veer constantly between meetings and discussions, symposia and forums, lectures and sermons, public relations and propaganda. We are hounded continually by radio and television, telephone and telegraph. We are the "talkingest" civilization in all of history. How desperately we need that *kaf ketana*!

Some time ago, Jewish leaders, all with good intentions – of enhancing the appeal for refugees and immigrants – announced to the world that Romania was opening its doors and letting its Jews out. And how tragically that torrent of words backfired, provoking the Arab states and causing Romania to shut its doors in the face of thousands of unfortunate Jews who must now remain un-reunited with their immediate families in Israel.

Only two weeks ago one of the most important leaders of Israel made the announcement that he expects Soviet Russia to open its doors in one to five years. Here were words that kindled a spark of hope in us, but at the same time caused a shadow of fear and the whisper of terror to pass over us. Perhaps those very words will cause the good news to be revoked. Perhaps because of the words, Russia will close its doors for more years to come.

It's about time that all of us, and especially Jewish agencies, learned that we ought not to be dominated by the public relations machines. It's about time that we learned to respect the *kaf ketana*. Moses himself was a stammerer and a stutterer, and so he spoke few words – but whatever he did speak was engraved in letters of fire upon the consciousness of the people. David told us, "Commune with your hearts upon your beds and be silent" (Psalms 4:5). Shammai reminded us, "Speak little, but do much" (*Avot* 1:15). Other rabbis told us that "The way to wisdom is through silence" (*Avot* 1:17). The Besht, the great Ba'al Shem Tov, meant the same thing in a comment upon God's command to Noah, "You shall make a light for the ark." The Besht pointed out that the Hebrew word for ark – *teiva* – means not only "ark" but also "word." Make each word brilliant, alive, shining, sparkling, and illuminating. Use it to enlighten, not to confuse. All of these individuals knew the secret of Abraham, that of the *kaf ketana*.

Words are important and powerful; therefore they are sacred. Because they are sacred, they must be issued with great, extreme caution. They must be tempered in the fire of one's character. And because they are holy and purified in fire, they must be few, choice, and scarce.

When we will have learned this, we will have learned a great deal indeed. So that ultimately, we will be able to say to God, with David (Psalms 65:2), "Almighty God, our very silence is praise unto You."

Frankness as Vice and as Virtue[1]

Most people have mixed feelings with regard to that uncommon quality called frankness or candor – and that is as it should be. It is something no doubt to be admired, and all too rare in human relations. And yet it can, in the wrong hands, be misused for the wrong purposes and prove dangerous and disruptive. On the one hand, frankness is based on *emet*, truth, and our tradition teaches that the very seal and insignia of God is truth (Exodus Rabba 4:3). Frankness is a prerequisite for clear and uncomplicated human and social relationships. Candor, while it may momentarily be annoying, ultimately proves to be the best guarantee of honorable living. It engenders a greater degree of truthfulness on the part of others as well. "Frankness," said Emerson, "invites more frankness."[2] And, on the other hand, it can be a tool of the smug, self-certain, and even the malicious who tyrannize friend and foe alike by their disarming bluntness which goes by the name of frankness.

Perhaps, then, in order to view the quality of frankness from a greater perspective, we ought to recall the ethics of Judaism as taught by

---

1. November 24, 1962.
2. Ralph Waldo Emerson, "Prudence."

Maimonides, in which he gives us a philosophy of character. In general, Maimonides teaches that we should avoid the extremes of character and keep to the *"derekh Hashem,"* "the way of God," which he also calls the *"shevil hazahav,"* "the golden path" (*Hilkhot De'ot* 1:7). In other words, one should generally follow the path of moderation, although in certain specific instances one may veer more toward one extreme than the other. So it is with the quality of truth-telling or frankness. The two extremes are, one, absolute candor even at the expense of another person's happiness, sensitivity, and peace of mind, and two, so much kindness and deference to the feelings of people that the truth is never spoken in its fullness, and untruth begins to prevail. Following "the way of God" as explained by Maimonides, we would say that in general one ought to be moderate in his frankness, tempering his manner of expressing the truth with gentleness and sensitive concern for the feelings of others, but that in certain very special cases one must veer toward one of the extremes – in the case of truthfulness to the extreme of greater veracity, more direct frankness, and forthrightness.

One of those special cases where frankness must prevail even at the expense of temporary unhappiness is hinted at in *Parashat Ḥayyei Sara*, according to the brilliant interpretation of Rabbi Naftali Tzvi Yehuda Berlin, the revered teacher at the Yeshiva of Volozhin, widely known by his initials, Netziv.

A great tragedy marred the lives of Isaac and Rebecca. The next *parasha* tells of the painful confusion with regard to the blessings Isaac offered to his twin sons, Jacob and Esau. Apparently, Isaac favored Esau, and Rebecca preferred Jacob. In order to reserve Isaac's blessing for Jacob and prevent its being wasted on Esau, Rebecca schemes with her son Jacob, persuading him to do something which runs against the whole grain of his character: to deceive his aged, blind father. The scheme is successful, but the end result is one of unrelieved anguish for all principals. Esau is left embittered, and more vagrant than ever. Jacob has soiled his soul and must flee from his brother into a long and bitter exile. Rebecca, the doting mother, is to die before she ever again sees her beloved Jacob. Isaac is confused and bewildered in the deep darkness that surrounds him in his blindnesss.

And yet, when we study and analyze the *sidra* carefully, we find that the tragedy is compounded by the fact that it was totally unnecessary. Isaac did not really favor Esau over Jacob. He merely wanted to prevent his total moral collapse. He wanted to salvage whatever shred of decency Esau still retained. He knew full well the difference in the characters of his two children. He, no less than his wife Rebecca, appreciated the saintliness of Jacob and suffered because of the wildness and sensuousness of Esau. He had never intended to give the blessing of Abraham to anyone but Jacob.

Why then the cross-purposes at which Isaac and Rebecca worked? If they were indeed in total agreement, why this deep and cutting tragedy that destroyed the happiness of the second Jewish family in all history? Because, the Netziv answers in his *Emek haDavar*, Rebecca never learned how to be frank with her own husband. She was possessed of an inner inhibition which, despite her love for him, prevented free and easy communication with him. It was a congenital defect in her character. If only Rebecca had been frank with Isaac, if only she could have overcome her inhibitions and shyness and taken him into her confidence, they would have discovered that they do, after all, agree on fundamentals – and how much heartache would have been avoided!

And the Netziv sees this quality of restraint and suspiciousness in the very first act the Torah records of Rebecca when she first meets her prospective husband. When she is told by Eliezer that Isaac is coming toward them, what does she do? She slips off her camel, and she takes her veil and covers herself. This was not, says the Netziv, so much an act of modesty and shyness as much as a symbol of a lack of frankness, an uncommunicativeness that was to hamper her happiness the rest of her life. In all her dealings with her husband, she was metaphorically to veil her personality. That veiling presaged the lack of frankness, the restraint between the two. The veil became, in the course of years, a wall which grew ever larger and kept them apart and prevented them from sharing their deepest secrets, fears, loves, and aspirations.

Indeed, that is why the Torah tells us of certain domestic and seemingly purely private quarrels between Sara and Abraham, and Jacob and Rachel. One might ask, why reveal for all eternity the domestic spats between couples? Sara laughs when she is told that she would have a child despite her advanced age and she denies it to Abraham. He turns to her in anger and says, "You did so laugh" (Genesis 18:15). Rachel wants children, and keeps urging Jacob for help. Jacob turns to her and seems quite irritated: "Why do you annoy me? Do you think I am God that I can give you children?" (ibid., 30:2).

We can now understand why these incidents are recorded: they are there for contrast. They show us how the other patriarchs and matriarchs exercised complete candor in their private lives. If there must be a slight argument, let there be one, but let husband and wife be perfectly honest with each other. Let there be no distance between them, no dissembling – no outer politeness which bespeaks an inner remoteness. How different was Rebecca from Sara and Rachel. There was so little frankness in Rebecca's relations with Isaac, so little straightforwardness – and therefore, so much agony, so much unnecessary pain and frustration.

Indeed, it would seem as if Eliezer, Abraham's servant whom he had sent to fetch a wife for his son Isaac, recognized this at the very outset. Charged with this grave and significant mission of looking for a wife for Isaac, a worthy mother of the Jewish people, Eliezer feels himself diffident and concerned. He prays for divine assistance, and twice he singles out one element above all others: *ḥesed* – love, kindness. "May God show my master Abraham *ḥesed*, may He grant that his son be blessed with a wife whose greatest virtue would be kindness, love, sensitive understanding, self-sacrifice" (see Genesis 24).

If I can find that kind of wife, Eliezer thinks to himself, who will bring *ḥesed* to her new home, then I will consider my mission successfully accomplished. And yet, after he has met young Rebecca, after he has satisfied himself that this is the right woman for his master's son, he offers a prayer of thanksgiving in which he surprisingly adds another quality: "Blessed is the Lord God of my master Abraham who has not forsaken *ḥasdo*, His *ḥesed* (mercy), and *amito*, His *emet* (truth), from my master." If we read between the lines we discover that Eliezer is quite satisfied that this young woman will bring *ḥesed* to her home. She will be a kind, devoted, loving wife. But what suddenly begins to disturb his innermost thoughts, perhaps only unconsciously, is that while there will be enough *ḥesed*, there will be a lack of *emet* or truthfulness in the sense of candor. There may not be enough frankness because she would be too kind, too fearful, too gentle to speak openly and lucidly with her own husband. How wise was that old and loyal slave of Abraham! Thank you, God, for the *ḥesed*; now help us with a little more *emet*.

Domestic life, then, is one of those areas where we ought to leave the exact path of moderation and incline toward one of the extremes, that of greater openness – greater frankness and honesty even at the expense of comfort and unperturbed peace of mind. Even to this day, before the *ḥuppa* we perform the *badeken*, or veiling of the bride, recalling the veiling of Rebecca. Yet, as if to emphasize that we intend thereby only the idea of modesty and not that of inhibition, we read the *ketuba*, in which we include the promise of the husband that he will act toward his wife in the manner of Jewish husbands, who work for, love, and support their wives, and then the key word: *bekushta*, in truth. *Kushta* or *emet* – truth – should be the dominant mood that prevails in the home. Without it, without full and free frankness, husband and wife cannot act in concert with regard to the great issues in life, especially with regard to the greatest gift entrusted to them: their children.

And yet, while frankness is so very important in domestic relations, and while it is a wonderful and indispensable personal quality in all human relations, there is no question but that frankness can be overdone. Truth has the greatest claims on us; but its claims are not absolute. That is why the Talmud specifically permits the *talmid ḥakham* or scholar to modify the truth in three instances, where complete candor would result in needless embarrassment. Not to tell a lie is a great virtue, but compulsively to tell all, to reveal all your innermost feelings without regard for others, is itself an unethical quality. When Abraham walked with Isaac to perform the *Akeida*, Isaac asked his father, "I see the fire and the wood but where is the lamb for the sacrifice?" Imagine if Abraham had exercised absolute frankness, unrestrained candor. He would have said: "Sorry son, but it is you I shall have to slaughter upon the altar." It would have been inhumanly cruel. That is why Abraham preferred to dodge the question with the reply, "God will take care of that." Or imagine if a physician who had just discovered that his patient is suffering from a terrible and incurable disease were to turn to him and, without any attempt to cushion the news, inform him bluntly of his imminent death. This kind of frankness is subhuman. It is living on the extreme edge of character, against which Maimonides counseled. That is why the halakha says[3] that if a person does not know his relative has died, and you do know it, and he will not learn of it during the next thirty days if you keep silent, then you must keep the information within and spare him the bad news.

Excessive frankness is, thus, a fault; a vice and not a virtue. When a friend begins a conversation with the words, "I want to be brutally frank with you," you may be sure that he intends brutality more than frankness. A whimsical poet once wrote, "of all plagues, good Heaven, Thy wrath can send, save, save, O save me from the Candid Friend."

Emet, then, is a virtue, if tempered with graciousness. *Emet* is important enough to be the connecting link between the Shema and the *Amida*. Yet we must remember that this *emet* is not mentioned alone. Along with it we enumerate a whole list of qualities which tend to make truth more palatable, which moderate frankness and make it human. *Emet* must also be *yatziv venakhon vekayam veyashar*, proper and straight; it must be *ne'eman ve'ahuv vehaviv venehmad vena'im*, loyally and pleasantly and attractively presented; even if it is *nora va'adir*, an awesome and powerful truth, still it must be *metukan umekubal*, prepared for and acceptable to human sensitivity, and above all, *vetov veyafeh*, expressed in a manner that is good and beautiful. Frankness, yes; but *mentschlichkeit* as well. *Emet* – but up to and including *tov veyafeh*.

Only then can we be sure that *hadavar hazeh aleinu le'olam va'ed*, that this truth will remain with us forever.

That is why the halakha maintained that the law of reproaching the sinner (Leviticus 19:17) must be executed with a great deal of delicacy and attention to individual feelings. There is, in Judaism, an ethic of criticism. A frank reproof may be in itself unavoidably painful, but one should minimize the anguish and the guilt and the feelings of inferiority and worthlessness that may needlessly result from it.

Too much frankness – candor with cruelty – is one of the causes of the lapse from religious faith as well. Sa'adia Gaon, in the introduction to his major work, *Emunot veDe'ot*, lists eight causes of heresy, of

---

3. See *Taz* on *Yoreh De'ah* 402:12.

skepticism. One of them is: *ha'emet hamara,* the bitter truth. Truth is often difficult to face, bitter to taste, and people may prefer to flee the unpleasant truth and satiate themselves with sweet vagaries of falsehood. I believe that in our day an even more frequent cause of the disdain some people feel for Judaism is that the truth, Torah, is presented as something bitter and terrible. When, instead of teaching Torah as an ennobling and uplifting doctrine, we force it down the throats of children as something dreadfully boring and meaninglessly restrictive; if it is advocated to adults as something dogmatic and irrelevant, if it is supported not by explanation but coercion, not by an appeal to conscience but by boycotts and smear-literature and stonings, then the *emet* becomes so bitter as to alienate large sections of our people from Torah. Torah is "sweeter than honey"; it is a crime to present it as dipped in gall. Frankness should not be confused with foolishness, and candor should not be confounded with crude, cruel coarseness.

Frankness, then, is a great virtue. In all of life, but especially in domestic life, is it an absolutely indispensable ingredient of happiness. Because she lacked it, because her personality and innermost heart was veiled, Rebecca's life was filled with misery. Yet, frankness must be attended by the grace of consideration, delicacy, and sensitivity.

Every morning, we begin the day with the following statement which sums up what we have been saying: *"Le'olam yehei adam yerei shamayim beseter uvegalui,"* one should always be God fearing, both publicly and privately; *"umodeh al ha'emet,"* let him always recognize and acknowledge the truth. But once he has acknowledged the truth, once he has learned it, it is always important not to blurt it out unthinkingly. For, insofar as speaking out the whole truth, let him be *vedover emet bilvavo,* telling all the truth only *in his heart.* When it comes to telling all that one considers to be the truth, exactly as one sees it and believes it – in all candor and frankness – one must also be judicious, and consider the secret fears and vanities of his fellows, their sensitivities and idiosyncracies. Complete and uninhibited frankness – only *bilvavo,* in one's own heart. Otherwise, candor must be wedded to considerateness, *ḥasdo* and *amito,* as Eliezer prayed, or *emet* and *yatziv* through *tov veyafeh,* as is our own devoted prayer every day all year long.

For this indeed is, as Maimonides called it, the *derekh Hashem,* the way of the Lord. And it is this way which has been bequeathed to us by our patriarch Abraham and which we were commanded to teach our children (Genesis 18:19): "For I have known him, to the end that he may command his children and his household after him, that they may keep *derekh Hashem*, the way of the Lord" – for in this way will righteousness and justice be achieved.

Toledot

Isaac – History's Thanksgiving Sermon[1]

T he life of Isaac, inspiring and pathetic in its tragic beauty, stands out as history's sermon to Americans, and especially American Jews, in this Thanksgiving season.

Tragedy seems to have followed this patriarch to the end. His early life was a magnificent episode. As a young man he accomplished the most glorious feat in Jewish history – his consent to be sacrificed for God when his father Abraham informed him that it was God's will. Here was a young man of thirty willing to be cut off at such a young age because it was the divine will that it be so. That God intervened at the last moment and rescinded His command to Abraham makes no difference. The fact is that Abraham surrendered his most beloved son; the fact is that Isaac made his decision to give his life; and the fact is that his beloved mother, Sara, died when she heard the news that Abraham had almost offered up her only son.

This great episode – known as the *Akeida* – is the theme we constantly recall in our prayers when we want to advocate the cause of Israel before God and plead for divine mercy.

---

1. November 27, 1954.

The early part of Isaac's life was gallant, glorious, and lofty. Our rabbis, however, with their customary bent for just and unprejudiced appraisals of our people's heroes, were quite critical of him. And they expressed this criticism in the form of an imaginary debate between Isaac and Moses. The Midrash (Deuteronomy Rabba 11:3) quotes Isaac as saying to Moses, I am greater than you, because I was willing to sacrifice my life by being bound on the altar, and thus, *"ra'iti penei haShekhina,"* "I saw the Divine Presence"; that is, I attained great religious insight. To which Moses answers, True, but I am still greater than you, because while you may have seen the *Shekhina,* you became blind soon afterwards – as we read in this *sidra,* "When Isaac became old, his eyes failed him" (Genesis 27:1) – whereas I spoke to the *Shekhina "panim el panim,"* directly (Exodus 33:11), and yet my eyesight never failed me.

Here is an interesting dialogue, although we must understand that since several generations separate the two, the midrash is not to be taken literally, and also that the arguments put into their mouths are not to be taken as typical of their characters – since they certainly were more humble than that. What our rabbis did mean to point out was that great sacrifice and the attainment of great vision are terribly important – but the vision must be sustained and the sacrifice repeated if necessary; that the vision must not be followed by failing eyes; that the insight should not be neutralized by blindness; that the moment of greatness should be followed by everlasting light and not by an eternity of darkness.

That is the tragedy of Isaac's life. To what great moments he rose when he lay down on the stone altar and calmed his father, directing him in his slaughter! At that moment, as the sages relate, as he was lying bound during the *Akeida,* face upwards, the very heavens split and Isaac saw the heavenly hosts and the ministering angels. He saw the Divine Presence – and, because of the brilliance of the vision, he was blinded. What a tragedy: from visionary to blind man! And even worse, as he grows older he becomes blinder. It is more than physical blindness, for while he remains the great and holy patriarch, one of the three fathers of Israel, he, in his old age, fails to discriminate between his evil son and his good son, between an Esau and a Jacob! Unlike Moses, who sustained his vision throughout his entire life, Isaac weakens with age, and turns blind – blind to Esau's treachery, blind to Jacob's piety (Deuteronomy

Rabba 11:3), blind to Rebecca's loyalty. How pitiful was that trek from *Akeida* to blindness!

This, then, is the intent of the rabbis in this midrash – history's Thanksgiving sermon expressed in the personality of Isaac. It is not enough to *have* a vision; one must *keep* it. It is not sufficient to *have made* a sacrifice, no matter how great; one must ever be prepared to repeat it. Vision and insight must be followed through with ongoing clarity.

I say that it is history's Thanksgiving sermon because now is the time for us Americans, and even more so us American Jews, to remember that the splendid visions of freedom and the noble sacrifices for democracy that our country made in its youth, and for which we now thank God – these visions and sacrifices can be lost, denied and belied in our time by the petty blindnesses that seem to be afflicting us as we grow older.

Let me give you two examples of great victories won through sacrifice and vision, and which are now being lost through "He became old, and his eyes failed him" – through a blindness that sometimes comes with age; two great freedoms which, one way or another, we are abandoning and allowing to atrophy.

First there is the precious American freedom, the freedom of speech. The American Revolution was the sacrifice our country offered for this great freedom for which we are so thankful. It was primarily Thomas Jefferson who had the great vision of completely free and unfettered freedom of expression. It was he who in 1779 insisted that "the opinions of men are not the object of civil government, nor under its jurisdiction ... truth is great and will prevail if left to herself ... errors ceasing to be dangerous when it is permitted freely to contradict them." This vision was, ten years later, to become part of the Bill of Rights as the First Amendment to the Constitution. It is one of the finest and noblest thoughts which men could envision and for which they might sacrifice.

If we had been like Moses, who could keep up a sustained vision, we would have insisted upon the sacred and inviolate character of that right. Instead, we have, with our increasing age, allowed that right of all free men to be gradually curtailed. During World War I, we allowed it to be legislated that to speak out against participation in the war is a crime. Since then, and especially since the Cold War, it has become a crime to advocate certain political thoughts. We are becoming blind, losing that terrific insight of our national youth that "truth will prevail if left to herself" and the errors will cease to be dangerous if we are free to contradict them. And now, just this week, we saw what is at one and the same time the most ridiculous and most dangerous of quirks of unintelligent congressmen. At the same time that certain national military schools forbade their students to debate the question of allowing Red China into the UN, a congressman from Virginia, who otherwise has been resting in fortunate obscurity, threatened students from a private college with turning in their names and statements to the FBI if they dare take the affirmative in this debate. Certainly, this is ridiculous, and many good Americans have rightly damned his statement. But it is a terrible symptom of impending blindness. This season, when we thank God for our freedoms, we have got to sustain them in a continuing vision of freedom of speech unblurred by nearsighted bigots.

A second, and even more important example, is that of freedom of religion. I need not recount to you the many sacrifices the Pilgrim Fathers and other early Americans had to make in order to assure this great freedom. It was not an easy task, because early America was not free from pernicious bigotry. Early American Jews found prejudice in New York and in Massachusetts and in other colonies. Freedom of religion was a noble vision and was hard-won, only with many sacrifices.

And yet, today, we have been somewhat untrue to those sacrifices and we have lost the vision. First, there is a tremendous abuse of this freedom – which includes the proposition that the state favors no one church or sect against another – right here in Springfield and in almost all of Massachusetts. Those parents who have children in the city's public schools are only too well-aware of the curtailment of religious freedom in our educational system. When Jewish children are forced to participate in reciting a prayer which comes from the Christian Bible; when our children are told that they must sing songs or carols which are most definitely Christian religious hymns; when these and many other such instances are public knowledge – and when these and similar matters are hush-hushed by our fellow Jews because they are afraid to be known as "troublemakers" – then I say that our democracy is decrepit with age and dying of blindness. If fighting for religious freedom makes one a "troublemaker," then I say that it is a mitzva of the Constitution to be a troublemaker. Being that kind of troublemaker puts one in the same category with Jefferson and Washington and Penn and Franklin. If we can allow such abominable conditions to go unchecked – because of the silly reason just mentioned, or because of a fatalistic, it-just-can't-be-helped attitude – then we are allowing our eyes to be dimmed and our sacrifice to prove vain.

But not only in this way are we losing the beauty of our early American dreams. I think that one of the main abuses of the freedom of religion is allowing religion to fall into disuse. Is it worth giving your life so that you can worship the way you want to, if you don't worship? By not practicing the religion for which you seek freedom, you blind the democratic insight, you make the sacrifice into a forfeiture and the vision into a pipe dream. If this Thanksgiving we thank God for the freedom of religion, let us by all means go ahead and practice it. Otherwise, there is little to be thankful for.

How can we, as Americans and as Jews, keep this vision constantly before our eyes? How can we vindicate the sacrifices, the American *Akeida*, and redream the American dream with unfailing clarity? By remembering that the Bill of Rights, our most precious political heritage, is not *given* to us by our government. It is *given* to us by God and only *guaranteed* by the government. When we remember that, then our insight becomes a vision, our vision a prophecy, and our sacrifices become an eternal vigilance and victorious struggle for Democracy.

In concluding, let me quote to you a similar-minded paragraph from Justice Douglas' splendid book, *An Almanac of Liberty*, which was recently published:

> The basic premise on which the Declaration of Independence rests is that men "are endowed by their Creator with certain unalienable Rights." That means that the source of these rights is God, not government. When the state adopts measures protective of civil liberties, it does not confer rights. It merely confirms rights that belong to man as the son of God.... To "secure" sometimes means to obtain, sometimes to safeguard. In the Declaration of Independence and in the preamble to the Constitution,

to "secure" means to safeguard … The rights and liberties "secured" were those which American citizens already had. Government merely underwrote them.

Therein lies the basic difference between democratic and totalitarian governments. In fascist, communist, and monarchical states, government is the source of rights: government grants rights; government withdraws rights. In our scheme of things, the rights of man are unalienable. They come from the Creator, not from a president, a legislature, or a court.[2]

These are the words of a wise judge. It is an American testament. It is something for which the Founding Fathers sacrificed, and which was already envisioned in the Torah, which declared that man was created by God, and that therefore all men are His children.

We are thankful that God has granted us these rights, and we are thankful that our country guarantees them. In appreciation of them, we will determine not to invalidate the sacrifices and demean the visions. As our democracy grows and matures, we shall strive to keep it from blindness. Instead, may it forever be capable of profound insight and ever-sustained vision.

2. William O. Douglas, *An Almanac of Liberty* (New York: Doubleday, 1954), 5.

The View from the Brink[1]

In a recent book by Norman Cousins, *In Place of Folly*,[2] there appears a most improbable obituary which is purely imaginary – and frighteningly real. It reads,

> RACE, HUMAN. Beloved father of science and technology, adored mother of the arts and culture. Departed this earth suddenly, but not without warning. Survived by no one.

What makes this obituary so very pertinent is the series of hair-raising events which, during the past month, took humanity to the very brink of annihilation. The Cuba crisis brought not only Americans but all human beings to the sharp edge of universal catastrophe, face-to-face with the ultimate terror.

The question that we must ask ourselves is what was or should be our reaction? We who have tottered on the rim of total horror, and have won a reprieve, we who have stared into the dread of the atomic

---

1. December 1, 1962.
2. New York: Harper, 1962.

abyss – what view do we now take of life? Have we undergone any inner transformation as a result of this experience? Do we view things any differently now?

For assuredly the brink represents a unique psychological situation. The knowledge of impending disaster, for mankind as well as for individual men or women, evokes a reaction which reveals all our inner qualities: personality, principles, and purposes – or lack of them. The more intensely we are aware of the end, of the limitation of life, the more we concentrate our essential character and aspirations into the time left to us.

Our *sidra* provides us with a clear contrast between two biblical characters in their reactions to the proximity of the end. They are for us an indication of what death tells us about life. Father and son, Isaac and Esau, were both concerned over the finiteness of life. Both based their lives on the fact that it ends. Both acted out of the knowledge that man is mortal and soon must pass on. Yet the same cause resulted in effects that were worlds apart. Listen to Isaac, the old father: "And he said, 'Behold now I am old, I know not the day of my death. Now therefore take, I pray you, your weapons … and make me savory food, such as I love, and bring it to me that I may eat, that my soul may bless you before I die'" (Genesis 27:2–4). Life is so short, says Isaac, and I am going to die any day now. There is so much left undone. I have taken care of Jacob – he is the sort of person who will always be a credit to me. But what of Esau? Must he always be condemned to play the savage – unwanted and unloved, feared and hated? Must he be eternally estranged from his heavenly Father? Shall it not be said of him that he did something noble in all his life? And so – because of his impending death – Isaac takes action, and sends Esau off on an errand that he can perform with competence, not for selfish purposes, but rather for a higher goal, that of the mitzva of *kibbud av*, honoring his father. Isaac is in a hurry to teach Esau to do something unselfish, something for others, something which can result in a blessing for him who was spiritually inferior to his brother.

Esau was motivated by the same consideration of the brevity of life and his eventual death. But look at how different a construction he places on this inevitable fact: "And Esau said, 'Behold, I am going to die, what profit shall the birthright be to me?'" (Genesis 25:32). Since life is short and must end, who needs or wants the spiritual mission implied by the blessing of the birthright?

For Isaac the imminence of death was an incentive to leave a blessing. For Esau it was a reason to feast on lentils. For Isaac death was a signal to reenforce the spiritual worth of a wayward child. For Esau it was an excuse for forfeiting a birthright. This is how death clearly defines the essence of personality – by making a man choose between a last blessing and a last fling.

All of us are acquainted with such cases of approaching disaster acting as the test to distinguish between the Isaacs and the Esaus. Two young men who seem remarkably alike in personality and background go off to war. One can achieve dignity and spiritual wholesomeness from this same experience which leads the other to immorality and a completely nihilistic outlook on life. One has found God in the fox-hole – and one has lost Him in the hail of frontline fire. The awareness of death has made one choose a last blessing and the other a last fling. That is why the last war turned some religious youngsters into cynical adults, and flighty youngsters into serious, dedicated, and pious adults. "Behold I am going to die" has forced upon them the ultimate choice of their lives – how to live in the face of death. It is the most fateful choice a man can make.

Indeed, the Talmud indicated that the same is true of old age in general – for advanced age is, in a manner of speaking, a euphemism for the sharpened awareness of the impending end. As we advance in years, we begin to concentrate, in the time left to us, on what we regard as truly significant and enduring, whether good or bad. So the rabbis taught: "*Talmidei ḥakhamim*, scholars and learned people, the older they grow the wiser they become," but "*Amei ha'aretz*, the ignorant, the older they grow, the more does their foolishness increase" (*Shabbat* 152b). This is the Talmud's geriatric test of character. What a man does with his old age is an expression of his whole life's values. If a man dreams of his retirement in the manner of most moderns – fishing, golfing, endless cardplaying – then it tells you something about his whole life, from the beginning and on. If his ambition is to retire so he can devote himself to voluntary work for yeshivot or hospitals or Israel, then it tells you something quite different about the meaning of his life. Most of a man's essential qualities, whether those of *hokhma* (wisdom) or *tipshut* (foolishness), are concentrated in his old age.

The halakha also reveals this insight. Thus, the Talmud (*Bava Batra* 175a) tells us that under normal circumstances if a man makes a public announcement acknowledging a debt to another, if he does not immediately appoint witnesses and instruct them to record his confession, the announcement is meaningless and the debt is not collectible. The reason is that he may argue, *"Meshateh ani bakh,"* "I was merely joking," I was not serious. However, if a critically ill person makes such an acknowledgment, even without appointing witnesses, the debt is regarded as real and collectible, as the words of a seriously ill person are regarded as written and transmitted. The reason? *"Ein adam meshateh besha'at mita,"* a man does not dissemble when death approaches. At a time of this sort, one is deadly serious. Then life itself is placed on the line, and all artificiality and empty conventionalism is discarded.

The Chafetz Chaim once said that all of life is like a postcard. When we first begin to write, we use big, broad strokes, and fritter away valuable space on empty, tired clichés: "How are you?" "How is the weather?" "Wish you were here…" But as we approach the end of the card, and realize that we still have not said anything of importance which we originally intended, we no longer squander our valuable resources of space, but write sparingly, in small letters, conserving our language and sticking only to what is truly essential. So it is in life itself. When we suddenly realize we are approaching the end of the card, we begin to abandon the petty and the trivial, and take up only that which we, in accordance with our basic character and in our hearts of hearts, consider as truly significant and abiding.

Perhaps in this manner we can understand an otherwise startling passage in the Talmud (*Berakhot* 10a). We are told that David contemplated the day of his demise and began to sing! How strange. One would think that entertaining this kind of morbid thought would result in sorrow or dejection, not song. Yet the rabbis have here given us a valuable key to the personality of King David – for he presents us with a historical paradox. Scripture describes him to us as possessing apparently two totally different personalities. Which of these is the real

David: the triumphant soldier, or the tender singer? The man of the sword, or the man of the Psalms? The general of the army, or the saint of the Almighty? The conqueror of Goliath, or the champion of God? He whose saber penetrated to the heart of the enemy, or he whose sweet singing reached the very heart of heaven? And the answer is: look at David when he realizes that the end is near, that life is so very limited. At that time you will find him revealing his true colors. And what do we find when David contemplates the day of his death? He does not plan a military campaign, but rather – another song to our Father in heaven! It is the song, not the sword, that symbolizes the real David. The essential, authentic David is the one of the book of Psalms, not the one that appears to us in the second book of Samuel.

Like David, we have stared death in the face. We have confronted the awesome possibility of universal apocalyptic cataclysm. The Cuba incident was only a single incident. Our world will never again be the same. During our lifetime, we shall have to live with that terror constantly. Henceforth all mankind shall have to walk and plod its way through the valley of the shadow of death. Psychologically, the new generation accepts the possibility of no tomorrow, of no future, as matter-of-factly as ours accepted automobiles and automobile accidents.

Our generation is even more aware of the end than that of twenty centuries ago when the Kingdom of God was expected momentarily. The H-bomb has made the possibility of universal destruction an immediate reality. The end of the world is no longer a matter of theological speculation. It is an overwhelmingly real threat, made possible by science and engineering and hanging on the thin threads of diplomacy and politics. "Behold, I am going to die" is of immediate importance even to a young man in the prime of health. The diplomats and statesmen are concerned with controlling the possibility of cosmic catastrophe and eliminating it.

The overarching problem for each and every one of us is, how shall we react to this dread threat of the End? Shall we dedicate ourselves to that which is important and sacred in life and try for a last blessing like Isaac; or shall we conclude that since death is near, nothing is any longer of importance, and hence sell our birthrights and take a last fling at a banquet of self-indulgence in the manner of an Esau? Shall we follow the rabbis who counseled (Deuteronomy Rabba 11:3): "Return to God one day before you die," and since you do not know which day that is, then return to Him every day; or that of the cynics quoted by Isaiah (22:13): "Eat meat and drink wine; eat and drink, for tomorrow we die"? Shall we emulate Moses who, before he died, left a *Vezot haberakaha*; or a Don Quixote who, expressing the sentiment of his age, advised us to "make hay while the sun shines"? Shall we turn to Shakespeare who informed us that "life is full of sound and fury signifying nothing"; or the Ba'al Shem Tov who, as his disciple the Koretezer Rebbe related, when he realized he had only a short time left to live, turned his eyes to heaven and said, "Almighty God, I make a gift to You of my remaining hours"? Shall we continue our wonted ways – of complaining that our luxuries are too few, of treating friends and family lightly, of pampering ourselves and grasping for more status; or shall we thank God for every new sunset and peaceful sunrise, for every clear horizon unstained by a mushroom cloud, for the security and comfort of familiar faces, for the privilege of striving for true stature rather than mere status? Which view shall we take back from the brink: that of Esau, and try to pack in all the "fun" we can in whatever time remains; or that of Isaac, and leave a blessing in the form of more Torah, more *Yiddishkeit*, more human decency and morality – and thus perhaps avoid the ultimate plunge over the edge of the Brink?

It is a crucial, fateful question. On our answer depends the future of humanity and of our very selves. May we opt for blessing, for return to God, for creativity. And from this choice may we emerge with the hope, the faith, and the confidence that there will indeed be a tomorrow, and tomorrows after that. In the words of Malachi in this portion's *haftara*, "My covenant was with him for life and for peace, and I gave them to him for fear, and he feared Me, and he bowed low before My Name" (2:5). If we wish to survive, and not only survive with life, but also attain true peace, then it must be through fear – not the fear of the bomb, but the fear of God. For only when man fears God can he have true confidence in hope for his own future and his inner self; and only when man bows low before the Name of the Almighty can he rise to the full stature of his own noble humanity.

Religion by Relegation[1]

In an almost casual, offhand way, our *sidra* tells us of a series of incidents in the life of Isaac that are apparently of no special significance, but in which our rabbis have seen the greatest importance.

Isaac lived in the land of Canaan, which suffered from scarcity of water most of the year, and he therefore decided to dig a well. We are told of three wells that he and his entourage dug. The first two involved him in difficulties with the people of Gerar, a Philistine nation. The first of these Isaac called *Esek*, because it was the cause of much strife and contention. He was no more successful with the second well; after his servants dug it, he incurred the hatred of the people about him. He therefore called the second well by the name *Sitna*, meaning enmity. It was only when the third well was dug that happiness prevailed once again; and so he called the third well *Reḥovot*, meaning: room, freedom, scope, peace, or joy.

Of what importance can these apparently prosaic matters be to later generations, who search in the Torah for matters of timeless significance and are not particularly interested in economic clashes and

---

1. November 27, 1965.

riparian rivalry in ancient Canaan? Nachmanides, following the principle of the rabbis that *"ma'aseh avot siman levanim,"* that the deeds of the fathers anticipate the history of the children, has taught us that the three wells of Isaac recapitulate the stories of the three great Sanctuaries of the people of Israel. The first well is a symbol of the First Temple, which was destroyed because of *Esek* – because of the battles and wars waged on the Jewish people by the surrounding nations. The second well, that called *Sitna*, represents the Second Temple, for this Temple was brought to ruins by the hatred and enmity that prevailed among the children of Israel during that period. However, the third well, *Reḥovot*, is the symbol of the Sanctuary that has not yet been built – that of the great future. It represents the *Beit haMikdash* which will one day be rebuilt in Jerusalem, and which will last forever in a spirit of *Reḥovot* – freedom, peace, and plenty.

However, the question remains: why indeed was Isaac successful with the third well, while failing with the first two? In what way was the third well, symbol of the Third Temple, superior to the others?

Permit me to provide an answer which has been suggested to me by my uncle, Rabbi Joseph M. Baumol, which not only answers this question but also provides us with a powerful moral for our own lives. If we analyze carefully the three verses which tell of how these three wells were dug, we will discover one significant difference between the first two and the third. The first two were dug by Isaac's servants, his hired help. Of the first well we read: *"Vayaḥperu avdei Yitzḥak,"* "And the servants of Isaac dug the well." With regard to the second well, we read: *"Vayaḥperu be'er aḥeret,"* "They dug another well." In both cases, Isaac relegated his duties and activities to others. Only with regard to the third well do we find the element of personal participation: *"Vayaḥpor be'er aḥeret,"* "And *he* dug another well" (Genesis 26:19, 21, 22). As long as Isaac was going to leave the performance of his duties to others, and not do them himself, there was bound to result *Esek* and *Sitna*, hatred and argumentation. It is only when Isaac, despite the many people ready to serve him, was willing to dig the well by himself, that he was able to achieve *Reḥovot* – the peace and plenty and freedom that he so very much desired. The Third Temple, that which will last unto all eternity, will come about only when every Jew will take it upon himself to perform the *"Vayaḥpor be'er aḥeret,"* the willingness to work by himself, to commit his own energies, talents, concern, and participation to the sacred tasks which we have been assigned.

Actually, Isaac's career from the very beginning reveals this tension between relegation and participation. Throughout his life we find signs of his struggling to learn this great principle of personal involvement. Even before he was conceived, the message came to his father Abraham that Sara would bear the child, Isaac. However, the message came not from God Himself, as it were, but through an angel. And so, when Sara heard it she laughed and ridiculed it – incurring Abraham's annoyance and God's irritation. Only afterwards do we read, "And the Lord said unto Abraham" – when God Himself addressed Abraham, by Himself and not through an angel, Sara began to believe in reverence and awe, and not doubt in mocking laughter, that she would be blessed with a child.

The great story of the *Akeida* also reveals this oscillation between relegation and participation. At first, Abraham decides to offer up Isaac himself. At the last moment, his hand is stayed and, instead, Abraham offers up a ram caught in the thicket nearby. The Torah puts it this way (Genesis 22:13): And behold, *"Ayil aḥar ne'eḥaz basvakh,"* which we normally translate: "A ram was caught in the thicket behind them." But this has also been interpreted in an equally valid fashion as: "Another ram was caught in the thicket" – that is, instead of Isaac, another sacrifice was discovered: the ram. Isaac's life was saved and a "messenger" was offered up in his place, the ram!

His very marriage followed the same pattern. Isaac did not himself go to look for a wife; his father sent the servant Eliezer instead. According to our tradition (*Tosafot* on *Ketubot* 7b), Eliezer was legally a *"shaliaḥ kiddushin,"* an agent to marry a woman for Isaac by proxy. No wonder, as the Netziv has pointed out,[2] throughout their married lives Isaac and Rebecca suffered from a sense of distance and remoteness between them, a lack of open communication and participation with each other. The Netziv sees this symbolized in the event that occurred when Isaac and Rebecca first met. There we read that at the moment

---

2. See "Frankness as Vice and as Virtue."

she saw him, Rebecca took her veil and covered her face. This veil is a symbol of a domestic curtain, an obstruction that prevented them from communicating freely. If there is no direct personal participation, then there is a possibility of misunderstanding and even enmity.

So it was with the wells. It took two difficult diggings until Isaac learned that you ought not send someone else to do your tasks. He then learned that only if "he dug another well," by himself and with his own effort, could he achieve *Reḥovot*, the peace and freedom and space that he needed for his full development.

This idea is especially important in contemporary society. As civilization grows more complex, each person grows less whole and less integrated, for he is less involved in the tasks that require his attention and devotion. With the division of labor, and the progressive concentration of expertise in narrower and narrower fields, we begin to suffer alienation, a sense of distance between ourselves and our fellow-man, a withdrawal from all of life to within ourselves. Especially in our crowded cities, this introversion and withdrawal takes place if only as a means to protect what little precious privacy we have left for ourselves.

And of course, to some extent, we must limit our involvement in society and the lives of others. We need the mechanics of the delegation of duties and tasks in order for society to function. A good administrator is one who does not do everything by himself, but sees to it that others do their parts. We cannot and should not attempt to do everything by ourselves.

The halakha recognized this idea and incorporated it in the institution of *sheliḥut*, agency. We are permitted to designate an agent to perform certain tasks, not only in financial law, but even with regard to such mitzvot as the giving of charity or the writing of a *sefer Torah*. Nevertheless, the principle of *sheliḥut* is not valid for every occasion. For instance, I cannot make an agent to eat in the *sukka* for me, nor can I appoint someone to listen to the sound of the *shofar* for me. If I do, I have failed to fulfill my religious obligations. How do I distinguish between those functions for which I can appoint a messenger, and those which I must perform myself? The famous author of the *Ketzot haHoshen* put it this way: I may make an agent to perform any commandment save a *mitzva shebegufo*, a mitzva which I am required to perform with my own body, my own self. Thus, charity can be given by anyone – the important consideration is the result, that the poor man be fed or housed. Anyone may write a *sefer Torah* for me, provided that I commission it and possess it and use it. But when the commandment is that *I* eat in a *sukka* or that *I* hear the *shofar* – that is a commandment relating to my body, to my person, and no one can take my place.

Thus, certain things cannot be delegated and relegated to others. Today, as we are threatened with the progressive depersonalization of life, we must emphasize as never before the *mitzva shebegufo*, the significance of the individual, of selfhood, of personal participation and responsibility. We must come to recognize that we are each of us not only a collection of assignable functions, but integrated, whole, unique individuals, who must act *by* ourselves and *as* ourselves.

This sense of participation and wholeness is important not only for our individual development, but also for the integrity of family and home. A family is the kind of unit which cannot exist when the people in it conceive of themselves as little islands of humanity who refuse to be involved with each other. A home is a place of people who are concerned with each other, not introverted ciphers. How relevant, unfortunately, to our modern condition is that caustic insight contained in the sarcastic story of a woman who was approached by a real estate agent to buy a home. She refused, saying: "What need do I have of a home? I was born in a maternity ward, raised in a nursery, cared for by babysitters, sent to kindergarten and then to a boarding school, spent my summers in a camp, lived in a college dormitory, moved to a hotel, I spend my vacations at resorts or cruises, when I am sick I am sent to a hospital, when I am old I will spend my time in a senior citizens' home and I will be buried from a funeral parlor. Who needs a home?"

Indeed, if we spend our lives assigning our activities to others, simply giving all of society the power of attorney over our lives, "home" becomes impossible. Modern life encourages "*Vayaḥperu avdei Yitzḥak*," the appointing of others as agents to do our own work, and therefore this same modern life produces an inordinate amount of *esek* and *sitna*, strife and hatred. Judaism, contrariwise, emphasizes the home by stressing "*Vayaḥpor be'er aḥeret*," the importance of personal participation and involvement – with the resulting *Reḥovot*, the sense of joy, release, and freedom.

Sa'adia Gaon, in his *Emunot veDe'ot*, asks: Why were not man and society created perfect so that there would be no need for Torah and mitzvot to help us on the road to perfection? He answers, because happiness and spiritual fulfillment require human work, personal effort, individual commitment, and participation. If perfection is given to us by God without our endeavors, it is impersonal, and it cannot help us to attain the highest levels of spiritual satisfaction. It is only when we, by our own participation and effort, can achieve spiritual growth through the study of Torah and performance of mitzvot, that we can rightly be said to have enjoyed and deserved what we have called *Reḥovot*.

This emphasis is indeed characteristic of Orthodox Judaism; it is indigenous to our whole faith. We believe that many religious duties *cannot* be delegated, and others *should not*. Prayer must be performed by the individual, not sung by the choir and chanted by the cantor and ground out by the organ. Torah must be studied by every individual Jew, by himself and in lectures, not left to rabbis and seminary professors. Kaddish must be recited by the mourner himself, not assigned to the sexton or some hired individual. *Kedusha* must not be confined only to the synagogue; from the synagogue it must extend into the home, so that even the Jewish table becomes an altar. No, there must be no vicarious observance, no religion by relegation.

It is all the more astounding, therefore, to learn of a prominent Orthodox synagogue, which boasts a distinguished membership, but which lacks that personal commitment to public worship which will enable it to have a regular *minyan* of members. This, despite repeated requests by its rabbis, almost to the point of mutual embarrassment, who are now reluctantly forced to conclude that their people lack the sense of personal action, and are almost ready to engage religious Hessians, hired personnel, others to do the work that really ought to be considered a *mitzva shebegufo*, a personal, nontransferable obligation.

This sense of involvement which we have been recommending is best symbolized by a rock that was placed into the coffin of the late, lamented Rabbi Yehuda Leib Maimon, the distinguished leader of religious Zionism and Israel's first minister of religion. When he was a young man, he preached throughout the length and breadth of Europe on behalf of religious Zionism. Once, when he was speaking in a synagogue in the Galician town of Kolomea, an opponent of Zionism threw a rock at him, one that was so large that had it struck its mark it would have brought to an abrupt and tragic end what turned out to be a great and eminent career of a founder of the State of Israel. Rabbi Maimon cherished that rock as a symbol of his utter devotion to the Zionist ideals, and he commanded in his will that upon his death the rock be placed in his coffin as an eternal memento of his personal dedication to and participation in the dream of Zionism based upon Torah.

May we too learn to apply our own efforts, energies, and personal talents to the great and sacred tasks at hand. May we dig hard and deep in the soil of Judaism and Jewish life. And may God grant that the wells of Torah open up, that they gush forth the living waters of Judaism and divine blessings, and that our lives become *Reḥovot*, possessed of new scope, new freedom, abiding joy and everlasting peace. Amen.

Vayetzeh

The Stone on the Well – Boulder or Pebble?[1]

In reading this *sidra* we are puzzled by some extraordinary incidents there recorded. Jacob, we read, had chanced upon a group of shepherds waiting to water their sheep from a nearby well. And on it there rested a stone – an *even gedola*, a stone big enough to cover the mouth or opening of the well (Genesis 29:2). When Jacob notices the shepherds lingering, he tells them, Why don't you go ahead, remove the stone from the mouth of the well and water your sheep? It all seemed so terribly simple to the naïve Jacob. But they answered: "*Lo nukhal,*" we cannot, it is impossible, until all the herds gather and the other shepherds help us. Jacob was puzzled by their attitude, and he thought he might be able to remove the stone – and, in the Bible's eloquent simplicity: "*Vayigash Yaakov vayagel et ha'even me'al pi habe'er*" – he went over and rolled the stone off the mouth of the well…just like that!

We can well imagine the attitude of the shepherds when Jacob walked over to the well. "Look," they probably sneered, "look who's going to play the big hero – Jacob, the *batlan*, the *luftmentsch*!" And we can also imagine their amazement – and their embarrassment – when

---

1. November 29, 1952.

this same Jacob walks up to the stone and effortlessly rolls it off. The stone appeared to Jacob, say the rabbis, *"kemelo pi kevara ketana,"* as big as the hole of a strainer. What to these mighty muscle men appeared to be a boulder, appeared to Jacob to be a mere pebble!

This narrative certainly is remarkable. Jacob's feat of strength and the shepherds' apparent weakness requires some explanation. Why could Jacob do it? And, even more important, why couldn't the shepherds? What does all this mean, and what is it that the Torah is trying to teach us?

The *be'er*, the well, was interpreted in many different ways by our rabbis (Genesis Rabba 70:9). Some said that it refers to Zion – the love for the Jewish home. Others would have it mean the feeling for Jewish ethics, when they say that it refers to Mount Sinai. Still others say that it is the well that accompanied our forefathers – referring to the tradition of the Jew and his sense of continuity. In essence, what our rabbis are trying to tell us is that the *be'er* is the well of the Jewish personality, the source of the forces of opportunity and accomplishment which well up in the Jewish soul and beg to be released. It is a man's talents and his innate abilities which seek expression. But we see so many people, you might say, who never amount to much despite the fact that they have a wealth of talent and ability. True – their talents are never released because there is a stone on the mouth of their well, there are difficulties – hard, cold, and rocky – which must be rolled away first. The stone represents the difficulties in the way of each and every person in his desire to set free the forces which lie in the great well of his personality and being. And it is his attitude to this stone, his approach to these difficulties, which determines whether he will be able to roll it away, like Jacob, or be forced to keep the well covered, like the shepherds.

Yes, it is the attitude which counts the most. It is the idea which gives birth to the fact. The reason the shepherds couldn't roll the stone away was that they were convinced they couldn't do it. Listen once again to the Bible's words: *"Lo nukhal,"* they said, "We cannot. It's impossible." When a man thinks that a particular task is impossible, then for him it *becomes* impossible.

Jacob, however, had no such difficulty. He didn't think that it was impossible. He thought that a man certainly could remove the stone from his well. He therefore went over and, without further ado, simply moved it out of the way. He thought it was possible, and so for him it *became* possible.

The same rule holds true for most of us. If we face the stone on our individual wells – the difficulties which keep us back from doing those constructive things which we want to do, and we imagine that stone to be a boulder – then that is what it is, and try as we might it cannot be budged. Our "*lo nukhal*" attitude makes of it an "*even gedola.*" Approach it, however, with the attitude that it is only "*kemelo pi kevara ketana,*" that the stone is only a pebble, and it can be rolled away as easily as a pebble. What you think is impossible becomes impossible. Think of it as possible, and the odds are that you can do it.

Here is a man who would like to get himself an education. He must continue at night school for two more years in order to get his degree. It is his opportunity to open up the well of his hidden abilities. But there is a stone which lies on that well and threatens to choke it. He must have time for his club, he must finish his office work, he must keep up his social contacts, he must have some rest. "*Lo nukhal,*" sorry, I can't do it – it's impossible. And so the stone becomes a boulder, and for him it is now a virtual impossibility to get a degree. The "*lo nukhal*" made a boulder of the stone, and he cannot surmount it.

On the other hand, take a man like the late President Roosevelt. In the prime of his life he was cut down by crippling polio. What a stone! What a rock! And yet we know, from the many biographies written of him, that his attitude was anything but that of resignation, anything but "*lo nukhal.*" He was going to beat it. It was for him only "*kemelo pi kevara ketana*" – and so the stone became not a boulder but a pebble, and he removed it, allowing all the world to benefit from the treasures stored up in the well of his personality.

The story is told of Marshal Ferdinand Foch, the famous World War I commander, who reported to his headquarters the following message: "My right flank is in retreat. My left flank is encircled. My center is caving. I am ready to attack." Here was a man who could not say "*lo nukhal,*" and so the stones became as pebbles, and he won.

And what is true for individuals is true for communities, and for this community in particular. Of course there are stones on our well. This is not primarily a residential area, the interest in religion in general is waning, and so on and so forth. Look at it that way, and the stone is as formidable as a boulder, and we might as well give up before we start. Think of it, however, as of minor significance, remember that within walking distance of this synagogue there live a minimum of over four thousand adult Jews, and your stone becomes not a boulder but a pebble. As long as we don't say "*lo nukhal*," "we can't, it can't be done, it's impossible," the well can be tapped to good use.

And so, getting back to Jacob, his show of strength was of the mind and not of the muscles; it was a matter of attitude, not sheer brawn. And it was this very same attitude, this "never say die" attitude, which made him perform such miracles all his life. Thus the ivory-tower scholar, the "*yoshev ohalim*," was able to turn shepherd for fourteen long years, to work for Rachel whom he loved. Thus the "*ish tam*," the naïve student, was able to outsmart Laban in his own game of trickery and deceit. Thus was he able to envision a ladder rising into heaven. All this – because he never said "*lo nukhal*," "impossible."

The Vilna Gaon, according to a folk legend, was once asked how one becomes a Vilna Gaon. And he answered, "*Vil nur, vest du zein a gaon*," "If you only will it, you can be a gaon." Just don't say "*lo nukhal*."

And Jacob's reward was ample. When he crossed the Yabok passage with his family and then went off by himself, an angel appeared out of heaven and began to grapple with him. The angel, who according to tradition represented "*saro shel Esav*," the patron angel of Esau, wrestled with him on those bleak Mesopotamian plains until morning. It was the battle for spiritual supremacy – who will ultimately control the destiny of the human race: Jacob, with his religion and faith and decency, or Esau, with his treachery and faithlessness and sinister intrigues? Jacob, fleeing from Laban after having been tricked into fourteen years of hard labor, and fearful of an uncertain future, could easily have been the pessimist and conceded to *saro shel Esav*. But that was not for Jacob, who rolled the stone from the well and never said "*lo nukhal*." And so, it is the angel who concedes to Jacob, and – and this is remarkable – in the very same expression of "*yakhol*." The Bible relates: "*Vayar ki lo yakhol lo*," the angel saw that he could not gain the best of him. Jacob would not surrender, Jacob had never learned the words "*lo nukhal*." How significant and how complimentary, therefore, the encomium which God bestows upon Jacob when, changing his name, He says to him, "*Ki sarita im elohim ve'im anashim*, you fought with angels and with men, *vatukhal*, and you won, you prevailed." There was no "*lo nukhal*" on your tongue; you did not regard any great and noble task as impossible – "*vatukhal*."

The limits of a man's ability are much greater than most men think they are. Tremendous forces churn incessantly in the well of human nature and particularly in the Jewish soul. The stone upon that well can either block it, or the stone can be cast away. What a man does with that stone depends on what he thinks of it. He can be a peasant and, in primitive fear, imagine it a boulder and choke off his life's mission. Or he can be a Jacob and understand that the stone is only a pebble; cast it off, and eventually grapple even with angels – "*vatukhal*" – and win.

Thank Heaven[1]

A thousand years ago, the great Rabbi Sa'adia Gaon taught that our Torah is reasonable and that the human intellect, by itself, can discover the great truths taught in Scripture. Given enough time and brilliance, the human mind can, unaided, arrive at the precepts and concepts revealed by God at Sinai. As an example of how reason can provide us with these principles, he gives: gratitude. The very first thing our reason tells us is that one ought to be grateful. Hence, from this principle of gratitude, we learn that a man ought to pray. It is reasonable that we pray to God out of gratitude to Him.

Certainly, therefore, intelligent people should not be ingrates. That is why Jews recite the *Modeh Ani* immediately upon arising, why they say the *Modim* as part of their prayer, why they recite *Birkat haMazon* after eating. That is why, too, Americans celebrate Thanksgiving Day every year. It is the first dictate of human reason.

It is all the more amazing, therefore, to learn of the remarkable statement of our rabbis in their comment on this *sidra*. We read of how Leah gave birth to her fourth son, and called him Yehuda (Judah)

---

1. November 18, 1961.

because *"Hapa'am*, this time, *odeh*, I shall thank the Lord." Our sages say, "From the day God created the world no one had thanked God until Leah came and thanked Him upon giving birth to Judah, as it is said, 'This time I shall thank the Lord'" (*Berakhot* 7b). Noah, Shem, Eber – all were prophets who discoursed with the Lord. Did they never thank Him? Abraham, Isaac, Jacob – the founders of the true religion – were they so callous and indifferent that they never acknowledged God's gifts to them? Were they, then, unfeeling, ungrateful brutes?

The answer, I believe, lies in a deeper understanding of gratitude or thanksgiving itself. For there are two kinds, or levels, of gratitude. Thanksgiving can be understood as courtesy or as conscience; as social gesture or as sacred grace; as a way of talking or as a state of the soul; as an aspect of personality or as a part of character.

The lower level, that of courtesy or social gesture, is one in which I give thanks only for goods received. It is a kind of verbal receipt – you give me, I thank you. It is based on a theory of compensation: just as I must pay in cash for what I purchase, so must I say "thanks" for gifts or favors. Instead of paying in dollars and cents, I pay in expression of sentiments. If you do not give me anything, naturally I do not thank you. This is an elementary human phenomenon. The compensation theory of thanks is also reasonable and rational. If I do not thank for what I received, I am an ingrate – unnatural, irrational, and unworthy. This is the *hodaya*, the gratitude, which Sa'adia Gaon believed to be a rational, universal principle even without the specific teaching of Torah.

But this is only minimal. It is not spiritual, not truly worthy; it lacks greatness and largeness of soul. This *quid-pro-quo* arrangement is a commercialization of human relations. It does not reveal any humaneness, any selflessness. Perhaps that is why the French philosopher Diderot said that "Gratitude is a burden, and every burden is made to be shrugged off." No one likes to pay, and if thankfulness is merely a payment, then it is no more than a necessary evil. Furthermore, this kind of thanksgiving can become debased and vulgar.

This week I noticed a sign in one of our city buses reading, "It Pays to Be Courteous." How materialistic, how truly cheap! If it did not pay, should one cease to be courteous? This is a selfish kind of thanks, it is gratitude with an "angle" to it. It is cut of the same cloth as the admonition, "Crime does not pay," or "Honesty is the best policy." At its worst, this kind of thank you is nothing more than a please in disguise: I am being courteous and saying thank you now in the hope and the expectation that I shall be the recipient of your largesse again in the future. A lower kind of gratitude indeed!

The higher kind of gratefulness is based not on compensation but on consecration – the consecration of one's whole character. It is a state of mind in which a man is so devoted to the Almighty, so dedicated to transcendent values, so elevated beyond petty, selfish concerns, that he feels himself grasped by a pervasive gratefulness even when he has not received some special favor in advance, even when not bribed into an expression of gratitude.

Perhaps these two kinds of gratitude can be differentiated as thanksgiving for the lower expression and thankfulness for the higher. In thanksgiving, I give thanks as I would give a tip; it is essentially impersonal and a mere discharge of obligation. Thankfulness, however, is a reaction of the total personality; deeply personal, profoundly human.

The most illustrious example of this nobler kind of gratitude, thankfulness, is our matriarch Leah. Her life's greatest ambition was to marry Jacob and to be sincerely loved by him. When our Torah tells us in this *sidra* that "The eyes of Leah were *rakkot*," dull or weak (Genesis 29:17), the rabbis tell the following story (*Bava Batra* 123a): What does "*rakkot*" mean? Rav says, actually dull, and this is not meant to discredit Leah but is said in praise of her. For she had heard people saying that Rebecca has two sons (Esau and Jacob) and Laban has two daughters (Leah and Rachel); the older will marry the older (that is, Esau will marry Leah) and the younger will marry the younger (Jacob will marry Rachel). She went about inquiring: what are the characters of these men? She was told that Esau is an evil man, a thief. Jacob is an "*ish tam yosheiv ohalim*," a decent, respectable, scholarly man. And she, therefore, was slated to marry the despicable but successful thief! As a result, she wept so much and so bitterly and so loudly that her eyes dulled, until her eyelashes fell off because of her many tears! Her red, dull, uncomely eyes were beautiful indeed, for they had become so out of protest against being mated to an Esau!

How pathetic is Leah's story! Her love of Jacob is so great that she even submits to her father's nefarious plan to substitute her for her sister Rachel, whom Jacob dearly loves, deceiving Jacob thereby. She is even willing to go to the *ḥuppa*, and throughout life, playing second fiddle to a more vivacious, dazzling, beautiful sister, married to the same husband. And when she finally is married to him – how tragic her frustration, the blow to her self-esteem! For Jacob does not love Leah at all, and he makes no attempt to disguise his true feelings. With dramatic simplicity, the Torah relates the stunning shock of Jacob when he discovers that he had been married, stealthily, to Leah instead of Rachel – and how crestfallen Leah must have been: "And it was in the morning – and behold it was Leah." It was only Leah, the plain-looking, uninteresting sister! Our rabbis let us in on the conversation which followed this discovery: Immediately Jacob turned to Leah and said, "Daughter of the deceiver, why did you deceive me?" And she answered, "But did you not deceive your father Isaac when you told him, in his blindness, that you were Esau and so took away your brother's blessing – and you accuse me of deceit?" As a result of these words of reproach that Leah directed to Jacob, he began to hate her (*Tanḥuma Yashan*).

Pathetic indeed – yet Leah does not give up hope. Her desire for Jacob's love and respect is too precious to yield so quickly. And so she has a son and feels that now he will love her, so she calls him Reuven ("see, a son"), adding, "Now my husband will surely love me." Does he? No, he does not. And so a second child comes, and she calls him Shimon, "For God *shama*, heard, how despised I am," and will make Jacob love me. And then a third child, Levi – this time, she says, I cannot fail. "Now my husband *yilaveh*, will draw close to me." But he does not. She has failed, and now she knows it. She cried her eyes out, quite literally, for this man, and he now openly rejects her. Now there is only resignation. The last flicker of hope is gone, the embers of promise for the future are cold and dead. She must reconcile herself to being scorned, unloved, unfulfilled. What would be the normal woman's reaction to this kind of marital problem, to this denial of her whole life's dreams? Despair, bitterness, being soured on life, becoming a misanthrope who hates the whole world, full of constant complaints.

And here is where the greatness of Leah shines forth in all its glory. Her fourth child is born – and she calls him Yehuda. Why? *"Hapa'am,* for this time, *odeh*, I shall thank the Lord!" This time, when I realize and accept the fact that the greatest, most overwhelming desire of my life will *not* be granted to me by God, this time I will thank Him! Despite all my failures and disappointments – I thank God! *Hapa'am* – this time, the first time in history, a great soul reached into the heights of the spirit and recognized that thankfulness is more than thanksgiving, that it is a way of reacting to God's very Presence, and not merely paying a debt for His favors. *Hapa'am* – this time, though my hopes are doomed, my love unrequited, my ambitions dashed, I am yet grateful. I do have a great husband nonetheless, I do have wonderful children. I do have the Lord's promise to be the matriarch of a great people.

This was not the thanksgiving of compensation but the thankfulness of consecration. This was not Leah's social gesture but her spiritual ascent. Would that all of us in our affluent society learn that even if we do not get all we want – and who does? – there is so very much to be thankful for. We ought to be grateful *"al nishmoteinu hapekudot Lakh,"* for the religious freedom we Jews enjoy in our beloved America.

Just compare our situation with those of our brothers and sisters in Russia, where the Jewish *neshama* is stifled cruelly. We ought be grateful for the hundreds of daily miracles from which we benefit – *"Al nisekha shebekhol yom imanu ...."* We ought to give thanks for life, health, family, friends. In our *Nishmat* prayer we speak of thanks *"al ahat me'elef alfei ribei revavot pe'amim"* – thousands and millions of thanks. For in this prayer, mentioned in the Talmud, we thank God for rain – for every single raindrop!

And gratitude is not only regarding things that we thank God for, but it is a state of mind, a psychological attunement to God, a climate of conscience; a matter not so much of *having something* as of *being someone*. For ultimately, the ability to achieve this higher form of gratitude is an integral aspect of character – it requires a humility based upon deep insight. That insight is – our own weakness and inadequacy in the presence of God. When we are grateful to Him we are cognizant of the infinite distance between us and Him, between our imperfections and His perfection, between our moral failings and His exalted spirituality. Basically, gratitude to God means acknowledging our dependence upon Him. We *confess* our need of Him, our inability to get along without

Him. No wonder that in Hebrew the word for thanks – *modeh* – also means: I confess! I confess my need of You, I thank you for coming to my assistance! The *Modeh* prayer we recite upon arising each morning means not only "Thank You, God," for returning my soul to me; it means also, "I confess, O God," that without You I would never wake up alive!

This gratitude, the kind we have called thankfulness rather than only thanksgiving, is what we Jews have not only been taught by our tradition, but what we bear as a message to the world by our very names – for the concept and the practice are deeply ingrained in the very texture of the Jewish soul, and this is reflected in the word "Jew." For the name "Jew" comes from Judah, which is the English for Yehuda – the name meaning "thank God," the name of Leah's fourth son, at whose birth our mother Leah reached the heights of sublimity in fashioning, for the first time, an expression of thankfulness issuing from a profoundly religious personality. It is a name that we ought, therefore, to bear with great pride and a sense of responsibility.

I conclude with the words of David: "*Hodu laShem ki tov, ki le'olam ḥasdo.*" Usually this is translated, "Give thanks unto the Lord for He is good, for His love lasts forever" (Psalms 118:1; 136:1). I would paraphrase that in a manner that is consistent with the syntax of the Hebrew verses: "Give thanks to the Lord, for it is good," i.e. it is good for the heart and soul of the thankful person to be grateful, "for His love is over all the world." Wherever man seeks, no matter how desolate the landscape of his experience and environment, he will find evidence of the great goodness of Almighty God.

The Edge of Innocence[1]

T he interpretation by the fifteenth-century commentator Don Isaac Abarbanel on the beginning of this *sidra* is more appropriate for a profound psychologist than for the accomplished economist and diplomat that he was. It puts Jacob's immortal vision of the ladder reaching to heaven in a new light, and yields insights that are highly relevant to the condition of modern man.

The vision of the ladder extending from earth to heaven, with angels ascending and descending it, and the Lord on the top of it, is obviously pregnant with symbolism; and God's address to Jacob in this prophetic dream is patently more meaningful than would appear at first glance. Otherwise, Jacob would not have trembled with awe and sacred terror upon awakening.

The interpretation of Abarbanel, unlike the metaphysical and mystical comments of the other exegetes, is completely personal and psychological, and comes to answer the question of why this vision took place at this time and in this place. Abarbanel tells us that the opening words of the *sidra*, "*Vayetzeh Yaakov*," that Jacob went out of the

---

1. November 19, 1966.

Holy Land, does not mean that he left as a tourist; Jacob was in flight, a refugee from his brother Esau who had sworn to kill him. The hatred of Esau for Jacob was a result of the fact that Jacob had deceived their father Isaac and taken for himself the blessing that Isaac had reserved for Esau. The major content of that blessing can be divided into three parts: the promise of *deveikut*, of communion or attachment between God and the object of the blessing; the promise of *zera*, posterity; and the promise that that posterity will inherit *eretz*, the Land of Israel. And now here he was – Jacob, the recipient of the blessing – without any of these three items! He was not in communion with God: Commenting on the biblical words, *"Vayelekh Ḥarana"* (Genesis 28:10), the rabbis expand on the second word and maintain that this was a place of *ḥaron af*; it reflected God's displeasure. Jacob had no *zera*, no children; not even brothers, or parents, or friends, for he was entirely alone and forlorn. He had no *eretz*, neither land nor the fruit thereof – nothing but the shirt on his back, reduced to using a rock for a pillow and sleeping in the open field.

And here, at this time, Jacob falls into self-doubt. He is nagged by guilt, and by the devastating thought: maybe I was wrong! Maybe I should not have listened to my mother and deceived my father. Maybe I should not have taken the blessing from my brother Esau. Maybe it was not God's will. Maybe I have brought upon myself not a blessing but a curse! In the last *sidra*, we read that Jacob was an *"ish tam,"* a man of wholesomeness, of ethical perfection; and no sensitive, ethical personality can fail to wonder at the rightness of his action. Hence, in this crisis of self-doubt, of ethical perplexity, of inner anguish, of moral torment, there takes place the immortal vision of divine encouragement. Yes, says God to Jacob in this prophetic revelation, you are right to question yourself. But rest assured that your final decision and your ultimate objective were right! The means you utilized were wrong; hence you must now suffer exile, poverty, and homelessness. But do not overstate your guilt. For it is inconceivable that the blessing of Abraham should be given to the likes of Esau. It was always the divine intention that Jacob be in the line of succession of the blessing of Abraham. Your goal, Jacob, therefore, is right. You may now stop torturing yourself, and you should remain firm in your self-confidence.

Thus, the vision confirms the three major components of the Abrahamic blessing. The ladder is a symbol of Jacob's attachment to God; like a ladder, he can make his way, step by step, until he reaches the highest point of communion. God tells him, "The land upon which you lie I shall give to you" (Genesis 28:13), which is the component of *eretz*. And then He gives him the promise of *zera*, or posterity: "Your seed shall be as many as the dust of the earth, and you shall spread out in all directions" (ibid., verse 14).

This vision, then, is addressed to a highly sensitive man, psychologically tormented by doubt and laden with guilt. It assesses this guilt both truthfully and realistically. Thus, Jacob reacts both fearfully – "*Vayira*"; and thankfully – with his famous vow, "*Vayidor Yaakov neder.*"

I say that this insight is pertinent to us, because the problem of guilt and self-doubt is more intense than ever in this complex, anxiety-ridden age; and because modern man, in his alienation and perplexity, lives not in an Age of Innocence, but on the edge of innocence. We are skeptical about ourselves, about our real worth, about our innate dignity. We question our own motives, our virtue, and our innocence. In our complicated society, life is shot through with ambiguities, riddled with contradictions, beset by intricate problems to which there usually are no simple answers. It is not that we do not want to do right; it is simply that we often do not know what is right. And so we walk the thin edge of innocence, and, all too often, cross the boundary and fall into the abyss of moral error and turpitude.

Of course, there are many ways – five, to be exact – in which individuals deal with guilt.

Some suppress it into their unconscious; they are simply not aware of it. It then reveals itself in the form of neurotic symptoms.

Occasionally we do something that is definitely wrong, we are fully aware of it, and we are filled with commensurate guilt – which is as it should be. For this, the Jewish tradition recommends *viduy*, confession, as part of *teshuva*, repentance. It is a healthy medicine for a healthy guilt.

Sometimes people are overburdened with guilt, their peace of mind destroyed – but the crime they regret is no crime; it is all an illusion, unreal! They suffer needlessly and punish themselves without reason. It often is my lot to speak with such people who blame themselves for business crises, for domestic difficulties, for children who go wrong – when it is all really due to circumstances beyond their control, and therefore no reason exists for any guilt. Perhaps the most poignant case of such illusory guilt occurred just a little over a year ago. At that time one youngster sobbingly confessed to his mother that he was responsible for an accident which caused misery to millions of Americans. The youngster was returning from sports practice and, as young boys sometimes do, swinging a broomstick, when he struck a utility pole. At that moment, the great blackout occurred. He was sure that he had caused the blackout by striking the pole! So we must be careful not to assume that we are the cause of some evil phenomenon, when it is really a matter of coincidence and independent of what we have done or said.

But in between the last two cases, there is a fourth category: the large number of good and decent people who, like Jacob, are less than perfect. But, because they are deeply moral and attuned to the divine in man, they question themselves, overreact, and suffer. Jacob, in this sense, is a modern man, caught up in complex dilemmas. Like Jacob, we are not always sure what we are. We are faced with difficult decisions, and we decide; yet we remain with a residue of nagging thoughts that maybe we should have done differently. We question how we have acted toward our father or toward our brother. In business affairs, like Jacob in his dealings with Laban, we sometimes barely skirt the borders of propriety. Again, like Jacob, in his dealings with Joseph, we may have mistakenly shown favoritism to one child over the other. But because of our fundamental decency, because we want to do what is right – like Jacob who is the *ish tam* – we often overreact and blame ourselves, and even hate ourselves. To us, therefore, this *sidra* is a reminder of the vision that Jacob once beheld in that forlorn and desolate field on that strange and cold night: *"Vehinei Anokhi imakh,"* "Behold," says God, "I am with you." As long as you are aware of your inadequacies, you will overcome them. As long as you consciously strive to be an *ish tam*, you are, in My eyes, both innocent and lovable. Banish the guilt, and get on with the business of making life more livable, and making man more true to the divine within him.

But this is not the end. I mentioned that there are five categories dealing with guilt, but I described only four. What is the fifth?

I feel that apologies are in order before I continue. If what I am about to say brings back evil memories – like removing the stone cover from a snake pit and watching the serpents and scorpions scatter – it is only because the Talmud (*Avoda Zara* 18a) warns us not to be one who is able to protest a wrong but does not.

Let it then be said that there are people today who fit into a fifth class: those who are clearly guilty, beyond a shadow of a doubt, but who disown and deny it. I speak, as you might by now suspect, of the recent news from West Germany.

I say what I say without denying the fact that there are some older Germans, especially those connected with the previous regime, who were brave and heroic in leaving Germany or risking life and limb in protesting Hitler's policies. I recognize that there are some young Germans who are thoroughly ashamed of their elders and who seek, in some manner, to do penance. And yet, I speak today not of individuals but of a government and the conscience of an entire nation.

One of the rudest shocks that any of us could have received was the news that a man by the name of Kurt Kiesinger has been nominated as chancellor of West Germany. This is a man who, in his maturity, was a card-carrying Nazi throughout the entire war. There is now talk of his name being withdrawn; but it makes little difference whether this is done or not. The fact that it was attempted by the leading circles of Germany tells us something significant and it speaks volumes. It means that only our protest can stop them, that nothing else matters. Furthermore, the possible withdrawal itself is not even related to the main fact of his past, but is merely a matter of internal politics.

For twenty-one years those of us who would not forget or forgive were told that we are undemocratic and illiberal and practicing guilt by association with regard to the Germans. Even the Ben-Gurions have pleaded with us to consider that this is a new Germany and that we must forget the past and look to the future.

And now eight out of ninety-six delegates to the state parliament of Hesse are old Nazis in new disguises. And the greatest insult of all is the effrontery to recommend as a leader of democratic Germany – a former Nazi! And consider the temerity of how blandly it is passed off. Kiesinger himself tells us that in his heart he didn't approve of Hitler's policies, and that he didn't pay his dues. The *Hamburg Welt* apologizes for Kiesinger on the grounds that he did much for Germany after the war, cementing its relations with France and Europe. The *Bild Zeitung* dismisses the entire matter as "a youthful error." What typical German arrogance, what ruthless *ḥutzpa*!

In antiquity, Nero fiddled while Rome burned; in our days, Kiesinger and the likes of him filed reports while the ovens of Auschwitz burned overtime, their obscene smokestacks belching forth the smoke of Jewish bodies.

This week the press told us about the attempts to extradite a German physician who was a "Selektions-Doktor" in Auschwitz, who with the motion of a finger could condemn a person to death or to unbearable life. A little over two weeks ago, the wire services told of another Nazi who was apprehended crawling from some hole. He was accused of lining up two thousand Jewish children between the ages of six and twelve and making them stay in formation, in their places, completely undressed for three days and three nights in the bitter December cold until they froze to death. I think of them often; they have not left me for one moment since I read the report. They were of my own generation. They would today themselves be fathers and mothers of children of the same age as when they perished – tortured to death by Nazis, whose organization included a Kiesinger, who nursed his private displeasure at such evil deeds – while continuing to draw a salary from the departments headed by Goebbels and Ribbentrop!

This people knows no guilt! And if we will not protest, who will? Do we have the moral right to keep silent? I say no, a thousand times no – *six million times* no! I am one of those who believe that we should never let them forget. I commend to you the suggestion of Pete Hamill in the November 17th edition of the *New York Post* who says that, "The streets of Germany should be plastered with the pictures of the dead. High school graduation ceremonies should be held in the ruins of the concentration camps. Someone should remind these people that they killed a lot of innocent strangers, that most of the killings were murder and that people are still living, scattered across the face of the earth [some in this very congregation!] who cannot sleep at night because of the fear that was placed in them because of Germans."

We cannot, must not, dare not, shall not forgive or forget. Let us never be distracted by apologists for West Germany. If we are told that considerations of "Realpolitik" should make us, keep in mind that there is a Russia to contend with; let us remind them that there is a Buchenwald to consider. When we are asked, "What does the young generation know?" let us answer: "What the old one bequeathed to it: a heritage of Treblinkas!" If the history-minded apologists tell us to remember Versailles, let us, in turn, remind them of Dachau. And if there is someone who puts forth the name of Adenauer, let us reply with the name of Kiesinger!

So there is a category of people who, beast-like, dismiss and disown their guilt. Compare them, if you will, to the people of Jacob who actually feel heavy guilt – for denying a spiritual blessing to a murderous and bloodthirsty Esau! Who feel nervous and uneasy because they had to defend themselves against a conniving Laban!

Perhaps this same overdeveloped Jewish conscience ought to move us to an *al ḥeit* about how we have allowed modern Germany to get away with it; how we have permitted Reform rabbis to preach reconciliation in Western Germany; how we have failed to protest the economic buildup of Germany by the United States; how we have failed to protest the reunification of Germany, which has become a sacred cornerstone of United States policy. And who knows – maybe Israel ought to feel guilt too because it has been going too far and too fast in the process of national reconciliation!

But I believe I owe it to you to leave you with a far more pleasant thought. Therefore, in conclusion, let me tell you the story of the Berditchever Rabbi, the great Hasidic "lover of Israel." It is told that one morning, while reciting the blessings at the beginning of the service, the rabbi, to the consternation of his followers, omitted the blessing, "Blessed are You, O Lord our God, King of the world, who has not made me a heathen." The Hasidim were troubled by this matter, and they finally decided to send the oldest among them to the rabbi to ask him for the significance of the omission. The rabbi explained that early that morning he awoke with a feeling of deep depression. He felt desolate, cheerless, deep in a blue mood, when the entire world seemed dispirited and forlorn, and a black cloud hovered over his heart.

He looked all about him for some opportunity to snap out of the doldrums. He found nothing and his sense of dejection increased. But suddenly he realized: "I am a Jew, a Jew! How wonderful, how happy, how marvelous it is – I am a Jew!" And out of sheer joy and overwhelming happiness, he cried out, "Blessed are You, O Lord...*shelo asani goy*" – You have not made me a heathen! "Therefore," the rabbi continued, "since I already made this blessing early in the morning, I did not recite it now in its usual place."

And so, when we read of a Kiesinger and his likes in Germany; when we compare the ferocious condemnation of Israel in the United Nations – no matter what one may think of the wisdom of the Israeli raid[2] – compared to the minor slap on the wrist administered to the Syrian murderers; when we contemplate every day the loss of conscience and the absence of elementary decency in the world all about us – then, let us all feel at peace with ourselves; let us all be proud, thank God, and offer a blessing to the Almighty: "Blessed are You...*shelo asani goy*"; let us be happy to be Jews.

---

2. The author is referring to the Israeli raid on the Jordanian-controlled West Bank village of Samu in response to al-Fatah raids against Israelis near the West Bank border.

Vayishlaḥ

Under the Terebinth[1]

A strange ceremony is enacted by Jacob in this *sidra*. After the unhappy incident of the violation of Dina by Shechem, and the destruction of the city by Dina's brothers, the sons of Jacob, Jacob calls his family together roundabout him. He scolds his sons for their excessive zeal and impetuousness in raiding Shechem, and they defend their actions. Then he turns to them, and commands them to put away all the "strange gods," the various idols that they had accumulated as spoils and souvenirs in the course of plundering the city. Put them away, he says, and purify yourselves and change your garments. They then give him all the strange gods they had in their hands and all their earrings (which contained figurines of various idols), "and Jacob hid them under the terebinth which was by Shechem" (Genesis 35:4).

What a dramatic scene that must have been! Jacob forces his family to purge itself of every vestige of idolatry. Here they stand around a muddy pit near a terebinth, or oak tree, near Shechem, and each member of the family tosses into the pit another figurine or idol or piece of sculpture, another token of the evil which had befallen them. And then

---

1. December 15, 1962.

the patriarch covers all these repulsive objects with earth, and they are forgotten, and the family is purified once again – ready to proceed on their great mission as the teachers of God's word, and to their destiny as the people of the Lord.

Now imagine if we were to do that, if we were to reenact Jacob's disposal of the tokens of evil under a terebinth now, in 1962. Imagine if we were all standing around a muddy pit, invited to toss into it all the tokens of what is undesirable, evil, and repulsive in our lives. The imagination is staggered by the implications. The possibilities are almost limitless! What a variety of objects, modern idols, would be thrown into that pit! Each one would be a symbol of another source of unhappiness in our lives. No doubt, someone would throw in a television antenna – symbol of that totalitarian machine which monopolizes the attention of our selves and our children to the exclusion of every form of real edification. Another might throw in a neon light – a token of sham, of the kind of bluster that preys on the gullible. Perhaps somebody would cast in a telephone, the one modern instrument which, above all else, has mechanized *lashon hara* and made of *rekhilut* a vocation rather than a mere diversion. Another person might toss in a watch, that little instrument which represents the tyranny of rigid schedules over our lives, preventing us from exercising freedom and spontaneity, and which casts its spell even over prayer, so that we engage in clock-watching during the services. There might come falling in a transistor radio, a symbol of all the ubiquitous noise that afflicts our ears and peace, and disturbs the silence so necessary for the creativity of the mind; the nose cone of a missile, which represents the perversion of values of those who concentrate on the conquest of outer space while so many insurmountable problems distress mankind here on earth; a mimeo stencil, the insignia of the public relations man and his artificial "image making"; a pair of theater stubs, tokens of respectable smut; a driver's license, the threat of the eventual atrophy of human feet. It requires no great stretch of the imagination to be able to add, here and there, a few status symbols of modern man. *Bekhol dor vador*, in every generation, people ought to take time out for a reenactment of that ancient scene under the terebinth by the city of Shechem. For our generation, no less and perhaps more than for any other, the reading of this *sidra* is the challenge to a spiritual housecleaning, to a cleansing of the soul from all the dross that life has accumulated over the years.

However, does this imply a rejection of modernity, a total condemnation of all its concepts as evil and its discoveries as infernal? It would seem so. And yet that is hardly the case.

As a matter of fact, Jacob seems to have been indirectly criticized for not engaging in a more vigorous annihilation of the tokens of evil. You will note that Jacob did not completely destroy these earrings and statuettes. He only buried them under the terebinth. The famed commentator, Nachmanides, protests that Jacob was not following the law strictly. Thus he writes, "All idols and auxiliary objects should not be merely interred, but must be ground and cast to the wind or into the sea."

The halakha demands complete destruction and not merely burial of idolatrous images. Nachmanides's criticism seems to be confirmed by the Jerusalem Talmud, where we read that Rabbi Ishmael went to Nablus [which is today the name for Shechem], and noticed some non-Jews bowing to the mountain. Rabbi Ishmael told them, you may not realize it, but you are not really worshiping the mountain but the images that lie buried underneath, as it is written, "And Jacob hid them under the terebinth which was by Shechem." So the Jerusalem Talmud also implies that Jacob was not sufficiently zealous in destroying the idols his family had gathered from Shechem; he should have ground them to dust and not merely buried them, where they might at some later age again become the objects of veneration by foolish pagans.

What was Jacob's opinion? And why may we feel sure that, indeed, he was right in what he did? Besides a halakhic justification, which the commentators present, what other, larger vindication of Jacob do we find?

What Jacob rejected was not earrings and sculptures, but the attitude that one brings to them. Had he completely annihilated these objects, he would have demonstrated his feeling that these articles are objectively evil. But when Jacob merely buried them, he showed that it is not they themselves that are evil – they are neutral, meaningless – but the human propensity for idolizing an image, the corrupt mentality of a person who venerates them; that is to be condemned. Of course, the sons of Jacob did not worship these things. The fact, however, that the people of Shechem *did* was sufficient to warrant their interment. Jacob thus taught his sons, and generations after them, that mute objects, the creations of man's ingenuity, can become things of exquisite beauty or great ugliness, objects of usefulness or abominations – all depending on whether the mind and heart of the one who uses them is pure or impure.

The Torah itself, in this *sidra*, indicates clearly though indirectly the approach of Jacob to this problem. Notice that before committing the tokens of idolatry to burial, he commands his family, "Put away the strange gods that are in your midst"; the idols that are perfected by man's hands are far less pernicious than the potent poison that spews from a perverse spirit, a wicked heart, and a twisted mind. The true culprit, the effective cause of idolatry, is: "the strange gods that are *betokhekhem*, in your midst."

And as if to emphasize this, the story is interrupted: after his command to remove the strange gods from their midst, and before his act of burying these gods under the terebinth, Jacob announces to his children that they will all arise and go up to Bethel and there build an altar "to God who answered me in the day of my distress, and was with me *baderekh*, in the way which I went." Jacob is here explaining his action. What is important is "the way which I went." The way, the approach, the attitude – that is what is decisive. Whether an engraving on a piece of jewelry is an ornament or an idol depends on the "way" which you adopt. If it is the way of God, then your life is pure and the artifacts are functional; if it is not, then these same artifacts are idolatrous and destructive. "And they gave to Jacob all the strange gods that were in their *hands* and the rings which were in their *ears*, and Jacob hid them under the terebinth which is by Shechem." All Jacob could bury physically were the physical objects – the ornaments "in their hands" and "in their ears" – the inner idolatry, the poisoned attitude, the corrupt approach – that each individual must purge by himself, from "*betokhekhem*," "your midst."

So it is with us. What we must protest is not the inventions of science and technology which have caused us, in so many various ways, unhappiness and even grief. Certainly we ought not to object to the insights and methods of science. Rather, we must fear and beware their misuse by dull hearts and narrow minds. Orthodox Jews sometimes rue and bemoan the advances of technology and yearn for "the good old days"; but that is as irrelevant and silly as the overzealous enthusiast of scientism who naïvely proclaims man's divinity and his imminent arrival at Utopia because of science. Both these attitudes attribute more power – whether good or bad – to the instruments of science than they deserve. The determination of whether science will lead us to a golden age or to a futureless age depends not upon what man's mind discovers in Nature, but what Nature will discover when it uncovers man's heart.

There is no doubt that the same objects which may cause us moral distress and psychological tension can be the agents of moral bliss and psychological relief. The same television screen which distracts a child with trite nonsense, and worse, can become the channel for education, a decent respite for a hardworking person, or a blessing for the shut-in. The watch can become the symbol of an ordered and hence efficient life. The same telephone which can be misused for malicious gossip and idle talk can be used for words of significance and exchanges of meaning. All modern inventions can spare people from a life of grind and allow them the leisure for creative personal activity. Above all else, nuclear power which threatens to destroy the world can also, as we read recently, be used as a new source of power to move mountains and make life more livable for man.

There are those who are amazed there exist such strange beings as religious scientists. They are astounded into disbelief when they hear of the existence and thriving activities of the Association of Orthodox Jewish Scientists. Yet there should be no surprise at all. On the words of Deuteronomy (4:6), that this Torah is our "wisdom and understanding before the eyes of the nations of the world," the Talmud (*Shabbat* 75a) comments that this "wisdom" refers to the study of astronomy. So important is this, the Talmud adds, that one who has scientific ability and does not use it for scientific purposes is not a worthy individual.

But what does Jewish excellence in the natural sciences have to do with "before the eyes of the nations"? Rabbi Jonathan of Lunel[2] explains that the Talmud urges Jews to study astronomy in order to show the glory and regularity of God's creation, and thereby refute the superstitious notions of the pagans for whom the constellations are the signs of

---

2. Quoted in *Ḥidushei haRan* on *Shabbat* 75a.

fate and destiny. When the Jew engages in astronomy, he discovers the truth, and denies thereby the falsehood of astrology.

So must it be in our day. Today, it is not astrology that is the problem, but a superstition far more pernicious because it sounds more sophisticated: the deification of science, the abandonment of God, the assumption that the world is a meaningless accident and history a cruel joke. When Orthodox Jews excel in science and remain not only confirmed but strengthened in their faith, it is the assertion of wisdom and understanding that issues from Torah; a proclamation that the greater man's knowledge, the greater his reverence for Almighty God; a declaration that all science – wisdom and understanding – is a hymn of glory to God. When the entire Jewish community lives in and with the modern world, when we do not allow modernity to distract us from divinity, and do not allow our countless gadgets to rule over us, but we remain in control, our personalities uncrushed, our aspirations noble, our goals sacred, and our *derekh* the way of Torah; then we purge the world and ourselves of the "strange gods" in our midst.

The Torah Jew, therefore, cannot and should not abandon the modern world. He seeks, rather, to master it while avoiding being enslaved by it. Just as Jacob taught by burying rather than destroying the ornaments of Shechem that they are mere tools that can be misused or used depending upon the "way" or attitude you bring to them, so must our approach be to the various inventions of modern science and to all of modern life. We must retain our moral freedom and our spiritual eminence, learning to master the implements devised by technology in order to further humane goals, to advance our spiritual purposes, to glorify our Creator from whom we derived the wisdom, in the first place, to conquer Nature.

It is in this sense that every now and then we ought to reenact the scene of Jacob disposing of the tokens of evil under the terebinth by Shechem. Let us purge ourselves of the strange gods which disturb our inner life. Let us, without seeking to escape from modern life and the responsibilities it places upon us, condemn to the pit of oblivion the various symbols of our moral distress that, because of our wrong attitudes, have been the cause of our ethical failings. Let us, then, rededicate ourselves to the God who answers us in the time of our distress and is with us in the "way" which we go, so that our ways will be blessed and we shall learn to live in the world as free men, created in the image of God, not manipulated by brute, mechanized objects.

For only by being truly the servants of God can we become the masters of our own destiny.

Sincerely Yours[1]

Hypocrisy is rightly a despised trait, and the word "hypo-crite" a harsh and contemptuous epithet reserved for vile people. It is all the more unfortunate, therefore, that the popular condemnation of insincerity is not always matched by a correspondingly universal absten-tion from this vice in the affairs of man in society. Every day many thou-sands of letters are written in which the writers employ varied devices ranging from subtle deviousness to outright deceit, and compound their crime by signing the letters, "I am, sincerely yours…."

What is a hypocrite? According to the dictionary definition it is one who pretends to be something other than what he really is (usually one who pretends to be better than he really is) or to feel what he does not really feel. Hypocrisy is feigning, acting a part, pretending. Perhaps a better word is the Hebrew *tzeviut* – literally: coloring, dyeing. Hypocrisy, then, is giving an impression which does not correspond with the facts. It is the incommensurateness of the inner fact and the outer appearance.

Our prophets stormed against hypocrisy. Our rabbis thundered against it. The Talmud quotes King Yannai advising his wife, Queen

---

1. December 11, 1965.

Salome, "Do not be afraid either of the Pharisees or of those who are not Pharisees; fear only those hypocrites who act like Pharisees, who behave like Zimri (an ignoble person), and who expect to be rewarded like Pinchas (the saintly priest of Israel)" (*Sota* 22b).

In that case, we are presented with a problem by the *sidra*. We read, in very few lines, that Reuben sinned with Bilha, the concubine of his father Jacob. If the Bible said so, it is the truth. Yet the Talmud (*Megilla* 25b) advises us that the story of Reuben should be read but not translated. It was once the custom that the Torah would be read as we read it, and then one person would be assigned to translate it publicly into Aramaic, the vernacular at that time. However, an exception was made of this story of Reuben, and when one rabbi insisted that it be read in the Hebrew but left untranslated, he was congratulated by his colleagues. But is this not insincere, even hypocritical? Is not the suppression of the truth hypocrisy, and is not every instance of hypocrisy deplorable?

The answer is no, it is not hypocrisy or insincerity, although it suppresses the broadcast of a true event. And, if one should insist that this is hypocrisy, then with full respect to all our honorable prejudices, certain forms of such insincerity are not malicious but wholesome and healthy. Not in all ways must one's appearances be thoroughly equivalent and correspond to his inner thoughts. To speak a conscious untruth aiming at personal gain or creating a favorable image and false impression is a foul act. But to refrain from telling all I know and consider to be true, either because I am unsure how that truth will be interpreted, or out of respect for the sensitivity and feelings of others – that is an act of civility, not insincerity.

Thus, in the affair of Reuben there were many mitigating factors, and varying interpretations are possible, as indeed many of them appear in the Talmud. A direct translation into the vernacular is, therefore, misleading and the cause of much misunderstanding. Furthermore, it is bad enough that the Torah preserves a sacred record of Reuben's misdeed, and there is no need to add salt to the wounds of a cherished forebear even if he is no longer in the world of the living.

It is a sin to lie; it is no mitzva to tell all I know, even if it is the truth. There is a law in the *Shulḥan Arukh* that if a man has, heaven forbid, lost a close relative for whom he must mourn, but he is unaware of his loss, then one ought not to apprise him of it within thirty days of the death, for then he would be obligated to observe all of the *shiva*. One may not give a false answer upon interrogation, but one ought not to volunteer this kind of information, and if he does he is considered a *kesil*, a fool.[2] A fool, indeed! Hypocrisy is not avoided and insincerity not served by mindless chattering and compulsive loquaciousness!

Too much cruelty has been practiced under the guise of honesty, too much frightful foolishness excused as frankness, too many assaults on the feelings of others carried out under the pretense of sincerity. Is it hypocrisy for a teacher to refrain from telling a slow student that he is unintelligent? Is it commendable sincerity to tell every homely person, "You are plain-looking and unattractive"? No, it is not. In fact, Hillel taught that one must even tell an unattractive bride that she is beautiful and charming!

The truth should be spoken, not blurted out. If you hear a performer or entertainer or artist, and have adverse criticism – even if it is constructive – then Jewish ethics and *derekh eretz* advise you: wait for a propitious time before offering your comments, do not offend the innermost feelings of another human being. If you apprehend a friend in embarrassing circumstances, performing an evil deed, it is a mitzva to reproach him. You are not free to withhold your comment. But the rebuke must be administered gently, considerately, delicately. The Torah commands us, "You shall reproach your friend" (Leviticus 19:17). And the rabbis add, "Even a hundred times" (*Bava Metzia* 31a). On this, one of the great lights of the *Musar* movement commented: this means that the single rebuke must be broken into a hundred pieces and offered in tiny doses, lest the person you seek to correct should become the victim of painful insult.

Furthermore, there is a decent, beneficial, and honorable kind of hypocrisy which is not insincere, and without which society might well collapse. There are certain conventional fictions that are apparently untrue, but that suggest a kind of truth far beyond the reach of normal comprehension. Jewish law, for instance, aims at producing perfect

---

2. For more discussion of this halakha, see "Frankness as Vice and as Virtue."

individuals and a holy society, yet it knows full well, as King Solomon taught, that no person in the world is perfectly righteous and blameless.

Halakha grants each person a *hezkat kashrut*, a presumption of innocence and virtue; yet it knows full well that, as the Bible teaches, "Man's innate disposition is toward evil" (Genesis 8:21). Is this hypocrisy? If it is, then we should all be in favor of hypocrisy! For without it, all law and religion must progressively be reduced and diminished to the lowest level of common practice. This spells the death of all ideals. A child who errs and stumbles, yet who is trusted by a parent and feels that the parent's opinion of him is higher than his poor reality, is inspired by this discrepancy to fulfill the higher image. Likewise the Jew and his halakha: he is imperfect and faulted, yet because he is granted the *hezkat kashrut* and told that he incorporates the image of God, and is expected to live up to it, he will strive to do just that, lest he suffer inner embarrassment and shame.

This week the Supreme Court has been deliberating on the problems of censorship and pornography. This brings to mind a fascinating article by George P. Elliot I read in a national magazine,[3] in which a principle similar to the one we have been discussing was put forth. The author believes that the law should banish pornography, but not enforce this regulation. He asks: is it not, however, hypocrisy to outlaw pornography if we know well that it will be sold surreptitiously? He answers: "The law should rest content with a decent hypocrisy," and ban obscene literature in the marketplace even if it knows that it will be sold under the counter, where the law will not and cannot bother with it. Law is the way that society approves and disapproves of certain acts. "A certain amount of official hypocrisy is one of the operative principles of a good society." Unenforced laws express society's goals, ideals, and visions. Law is meant not only to punish, but also to educate to higher standards. "Civilization behaves as though men are decent in full knowledge that they are not."

Judaism cannot take exception to this doctrine. When, at the beginning of the Emancipation, non-Orthodox Jews did adopt an opposite point of view, they began to prune the laws and cut down the halakha to fit current, prevalent practice. As a result, they discovered –

---

3. *Harper's*, March 1965.

as we well know in our days – that when you do this Judaism begins to crumble and Jews begin to vanish. If Jewish laws are abandoned because they are not universally observed, Judaism becomes nothing but a sanctimonious self-approval for spiritual failures, a vacuous *"hekhsher"* for not-so-kosher Jews.

That is why we ought not to be impressed or depressed at the cries of hypocrisy often hurled at Orthodox synagogues that disapprove of travel on the Sabbath, though many of its members violate that standard. We rightly insist upon full and meticulous observance of *kashrut*, though some members in the privacy of their homes or when away from home do not live up to this ideal. If a standard is set, the congregation must live under the impression that the ideal is a reality; and all who fail to conform must suffer the pangs of guilt. If that is a fiction, it is a splendid and sublime fiction, on the way to becoming a luminous truth.

Finally, there is a form of feigning or pretense which is not only necessary and permissible, but the highest rung that men can reach. We read in the previous *sidra* that Jacob, after twenty years with Laban, decided to return to Canaan and the inevitable confrontation with his vengeful brother Esau. This came about, the Torah tells us, immediately after the birth of Joseph. Why just then? The Talmud (*Bava Batra* 123b) answers, referring to our present *sidra's haftara*, that the House of Joseph is regarded as a flame, and the House of Esau as straw; in other words, that Joseph for some reason is the ideal antidote to Esau's hatred. The Midrash (Genesis Rabba 73:7) introduces this answer with the following four words which are most significant: *"Mishenolad sitno shel Esav,"* upon the birth of Joseph who was the "Satan" of Esau! Joseph is considered the "Satan" – the adversary or antagonist – of his uncle Esau. One of the great Hasidic rabbis of the Sochatchower dynasty explained this as follows: Esau was a hypocrite. Outwardly, he was a pious individual. He would approach his blind father, Isaac, with such questions as: "How does one offer a tithe of salt or straw?" although he well knew that such objects do not require any tithe. He put on an act; he pretended to be pious and observant. At the same time, inwardly, he was a *rasha*; vile, wicked, and cruel.

Now, Joseph was also guilty of pretense – but in the exactly opposite way! Outwardly, our tradition tells us, he was a callow youth. He was the sort of youngster who would stand for hours in front of a mirror teasing his hair. He occupied himself with the latest fads and fashions of the contemporary youth. An outside, objective observer would gather that he was nothing more than a shallow, childish youngster with nothing better with which to occupy his mind than the style and length of his hair! Yet, as we know with the benefit of hindsight, this young Joseph was anything but a biblical beatnik; he was a true *tzaddik*, a man of utter piety and complete self-discipline, who incorporated within his conscience the spiritual image of his saintly father (*Sanhedrin* 104b)!

This too, then, is a form of pretense – but how delightful and noble! To achieve inner dignity and not brag about it; to attain greatness and not exhibit it; to reach spiritual heights and not display them – this, if it be hypocrisy, is the saintliest insincerity, the most precious pretense within the capacity of man to attain.

This gem of character recommended by the Talmud was incorporated in the famous legend of Jewish tradition about the *Lamed Vavniks* – the thirty-six hidden *tzaddikim*, or righteous men. In every generation, according to this legend, there are thirty-six righteous people of whom no one knows; sometimes they themselves are not conscious of it. Yet it is because of their inner, hidden, disguised saintliness that the world is sustained. Without them, divine wrath would turn all the world into primordial chaos. These *Lamed Vavniks* are patterned on the character of Joseph: outwardly mediocre, ordinary, plain, and unimpressive, while inwardly made of the finest spiritual stuff; righteous, self-sacrificing, and utterly moral.

An interesting consequence of this teaching about Joseph and the legend of the thirty-six righteous people is: one must never scorn or slight any human being no matter how ordinary he appears. One must never disdain or underestimate any fellow-man no matter what the provocation. You can never tell: he may be a hidden *tzaddik*, one of the thirty-six! He may be a Joseph whose shallow exterior disguises inner greatness! How often has a teacher found that a student who is quiet, withdrawn, and retiring will suddenly, at the end of a term or a year or an entire school career, rise to the greatest intellectual heights. How often have parents found that children whom they did not suspect of anything beyond the average demonstrate, as they grow older, inner resources that amaze and delight their parents. Our rabbis (*Avot* 4:3) put it this way: "Never scorn any person." You can't be sure of what they really are like!

In sum, hypocrisy is a contemptible vice, and sincerity a glowing virtue. But while sincerity calls for no falsehood, neither does it call for telling all that is within us, even if it is true, if telling this truth can hurt others. Secondly, sincerity is not a reason to abolish unpracticed ideals and laws. Thirdly, there is a kind of pretense which is saintly: that which urges me to develop my inner life without deriving the benefit of society's applause and approval.

We live in an *alma diperuda*, an imperfect and fragmented world. For truth to be triumphant, it must proceed cautiously. We must give no quarter to falsehood, but we must remember that truth must often disguise itself in a thousand different garments – until that blessed day, the "day of the Lord," when man and society will be redeemed; when truth will be revealed courageously and fully; when this world will become transformed into an *olam ha'emet*, a world of truth; when God's unity will be expressed in living the whole truth and nothing but the truth; and when men will confront their own selves in truth, and be truly devoted to each other, so that each man will be able to address his brother and say, in full and genuine honesty, "I am, sincerely, yours!"

Growing Pains[1]

I n one chapter of our *sidra*, the Torah mentions no less than four times the relationship between Esau and Edom (*"Esav hu Edom"* – "Esau is Edom") – either describing their mutual identity, or pointing out that Esau is the ancestor of Edom. The commentators seem not to have noticed this repetition.

Is there any special significance to it? I believe there is, and that it lies in the fact that these references follow the chapter in which God affirms that Jacob's name shall be changed to "Israel." In this juxtaposition of *Esau = Edom* to *Jacob = Israel*, I believe we find a most important Jewish insight. Esau was born precociously mature: "Full of hair" (Genesis 25:25), and, as Rashi points out, the newborn infant was, in his covering of hair, as mature as a young man. Rashbam indicates that this is the significance of the name Esav (Esau): *"adam asuy* [from the same root as Esav, meaning, "made" or "done"] *venigmar."* He was mature, developed, complete. And what does "Edom" mean? According to the Torah, the name was given to Esau when he approached Jacob, who was preparing a meal of red lentils, and said to him, *"Haliteini na min*

---

1. November 25, 1972.

ha'adom ha'adom hazeh," let me have some of this *adom*, red, food. The food was processed, cooked, done. Edom thus implies the same idea: completion, maturity, finished development. Therefore the equation of Esau and Edom is symbolic of the static, of one who has arrived, who experiences no development or growth, who has no place further to go.

The exact opposite is true of Jacob. He is born as a straggler: "And afterwards his brother came out" (Genesis 25:26). He follows Esau out of the womb and into life. He hangs on to his brother's coattails, or, to use the original biblical idiom, his hand holds the *akeiv*, the heel, of Esau: hence his name Yaakov (Jacob). He is hesitant, diffident, backward. His insecurity and weakness plague him all his life. And therefore he must always struggle. And struggle he does! We read of Jacob's wrestling with the angel, a crucial incident in his life. As a result of this encounter, his name is changed to "Israel," as we read: *"Ki sarita im elohim ve'im anashim vatukhal,"* "Because you fought with angels and men and you prevailed" (Genesis 32:29). Notice that the name Yisrael does not incorporate the word *"vatukhal,"* the concept of triumph and victory, important as it is, but rather *"sarita,"* the concept of struggle. The identification of Jacob and Israel symbolizes development, growth, progress, the good fight to grow and transcend oneself.

Hence, the proximity of the two portions (i.e. the identification of Esau with Edom and the renaming of Jacob after his fight with the angel) presents the student of Torah with a study in contrasts between the one brother who arrives on the scene already finished, and leaves it in the same manner, experiencing no change or growth; and the other brother, who begins very low indeed and then, by sheer will, resolve, and determination, struggles to superiority and triumph.

I mention this not only as the explanation of a number of biblical verses, but because it incorporates a major insight of Judaism. Judaism is predicated on man's self-transformation. The concept of *teshuva* or repentance does not merely mean to experience regret and mend one's ways, as much as it implies the concept of spiritual movement, of growing, of changing for the better. Scholars have already pointed out that whereas Judaism emphasizes *becoming*, the Greek philosophers, from Parmenides to Plato and beyond, have idealized the concept of *being*, the perfect state in which no change occurs.

In the Jewish tradition, angels are referred to as *omdim*, as those who stand, or are static; whereas man is called a *mehalekh*, one who goes and progresses. Thus, in the vision of the prophet Zechariah, God promises Joshua the high priest that if he obeys the will of the Lord, "*Venatati lekha mahlekhim bein ha'omdim ha'eleh*," I will give you the capacity for going, for moving, walking, progressing among these (angels) who stay in one place (3:7).

There is an interesting if quaint controversy among great Jewish authorities about the relationship between angels and humans. Maimonides and Ibn Ezra maintain that angels are at a higher level than man, because angels are purely spiritual whereas man is subject to all the weaknesses of the flesh. Sa'adia Gaon maintains, on the contrary, that man is superior because he is possessed of freedom of the will. Rabbi Chaim of Volozhin offers a compromise in an attempt to resolve this controversy. Angels, he maintains, are initially on a higher level than man. But man, if he properly exercises his free will, can grow from a much lower station to a much higher one. By virtue of spiritual struggle he can achieve an eminence that is greater than that of the angels.

This capacity for growth, for emerging from "Jacob" to "Israel," should be the source of great encouragement for parents. As one who often listens to parents unburden themselves of worries concerning their children, I strongly recommend the biblical figure of Jacob to your attention. Parents sometimes are concerned that children show no motivation, that they seem to be limited in their talents and in their will. Certainly we must do whatever we can to help them. But there is often a danger of over-intervention, with the resultant resistance and conflict that it engenders. But, after having done all we can and should, parents also should have a measure of confidence that as human beings, and especially Jewish human beings, it is possible and even probable that our young people will eventually struggle, transform themselves, and grow. They will reenact the adventure of Jacob-Israel.

Of all the things we must give thanks for in this great country, it is that growth has been characteristic of America as well. It is true that in recent years the counterculture has vigorously objected to this country's lack of sufficiently rapid growth. Of course, in its violence and its extremism, this counterculture often was destructive rather than constructive. But now that the movement seems to have spent itself, and America is getting back on an even keel, it is well to remember that if we stop growing and changing and moving in the right direction, we will be false to our own heritage.

The same principle reminds us of the Jewish community that we must not be satisfied with what we have. Any organization or institution that refuses to look upon itself critically and to experience change, thereby condemns itself to paralysis, and dooms itself to enshrine its faults and failings as a permanent part of its constitution. The survival of the Jewish community can take place only if there is viability, if there is the capability and the will for institutional change.

Of course, all this is not simple, not effortless, and not painless. Spiritual growth is always accompanied by anguish. That is why the Torah in this portion tells us that Jews are not permitted to eat the *gid hanasheh*, the thigh-vein or sciatic nerve which is situated on the "hollow of the thigh," because the angel struck Jacob on the hollow of the thigh in the thigh-vein. In other words, because in their struggle Jacob was wounded by the angel and suffered a dislocated hip, therefore we are not permitted to eat the sciatic nerve of animals.

Now, that sounds more redundant than explanatory. So what if the angel struck Jacob? Is it out of sympathy with Jacob as a victim that we refrain from eating the *gid hanasheh*? Is it out of a sense of celebration of his triumph?

I believe it is neither. Rather, we are commanded this halakha out of admiration for Jacob's struggle, because we are proud of his growing pains. It is a commitment to embrace such growing pains for ourselves as we attempt to emulate his adventure of growth from Jacob to Israel.

Similarly, the Netziv in his commentary tells us that the *gid hanasheh* is associated with the hip – it is situated at the top of the organ which moves as man walks. What he means to say, I believe, is that the thigh-vein is related to motion, going, progress, growth. It is a symbol of dynamism and the price one must pay for such struggle. Judaism has taught us through Jacob to be a *mehalekh*, even if it hurts, unlike Esau.

It is a happy coincidence that we read this portion of Jacob's growth on the nineteenth day of Kislev. The nineteenth of Kislev is a great holiday not only for the Ḥabad community, which celebrates the release from prison of the founder of the Lubavitch movement, but it has wider significance as well. For this very day, the nineteenth of Kislev, is the *yahrzeit* or anniversary of death of Rabbi Dov Ber, the "Great Maggid" of Mezeritsch. Whereas Rabbi Israel Ba'al Shem Tov was the founder of the Hasidic movement, Rabbi Dov Ber was primarily the charismatic figure who inspired others. The brains of the movement, as it were, the man who became the great teacher of the most eminent spiritual personalities of his time, the one who formulated the worldview of Hasidism in a transmissible manner, was the Great Maggid. What he and the Ba'al Shem Tov and his students did is a tribute to the Jewish capacity for growth. Through Hasidism, Judaism experienced an infusion of vitality; it relearned the principle of self-transformation and renewal.

But what growing pains they experienced! There were recently published two bulky volumes of all the literature – theological, polemical, and vituperative – written against the Hasidim.[2] Reading Professor Wilenski's collection of Mitnagdic writings is no pleasure. The Maggid and the Hasidic movement had to fight not only *anashim*, human enemies, not only poverty and small-minded people, but *"ki sarita im elohim,"* they had to struggle against veritable angels – the Vilna Gaon, by the unanimous consent of all Jewry, whether friend or foe, was the most unique personality in many, many generations, not only for the sheer genius of his intellect, and not only for the richness of his mystical visions and the voluminousness of his kabbalistic and halakhic writings, but also for the purity and saintliness of his character. He was the leader of the struggle against the Hasidism. And yet, the Maggid and the Hasidim had to struggle against him as well, and as a result, *"vatukhal,"* it was Judaism itself which triumphed and benefited. In the struggle, as history was later to show, each side gave a blessing to the other, so that Judaism today is an amalgam – or, better, a mosaic – of the various lifestyles and viewpoints of the many authentic expositions of classical Judaism.

So let us dedicate ourselves in the spirit of Jacob and in the

---

2. Mordecai Wilenski, *Ḥasidim u'Mitnagdim* (Jerusalem: Mosad Bialik, 1970; revised and updated, 1990).

memory of the Maggid to this principle of spiritual growth, of dynamic development; even if it hurts.

For this is implied as well in the festival of Ḥanukka which we celebrate this week. The halakha decided with the House of Hillel and not with the House of Shammai (*Shabbat* 21b). We light candles, not to begin with eight and to end with eight for that is completely static; not to begin with eight and to reduce to one, as the House of Shammai would have it; but rather the law is *"mosif veholekh,"* according to the House of Hillel – we must always add. We begin with one candle, and every day add another until we reach the climax, the conclusion, of eight burning candles.

The concept of growth in the Ḥanukka lights is the symbol of higher and emergent development in the spiritual life of the Jew: *"Ma'alin bakodesh ve'ein moridin."* May we incorporate into our own lives this governing principle of never declining in sanctity, but always growing and increasing in the realm of the spirit.

Vayeshev

The Silence of Jacob[1]

S ilence, it is said, is golden. Our rabbis taught that it makes for wisdom (*Avot* 1:17).

Yet, the wisest of all men preached that while there is a time for silence, there is also a time to speak up. *"Eit laḥashot ve'eit leddaber"* (Ecclesiastes 3:7). Just as there is a time for passivity and restraint, so is there a time for activity and protest.

Let us speak of the importance of *eit leddaber*, of speaking out, and of carrying the virtue of silence to an excess.

In the previous two Torah portions, we read of three occasions when Jacob could have spoken up but did not. In each he revealed remarkable self-control, a fully disciplined spirit. Jacob, the *ish tam*, stands out as a man who is pure almost to the point of innocence. He has an abiding faith in humanity that ordinary men perhaps do not deserve. So distant is he from evil that he no longer truly believes that it is a real factor in the life of man and the constitution of society. And the Torah, in recording Jacob's silences, suggests an indirect criticism

---

1. December 2, 1961.

of him. The Torah reminds us that just as there is a time to be silent, so there is a time to speak.

One such case occurs in our *sidra*, where we read: "And [Joseph's] brothers envied him, but his father kept it in mind" (Genesis 37:11) – the brothers were jealous, and Jacob merely made a mental note of it. Imagine if instead of merely passively observing the budding hatred and envy that was developing among his children, Jacob had actively stepped into the picture and reproached the oldest brothers, saying: You are all older and mature men. How can you keep your self-respect while envying a mere teenager because of his adolescent daydreams and ambitions? But Jacob wanted to spare their feelings. He was himself a sensitive individual. Furthermore, he didn't believe that this kind of emotion could last long in the hearts of his beloved children. Had he not been addicted to periods of silence, had he spoken up, he might have stopped then and there the envy and animosity which was beginning to develop among the brothers, and which was fated to result in the Egyptian exile, and to remain a factor throughout history when the Jewish people split up into two warring kingdoms.

A second case is the silence of Jacob in the episode of the kidnapping and violation of Dina by Shechem. When the reports of this disgraceful act came to Jacob, we read: "And Jacob held his peace until his sons came home" (Genesis 34:5). When the sons did come home, they naturally were deeply grieved and connived to destroy Shechem, punish his partners in crime, and rescue their sister. Jacob was unhappy over the methods they employed. Yet, if Jacob had not kept his peace but had spoken up at once to Shechem and his father and demanded the immediate safe return of his daughter, the whole sordid and heartrending episode might never had occurred.

The third and perhaps most interesting case is that which occurred after the death of Rachel. We read in the Torah: "*Vayelekh Reuven vayishkav et Bilha pilegesh aviv, vayishma Yisrael*" (Genesis 35:22). The understanding of this verse, according to the Jewish tradition, is that after the death of his beloved Rachel, Jacob made his home with Bilha, her maid whom she had given to Jacob as a concubine. Reuben was outraged that Jacob gave preference to Bilha, a mere concubine, just because she was close to Rachel, over Leah (Reuben's mother), who was a full-fledged wife of Jacob. And so Reuben forcibly removed Jacob's permanent quarters from the tent of Bilha to the tent of Leah – an unwarranted interference by Reuben in his father's personal affairs.

What did Jacob do? Did he say anything? No. "*Vayishma Yisrael*," "And Israel heard of it." He heard, he noted, and he probably grieved deeply within at the brazenness of his son and the fallen state of his domestic life.

Was Jacob right in refraining from censuring Reuben? It is interesting that the *parasha*, the section, ends after the words, "And Israel heard of it," but this is in the middle of a verse! The new section continues with the second half of that verse, indicating an inner connection between the two recorded incidents. What is the beginning of that new section? "Now the sons of Jacob were twelve." Why this strange arrangement of the verse? And what new information is there in the Torah's mention of the twelve sons of Jacob?

I believe that the sin of Reuben is not only his audacious interference in his father's personal matters, but, what is worse, his taking advantage of Bilha's defenselessness. Bilha was a concubine, not a full wife. Reuben was the eldest of the sons, the heir apparent. He was strong, she was weak. During the time that Rachel, her protector, lived, Reuben would not have dared to do what he now did. For Rachel was the favorite of Jacob and he never would have countenanced any insult or injury either to her or to those close to her. But now that Rachel was gone – the incident of Rachel's death immediately precedes this episode – Reuben immediately began to exploit Bilha's new weakness. He asserted himself in total disregard of Bilha's sensitivities. Yet Jacob did not speak up. "And Israel heard." He probably considered the distress and inner anguish of Reuben. He did not want to hurt him anymore. He believed, no doubt, that this was a singular affair and never would Reuben do such a thing again. And yet the Torah calls out to Jacob: Remember, "The sons of Jacob were twelve" – you have twelve sons, not just one. It may be very virtuous of you to suffer in silence and refrain from rebuking your elder son, but if you let him get away with it, he, as the eldest son, will set the example for the others; they will learn from him how to act the role of the bully! And indeed, that is just what happened. Only a short time later when the envious brothers see Joseph approaching, without the protective custody of his loving father, they pounce on him, taking advantage of his weakness. They had learned their lesson from Reuben very well. They too would now gang up on a defenseless fellow-man. If only Jacob hadn't kept his peace!

So Jacob, the *ish tam*, was too good, too kind, too patient, too unwilling to believe the worst, too considerate of the feelings of others. He could not bring himself to believe that all his children were anything but *ish tam*, people of the highest and noblest perfection. No wonder he is so severe with them on his deathbed: he was a disappointed father. They were only human, but his expectations had been so great. He erred in projecting his own faithfulness to others. And when the Torah records these silences of Jacob, it reminds us to emulate his saintliness, but not his silences; his nobility of soul, but not his extravagant and unrealistic faith in frail and inadequate man.

It is an old Jewish trait to be over-confident in man's goodness, to ascribe to others the innate decency that you possess yourself. King Saul, when he captured Agag, the Amalekite king, could not bring himself to believe that this man was a thorough scoundrel and should be put to death according to the word of the prophet. So he turned passive instead of active, and in the process lost his own throne. Queen Esther, apprised of the nefarious plans of Haman, probably considered them the rantings of a madman. He could not possibly really mean to do what he proclaimed he would! It was only when Mordecai spoke to her in words as strong and cold and cutting as steel that she came to her senses and averted a great tragedy. The democracies of the West similarly did not believe that Hitler meant to do what he announced in his *Mein Kampf.* They did not believe it; they were silent, and eighteen million people killed are testimony to that silence.

This past year we listened with rapt attention to the Eichmann trial. And in the course of the trial we have been plagued by a nagging question: "Why did European Jewry not react violently to these plans of destruction?" An answer seems to be crystallizing from all the mass of data: the Jews, because of their own innate character, simply never believed the reports they had been receiving of death camps and crematoria. It could not be true. And so they were silent…

One of the major teachings of Ḥanukka is that when the crucial moment came, our ancestors finally did learn to speak up and to act. Over two thousand years ago, an old man realized that the time had come to throw off the shackles of the oppressor and to react to the treason of the Jewish Hellenists. And so Mattathias struck the traitor to the earth, and the episode of Ḥanukka was begun. An end to silence – *"eit leddaber."*

The founding of the State of Israel, an active and creative protest against the bestiality of one-half of the world and the inhuman indifference of the other half, was in the tradition of Ḥanukka. When, recently, the Israeli government confirmed its protest against racial violence and bigotry in the Union of South Africa, despite the exposed position of that very important Jewish community in South Africa, it was again following in the great and historic footsteps of the Ḥanukka triumph.

But just as we are delighted with the activism of the State of Israel with regard to specific problems, so must we not surrender our critical functions regarding the country itself. The Jewish religion must ever be the conscience of the Jewish state and the Jewish people. For the spokesmen of Judaism to keep silent at crucial moments would be a sin against their most preciously held tenets and against the very people and state whom they profess to love. It is in this sense, and in this sense only, that we voice our displeasure at a recent decision of the prime minister of Israel. That he is truly a great man, that he deserves our gratitude, and that he has won an honored place in the history of our people – this no one can, will, or wants to deny. But he is not immune from the judgment of his peers or his tradition.

Whatever Mr. Ben-Gurion's motives, whatever his personal predilections, we were distressed and embarrassed to learn that he would be spending his vacation in a Buddhist monastery in Burma. The original announcement made to the press was later modified. He would, of course, not worship in the monastery, but merely go there as a guest of Premier U Nu and meditate while U Nu would teach him advanced techniques in Yoga.

It makes little difference whether Ben-Gurion's real motive is to learn Yoga, to learn philosophy, to get a good rest, or to negotiate diplomatic problems with the prime minister of a friendly country. What does matter is that we have here a dramatic contempt for the entire community of Jewish believers. What does matter more than all else is that because of his fame and popularity he has a profound influence upon a very impressionable young generation in the State of Israel. And when they will see that their hero and idol, who never set foot into a synagogue, allows himself the luxury of a vacation in the monastery of another faith, we fear most profoundly the effects and consequences upon world Jewry and especially upon Israeli Jewry. We dare not fall into the same trap of Jacob, that of "And Israel heard" – and do nothing about it. We must remember that "The sons of Jacob were twelve," that here we may have the beginning of a new fashion and a fad for the young generation of Israelis, so that while American youngsters do the twist, Israel's may go Buddhist.

A true friend is not one who is always carping, critical, and captious. But it is equally true that a real friend is not one who would never apprise you of your own mistakes, who will hide from you things that are apparent to others but that you may not be aware of. The same holds true for our beloved Israel and its distinguished leaders. Our rabbis taught: "Love that does not contain in it a critical element is not really love" (Genesis Rabba 54:3).

On Ḥanukka we emphasize the education of the children of Israel, from the pious silence of Jacob regarding his children to the more pious activism of Mattathias and his children. In the words of the prophet Isaiah (62:1), "For Zion's sake I will not hold my peace, and for Jerusalem's sake I will not keep silent, until her triumph goes forth as brightness, and her salvation as a torch that burns."

Fulfillment[1]

Several times in the book of Genesis, the Torah summarizes the biography of a protagonist of the biblical narrative, introducing this spiritual profile by the words "*Ve'eleh toledot*," "And these are the generations of," or, in more colloquial English, "This is the story of" so-and-so as an individual. Four such instances are particularly worthy of our attention: those referring to Esau, Noah, Isaac, and, in this *sidra*, Jacob. The differences between them are noteworthy, for these are four archetypes that are still very much with us, and they represent four attitudes toward spiritual fulfillment.

The first of these, and the one who is of least concern to us, is Esau. Of him we read, "And these are the generations of Esau, he is Edom; he took wives from the daughters of Canaan" (Genesis 36:1). Esau is a man whose life begins and ends in the satisfaction of his own concupiscence; the "*Ve'eleh toledot*" of Esau is Edom, which implies the redness (*adom*) of heat and passion. He is a man who believes that one's manliness can be expressed only in the number of wives he amasses, in the harem that he builds for himself, in the natural appetites that he succeeds in indulging,

1. December 3, 1966.

in the conquests that he makes. He has no spiritual pretenses; he lives only as an animal in human form. We need not belabor the point about the prevalence of this type of personality in our own society.

Noah, the second of the four, is a much higher type: "And these are the generations of Noah – Noah was a righteous man, whole in his generation, a man who walked with God" (Genesis 6:9). He was a man who saw his destiny not in the satisfaction of every personal impulse and erotic whim, but rather in transcending these material desires. However, the problem with Noah is that his spiritual aspirations are entirely self-centered. We look in vain in Noah's biography for some hint that there are human associations that enhance his spiritual ambitions. Did he perhaps have a special relationship with his father? Apparently not. How many of us recall that his father's name was Lemekh? It is a rather unimportant fact. Was he especially concerned with his children? It appears that he had no special fatherly relation to them. One of them, Ham, had utter contempt for Noah; the others were better: they did not have contempt for their father, or, if they did, they didn't show it. No wonder that at the beginning Noah is not described as the father of his three sons, but rather, quite biologically, "*Vayoled Noaḥ shelosha banim*" – he sired or begot three sons. He is a pious man, a fine individual, but he does not relate. He is unconcerned with the past or the future, or even the present of others. "And these are the generations of Noah – Noah"; the story of Noah is – Noah!

This type is still available today. There are people who are religious, observant, even aspiring to some knowledge in Judaism, but they are insular and isolated. They are people of small sentiments and little concern for others. They are spiritually egoistical, though not egotistical. Like Noah, their selfishness is of a spiritual kind and not obnoxious; but it remains selfishness nonetheless. "And these are the generations of Noah – Noah!"

The third type is yet greater in importance and is represented by Isaac: "And these are the generations of Isaac the son of Abraham, Abraham was the father of Isaac" (Genesis 25:19). The self-image of Isaac was inextricably bound with his father. He saw his own life and his own destiny as the fulfillment of Abraham's spiritual career. At the time of the *Akeida* he was a very young lad – Maimonides does not accept the midrash relating that Isaac was already thirty-seven years old at the time – and so he was the young object of the great episode in which his father Abraham was the heroic subject. All his life he lived under the giant shadow of a great father. His greatest ambition was to realize in his life his father's unrealized dreams, to make his father proud of him retroactively – even after his father had long since died. Hence, Isaac remained in Canaan all his life, because his father came there. He married Rebecca, because his father chose this wife for him. He was a shepherd and he dug wells, because that is the career Abraham outlined for him. All Isaac asked of life, his entire "And these are the generations," was that he, Isaac, be worthy of the title "*ben Avraham,*" the son of Abraham.

Such parent-oriented individuals are fully authentic Jewish spiritual types. We meet them occasionally, though not often enough. You can recognize such a person by his conversation. It is frequently peppered with such remarks as, "My father used to say…" or "My mother of blessed memory would do such and such…" It is a marvelous, heartwarming thing to encounter such an individual who dedicates his or her life to the fulfillment of the life of a beloved parent.

Most of us are not that type. Our parents were either immigrants or first-generation American Jews, busy surviving and unable to achieve distinction as religious personalities or Jewish scholars. We love them, we respect them, we want to continue their traditions; but, speaking objectively, we do not see them as distinguished spiritual giants whose destinies we must dedicate our lives to consummate in our own experience as believers.

And not only are we not the Isaac type, we are not even the Noah type. We ourselves are too busy proving that it is possible to live as a full participant in modern culture and Western civilization and still remain Orthodox, loyal to Torah. We are therefore spiritually unfulfilled, and, if we are honest, we cannot disguise the thirst and the hunger. We therefore seek this fulfillment which has eluded us in our own experience, in the lives of our children. It is in our children in whom we place our hopes, our trust, our dreams for the unrealized religious greatness and the untapped spiritual resources of our own lives. And this type of personality is represented by Jacob.

In our *sidra* we read, "And these are the generations of Jacob – Joseph was seventeen years old…" (Genesis 37:2). Jacob was a man who no doubt loved and revered his father; but their relationship was not remarkable. Isaac was actually ready to give the blessing to Esau! Jacob himself knew full well that he could not completely realize his own spiritual potential. He was always on the go, always running away, always a fugitive, always in exile. At the very beginning of the *sidra*, on the opening words *"Vayeshev Yaakov,"* "and Jacob dwelt," which literally means that he sat, our rabbis commented (Rashi, Genesis 37:2) that when Jacob finally thought he would find some peace of mind, some equanimity in which to grow spiritually, the entire Joseph episode erupted in his life and placed him in eclipse. How then did Jacob hope to achieve his spiritual fulfillment and immortality? "And these are the generations of Jacob – Joseph"! The consummation of the story of Jacob can be found in the story of Joseph!

If a child vindicates his parents' faith in him it is a sublime achievement of unparalleled proportions. But it involves a great risk on the part of the parent: to place one's very destiny, one's whole immortality, in the hands of another human being, even one's own child!

It is therefore good for us to examine Jacob's conduct toward Joseph, to analyze both his weak points and his strong points, in order to learn for ourselves how to be sure, to the best of our ability, that our children will carry out our mandate and fulfill our most cherished dreams and prayers.

Jacob made one great mistake – and we are prone to repeat that same error. Sometimes we are so enamored of a child, so much in love with him, that we develop a sense of over-confidence. We take the wish for the reality, we substitute the dream for its own realization. Thus we take a young, promising child, and treat him as if he were a fully safe and completely mature adult. That is the gist of Jacob's error: he so loved his Joseph that he treated him as an equal, and he sent this young and impressionable lad of seventeen into the company of brothers who were ready to devour him and sell him down the river!

Indeed, the Malbim analyzes Jacob's reaction to the news of Joseph's reported death and finds that Jacob realized his mistake. For when the brothers presented to their father the bloodied shirt of his favorite child Joseph, we read that "Jacob rent his garments," and "He placed a sackcloth on his loins" (Genesis 37:34). These, says the Malbim, are two separate acts. The first one, that of the rending of a garment, is the traditional sign of mourning. It is a Jewish expression of grief upon the death of a loved one. But the second act, that of wearing the sackcloth, is an act of *teshuva*, penitence. In our responsa literature we read that if a man sends a deputy into a condition of danger, and the agent is injured as a result, then the sender must feel himself at least morally responsible to the extent that he is required to perform *teshuva*. Jacob realized that he had no right to expose young Joseph to such danger; hence the sackcloth as a sign of *teshuva*.

We, too, tend to the sin of over-confidence, and expose children to danger prematurely. I do not fail to be amazed when sensible, intelligent, and religious parents will take a child of eight or nine and send him to a summer camp which will, by omission and commission, destroy every shred of religious upbringing which we try to give to a child during the remaining ten months of the year; or when parents will send a child of fourteen or fifteen on a crosscountry trip or to Europe in the company of others his own age, when he has not yet learned the art of self-control; or when parents will send a young lad of seventeen to an out-of-town college where there is no Jewish community, no Jewish environment whatsoever, when he is not yet prepared for it. Of course, such determinations largely depend on the individual child and his special circumstances. Of course, too, it is possible to be over-protective and harm a child in that manner; no young man or woman should forever remain tied to the apron strings of either mother or father. But we usually sin in the opposite direction. And when we are over-confident and expose the children to danger, we risk the tragedy of receiving that calamitous report: "*Tarof toraf Yosef*," "Joseph is devoured"; all our work is in vain, all we have put into the child has been undone because of one foolish move. And when that happens – we must do *teshuva*.

If we seek our own spiritual fulfillment in the lives of our children, we must not only, negatively, refrain from exposing them to risk prematurely, but we have a sacred obligation to prepare them well for the confrontation with a hostile world. It is our holy duty to intensify the religious training of our children. I am therefore amazed when certain parents send their children to day schools that have superb departments of general education, superior to all public schools and to most private schools – and yet they complain that the school is "too religious"! I have yet to hear a patient complain that the hospital pays too much attention to health, or a businessman complain that his accountant saves him too much money. Yet there are some parents, otherwise fully intelligent and perceptive, who bitterly complain that the day school takes its job seriously.

To parents of such children, permit me to give you some unsolicited advice and prediction: do not worry about your children becoming too "*frum.*" They will not remain that way for too long! May God grant that ultimately they will be as religious as we are – and God knows that we are not pious enough! In the kind of world in which we live, there is an inexorable attrition, an inevitable erosion and corrosion of religious loyalty and steadfastness. Our main task is to prepare our children well not only intellectually, but, primarily, emotionally. Before we turn them loose into the world, in the company of enemies and even of brother-Jews who are ready to strip them of every vestige of Jewishness, our task is to concentrate not so much on an extra portion of Ḥumash or another page of Talmud, but more than anything else – on "*davening.*" Is it conceivable that parents should complain that children are given too much inspiration to pray? What is the purpose of studying Ḥumash and Talmud and everything else if not that we shall thus thereby raise a child who will be ready for the sublime religious experience of contemplating his or her own mortality in the face of the Infinite God of all the universe? Of course, we must give them as much information as possible; but the experience of piety, the sense of religion, is far more important.

Finally, let us learn also from Jacob's strength, from his great merit – though he was not conscious of it at all. Jacob thought that Joseph had died. He mourned for him for much longer than the one year that the Jewish tradition prescribes. When his sons and the rest of his family tried to console him after this year, he proved inconsolable. He refused to be consoled. His mourning continued unabated, his grief without cease. Why so? Is it not normal and advisable to allow one's mourning to abate after a year? The rabbis, quoted by Rashi, answer that one does not accept consolation for the living. It is possible to listen to the advice of friends and dear ones who ask us to reconcile ourselves to the loss of a dead relative, but no one can reconcile himself to the loss of one who still lives. And Jacob knew, by virtue of his *ruaḥ hakodesh*, his holy spirit, by some prophetic intuition below the level of his consciousness, that Joseph was still alive! In his bones, in his heart, in his soul – though not in his mind – he knew that his spiritual posterity, his beloved Joseph, his favorite child, was eclipsed – but not forever lost. That is why he refused to be reconciled to the eternal loss of this child.

Many of us find ourselves, unfortunately, in a similar situation. We do all we can for our children, we try our very best. We sacrifice comfort and convenience, and express our devotion in every way we know. But then we find that we have failed. The Josephs leave, and they are gone – seemingly forever. We spend our lives in all kinds of difficulties in order to continue the tradition of our forebears, only to discover that our children have betrayed our way of life. Shall we give up hope? Shall we, in our heart of hearts, declare them lost to Judaism? The answer is: No! Change techniques, try a different method, above all use the advice and counsel of the sainted Ba'al Shem Tov: "Love him more!" Do not give up hope for any child. We do not have the moral right to do so. Of course, it happens often, much too often, that these Josephs are lost to us, and do not return. But there are some who do. For their sake, we must never give up hope in our own individual cases as they touch our lives.

If we wait, if we try, if we hope, if we pray – we may yet hear those blessed words after so many years: "*od Yosef ḥai*," "Joseph still lives!" We may find that – miracle of miracles! – Joseph will seek reconciliation with Jacob, and that if Joseph does not then Joseph's children will. Somehow, sometime, somewhere, they will return and we will find our fulfillment in the generations that follow us. "*Ki lo yidaḥ mimenu nidaḥ*" – we do not give up hope for any Jew! We are stubborn in our love and relentless in our loyalty and adamant in our refusal to succumb to despair.

It is this hope which will give us the strength to continue. For it is this hope and this prayer and this dream that define the "*ve'eleh toledot*" of each and every one of us.

Afterwards[1]

I n the whole sordid story of the selling of Joseph, it is the oldest brother, Reuben, who comes out better than all the others. "And Reuben heard, and delivered him out of their hand, and said, 'Let us not take his life.' And Reuben said unto them, 'Do not shed blood; cast him into this pit that is in this wilderness, but do not lay hands upon him' – that he might deliver him out of their hand, to restore him to his father" (Genesis 37:21, 22).

Yet, Reuben's plan comes to naught. At the crucial moment, Reuben fails. When he is most needed, he is not there. For by the time he has returned to the pit in order to release Joseph, the brothers have already sold him into slavery. "And Reuben returned unto the pit, and behold, Joseph was not in the pit; and he rent his clothes, and he returned to his brethren, and said, 'The child is not there; and as for me, where shall I go?'" (Genesis 37:29, 30).

Where was Reuben? Why wasn't he there in time to avoid the tragedy? The rabbis (Genesis Rabba 84:29) give a number of answers, one of them somewhat surprising: Reuben was preoccupied with doing

---

1. December 7, 1974.

penance because of his previous sin of "changing the bed of his father"; in taking up the cudgels for his mother Leah, he offended his father Jacob by removing Jacob's bed from Bilha's tent, into Leah's tent. He meant to establish his mother's primacy as chief wife over her co-wives. But in so doing, he deeply hurt Jacob. Reuben was seized by remorse and contrition. He was so engrossed in his own spiritual rehabilitation that he missed the opportunity to save Joseph.

Reuben meant well, but it came out all wrong. His priorities were jumbled. He failed to appreciate that life and survival come first, and only then can one attend to his own spiritual growth and religious development. *Pikuaḥ nefesh* (saving a life) takes precedence over *teshuva* (repentance).

At the recent national convention of the Union of Orthodox Jewish Congregations of America, which I attended along with a number of leading members of the Jewish Center, the focus of debate was the problem whether or not the UOJCA should secede from the Synagogue Council of America, in which are represented both the rabbinic and lay organizations of Orthodox, Conservative, and Reform groups. The point of view that I advocated was that we should stay in. But the secessionists too had a point, and they pressed their argument vigorously. Fortunately, the convention decided that now is not the time for divisiveness and factionalism. In order to avoid an open battle, it was decided to postpone the issue for three months. But the sentiment of the majority was clear. It was for staying in, not pulling out.

When all the House of Israel is threatened, you do not go off in a corner by yourself. When everyone else seems to be against you, you do not divide yourself against yourself. When Jews are in danger of being sold out; when supposed friends and allies and brothers stand by impassively; when "an evil beast has eaten him" – when the PLO is acknowledged as a legitimate group in international forums[2] – this is not a time to go away and brood over spiritual problems "because he changed the bed of his father," worrying lest innocent Jews will confuse Conservative and Reform for Orthodox and vice versa.

In Israel too the same principle of priorities must hold. Now is

---

2. In 1974, the PLO was granted observer status in the United Nations.

not the time for political bickering and interparty sniping. Now is not the time to insist upon the purity of the principles of each individual group. Now is the time for all factions to work together, and to postpone individual self-assertion and ideological pursuits. Would that the government be broadened to include all groups in a national coalition!

The same message is subtly woven into the very structure of our Ḥanukka prayer, *Al haNissim*. We say that in the days of Mattathias, when the evil Greek-Syrian government oppressed Israel "to cause them to forget the Torah and to violate the commandments," the Lord miraculously saved us. We would expect that our song of praise would indicate immediately that the Lord came to our rescue by allowing us to study the Torah and observe the mitzvot. The rational assumption is an immediate resumption of spiritual and religious activity. Instead, we read a rather long passage:

> And You, in Your great compassion, stood by them in the time
> of their woe,
> You fought their battles and championed them in
> judgment and avenged them.
> You delivered the strong into the
> hands of the weak, the many into the hands of the few...
> And for Your people Israel did you perform a great salvation
> and redemption on this day.

And only then do we read:

> And *afterwards* (*ve'aḥar kein*), Your children
> came into Your holy house, and cleaned Your
> sanctuary, and purified Your Temple, and
> kindled lights in Your sacred court, and
> established these eight days of Ḥanukka...

What this prayer is telling us by its very construction is that before all else, the very first item on the national agenda is survival against the common foe. The Greeks must be repulsed, their armies scattered, and military triumph assured. Only then, "*ve'aḥar kein,*" "afterwards," will they attend to the fulfillment of their ideological commitments, to "cleaning house" internally.

If this is true of principles, especially of religious principles, how much more so is it true of purely personal concerns, of luxuries, conveniences, and comforts! All these must take a back seat to our central and foremost concern: the survival of the people of Israel, which in our days is to such a great extent contingent upon the survival of the State of Israel. We therefore expect that all members of the Jewish Center, without any single exception, will subordinate their personal needs and considerations to support Israel *"be'eit tzaratam,"* in their time of woe, in greater measure than ever before.

Yet, this principle of *"ve'ahar kein,"* "afterwards" – that first must come the fact of survival and only then can we attend to the quality of that survival and the purity of Jewish existence – holds true only where indulgence in one's own ideals may jeopardize *klal Yisrael*, the totality of Israel. It is an institutional, not a personal priority. The priority of a life-and-death question is valid only in the area of organizational activity, in the arena of practical undertakings.

Each man must realize at the very outset that without *emuna* (faith), without the Holy One, all is lost. Fundamentally, our struggle for survival itself begins with and is contingent upon an act of will and faith. The taking up of arms – "You fought their battles and championed them in judgment and avenged them" – must be undergirded by a pervasive awareness that the battle is "the evil in the hands of the righteous, the wicked in the hands of students of Torah." It is not only a military battle of unequal odds – "the strong into the hands of the weak, the many into the hands of the few" – but also one of moral confrontation.

The State of Israel – its founding and survival these past twenty-six years – as well as the persistence of Jews for over two thousand years in enduring the exile, is irrational, improbable, and unpredictable without the spiritual-historic dimension. There is more than a grain of truth in that famous anecdote about a rabbi who turned to his people during the War of Independence in 1948, after noticing the poverty of Israel's arms and the multitude of its enemies, and called out, "*Yidden*! Do not rely upon miracles! Recite Psalms!"

To rely on the UN or the United States or even one's own armed forces is to rely naïvely on miracles. To rely on God, to act with hope and confidence and *emuna* and *bitaḥon*, is the only sane and rational course. With all prior attention to the exigencies of economics, arms, and politics, underneath all and before all else, the issue of success – or failure, God forbid – will hang on faith: faith in God, faith in Israel, faith in the justice of our cause, faith in ourselves, faith in our future.

A recent issue of the Israeli newspaper *Ma'ariv* relates that there was an old Breslover Hasid in Jerusalem. He came to Israel, then Palestine, at the end of the 1920's, when Russia forbade emigration and the British let no one in to the Holy Land. The late Rabbi Elimelech Bar Shaul tells that he once asked this old Jew how he managed to cross the international borders at such a difficult time in order to get into Palestine. The Hasid answered, "What kind of question is that? I knew that a Jew must come to the Holy Land, and so I wanted to come, and so I came."

"But how about the certificates?"

"Bah, that's nothing. I knew that if I wanted to come, that if I believed that I must come to *Eretz Yisrael*, then I will with the help of God reach it. Indeed, I once stole across the border in Syria, but the British caught me and sent me back."

"And after that you did get a certificate?"

"No, not at all. I knew that something must be wrong with my faith, that I did not believe with my whole heart, and that is why I did not succeed in stealing across the border. So I sat in the *beit midrash* and I worked on my faith. Again I tried, and again I was caught. So again I returned to the *beit midrash*, to strengthen my faith and my trust. I thought that if I believed with all my heart and all my might, that I desired with every bone in my body to reach *Eretz Yisrael*, that the Holy One would help me. So I tried a third time, and then I believed as one must believe, and that is why I am here."

As we enter Ḥanukka we reaffirm our priorities. First, we must strengthen our own *emuna*, our own faith and hope. Secondly, we must dedicate all our efforts to save *klal Yisrael* and the State of Israel. Afterwards, *ve'aḥar kein*, we must make sure to rid ourselves of the desecration of contemporary Hellenism, of the flippancy to Torah and halakha, of the insinuation of assimilation and quasi-assimilation into our religious life. Then must we clean the sanctuaries of Judaism, purify its temples, kindle lamps in its courtyards, and, with the light of God and Torah, illuminate the life of all Jews, and through them become *or lagoyim*, a light to all the nations.

Miketz

On Being Out of Touch[1]

I
t is no great news that our world is a rather unhappy place. Judging by the quantity of sleeping pills sold, peace-of-mind books on the best-seller lists, and lectures on how to overcome all sorts of personal problems, most of us are in a pretty bad shape. And the sleeping pills, the best-sellers, and the lectures do little to help us in our unhappiness.

Most recently, one book has appeared that is different from the rest. It is different because the book itself is far more profound than anything the eager salesmen of Instant Happiness offer us, and because the author is one of the outstanding psychoanalysts of our day. Dr. Erich Fromm's latest thought-provoking book is entitled *The Sane Society*,[2] and addresses itself to the problem at hand: why is ours such an unhappy world? According to Fromm, contemporary man's profound unhappiness can be traced to the *alienation* of the individual from the basic and essential forces of life. The alienated person experiences his very self as an alien, an outsider. He is out of touch with himself as he is out of touch with any other person. The individual has become only a cog in

1. December 17, 1955.
2. New York: Rinehart, 1955.

the great machines of production and consumption. We do not know how bread is made, how cloth is woven, how a table is manufactured. We live in a world of "things," and our only connection with them is that we know how to manipulate or to consume them. Our lives have become depersonalized, and we have given up every vestige of selfhood in order to achieve the thin and shallow Success which everyone is expected to strive for. Our people are educated, well fed, and profess a belief in God. But underneath it all is a threatening spiritual void and religious bewilderment. Modern man is an alien in his world.

This is the analysis Dr. Fromm has to offer. We are unhappy because we are alienated from life, and out of touch with both ourselves and others. It is a brilliant analysis, and you can convince yourselves of it by reading the book.

Now, what is the solution? Stop deifying the machine, Fromm tells us. Be done with this hollow glorification of power and success. Create the Sane Society "in which man relates to man lovingly, in which he is rooted in bonds of brotherliness and solidarity." No one can disagree with the intention of this solution. But we may take exception to its practicality.

First, it is difficult for individuals to rid themselves of alienation in their own lifetimes, because it takes more time than that to remake all of society. It is perhaps too much to ask of us to enter into a relation of immediate brotherliness with others when the others are not prepared for it. Second, it is very possible that the lack of brotherliness is partially a *result* of our alienation and aloneness, and not the cause of it. So prescribing brotherliness for the disease of alienation is no more than removing a symptom, not going to the root of the malady.

But third, and most important, is that even if we grant all other objections, the solution will not work for us Jews. It may be bold and unpopular to say so, but the fact is that we Jews were, are, and always will be regarded and made to feel like aliens – no matter where we are. It is not of our own choosing; it is a hard, stubborn, irreducible fact that no matter how extensive our political rights, no matter how deep our loyalty to the nations of which we are citizens, no matter even how much we want to be accepted completely and not as aliens, our very differentness makes us just that – aliens. Except by suicide, we cannot rid ourselves of our Jewishness, and that Jewishness always marks us off from all others; it makes us aliens. And let me make myself clear: not only do the half and three-quarter anti-Semites regard us as being alien. The finest gentile thinkers, people of great moral and intellectual substance in their own right, do so as well. The renowned Protestant theologian Paul Tillich recognizes the differentness of the Jew when he asserts that there must always be a Judaism if only to act as a corrective against Christianity's relapsing into paganism. That great economist Thorstein Veblen said of us that the Jew is "an alien of uneasy feet... a wanderer in the intellectual no-man's-land... seeking another place to rest, further along the road somewhere over the horizon." It is the Jew's differentness, his being an alien, which is responsible too for the fact that he has shown himself a leader in all kinds of progressive movements – in politics, in labor, in economics. Whether that alienation has evoked admiration or condemnation of us or by us, the fact remains that we are aliens, and that even if the rest of society should become, in Fromm's words, "sane," we would remain the outsiders, the aliens.

Now, if that be so, we are faced with a very unappetizing conclusion. If alienation is the root cause of modern man's great unhappiness, and if the Jew must forever, in the Diaspora, remain an alien, then it would follow that the Jew must forever be doomed to unhappiness. Must it be so? Must we, in all truthfulness, concede that to be a Jew is to accept the fate of unhappiness and misery?

I do not think that it must be so. And allow me to explain by an illustration, drawn from this *sidra*, in comparison with the predicament of most of us American Jews.

The rise of Joseph in ancient Egypt is a biblical Horatio Alger story. He starts out as an immigrant, a slave, and a prisoner, unknown and unwanted. Within a short time, by the use of a lot of brain power, he becomes a powerful figure in government – second to Pharaoh alone – and a man of great personal wealth with a reputation as a wizard of finance. He marries into an important family and literally has the world eating out of his hands. Most American Jews have experienced a similar rise in political power, economic well-being, and material success in this blessed country.

But the picture is not complete until we add the anticlimax, the one that the Bible tells of Joseph and which we recognize as applying as well to our own situation. For all his success, for all his eminence, for all his fame, no Egyptian would eat with him: "For the Egyptians would not break bread with him, for they considered it an abomination" (Genesis 43:32). The great viceroy of Egypt, savior of their empire and favorite of Pharaoh – he was abominable to the most menial Egyptian, because he was, after all, a Jew; an outsider, a foreigner, an *alien*. Is it not so to with the American Jew? Despite all his attainments in the world of commerce or science or the professions, despite all his patriotism and sacrifice for America, he remains a Jew, an alien, whether for good or for bad, whether it results in his being tagged as a man with drive and ambition, or as a subversive and either capitalist or communist, or, ultimately, as the descendant of those reputed to have crucified the Nazarene.

But here is where our comparison ends, and with great abruptness. Joseph is above all a happy man. He doesn't care one whit whether or not he is socially acceptable. He doesn't bother with worrying about not being invited to dine with his Egyptian peers. Loyal to Egypt, yes. But forcing himself upon them – not necessary. He has been successful in his undertakings and he is happy. He has two children, and names the first Menashe in recognition of his gratitude that he has forgotten the grudges against those who made his youth one stretch of uninterrupted misery, and the other Ephraim in thankfulness for his great success. He is an alien, he knows it, and yet he is supremely happy.

What of our American Jew? You know the answer as well as I do. He can be a major industrialist, a millionaire, happily married, in good health, and a man of influence. But if, heaven forbid, he is not invited to the gentile country club, if he sees a "restricted" sign on a hotel billboard, if he detects the least sign of his own social unacceptability in gentile society, he is ready to commit suicide! All his other real successes are hollow for him. He is resentful, he is anxious, ready for the psychiatrist's couch and, as a result of his alienation, a miserable, forlorn, unhappy man. This alienation has transformed and ruined his life as no failure in business could do. Life's pleasures have no real allure for him beside this great tragedy of social alienation.

So, while this alienation which we Jews must experience whether we like it or not has caused much unhappiness in the ranks of American

Jewry, it is not a situation which must necessarily continue to exist. It is still possible to find happiness, as did Joseph under similar conditions.

Wherein lies the difference between the Josephs and the great majority of our fellow Jews? It lies in this: that the American Jew – the kind we are discussing – is a *complete alien*, utterly without roots, whereas Joseph has roots which run deep, and his roots are – in heaven! He is spiritually anchored, religiously fastened; he is not an alien to God, and hence his happiness is confirmed, much greater than the kind of happiness society would experience even if it did adopt Erich Fromm's advice. Whereas the Josephs are close to God, rooted in Torah, in touch with the Almighty, the American Jew, that composite being, is estranged from his Maker, has no roots in a spiritual realm, and is out of touch with God just as he is out of touch with his fellow humans and hence himself. The brotherliness – to all people – the creativeness, the relatedness which Dr. Fromm preaches as the solution to alienation, is found in Joseph and all the Josephs who have roots in heaven and are not aliens to God. Having this greater, deeper, and more permanent companionship and relatedness, the social alienation they experience on earth is not only tolerable, but, what is more, becomes creative. Not unhappiness but happiness, not anxiety and neurosis but tranquility and creativity, are the lot of those who are not alienated from God. The true Jew has never been like a tree, with roots in this material world, but like a hanging vine whose roots are in heaven and who can enjoy the earthly atmosphere all the more because of it.

Philo, the great Jewish philosopher of the bustling metropolis Alexandria of two thousand years ago, wrote that those whom the Torah calls wise are always represented as sojourners – aliens! "Their way is to visit earthly nature as men who travel abroad to see and learn.... To them the heavenly region, where their citizenship lies, is their native land; the earthly region in which they become sojourners is a foreign country."[3] That is the point we are making: when a man is deeply religious, truly pious, when he is in touch with God and a citizen of heaven,

---

3. Quoted in Hans Lewy, ed., *Selections from Philo* (Oxford: East and West Library, 1946), 37.

then his alienation from petty little societies is not worthy enough to make him unhappy.

As we American Jews begin the fourth century of our history, let us remember that the sense of alienation does not reflect unfavorably on the hospitality of America or the loyalty of Jews; and that such alienation can undermine our happiness unless we end the estrangement between ourselves and our Father in heaven, unless we reaffirm our citizenship in heaven, our relatedness through Torah, and our brotherliness with all humans because they were created in the image of God. May that supreme happiness be ours as we keep ever in touch with the Almighty.

It's Dark Outside[1]

The enemies of Israel are in a state of exultation, grinning from oil well to oil well. Former friends are now hostile, or at best turn away from us. Israel's one great ally, the United States, is showing signs that she is beginning to desert her. Economically we are in deep trouble. Psychologically we are anxious and depressed. The situation of the Jews in the Diaspora, because it is to such a great extent contingent upon the State of Israel, gives cause for much concern.[2] It's dark outside.

What does a Jew do when it is dark outside? "It is better," goes an old saying, "to light one candle than to curse the darkness." Judaism has institutionalized that wise insight. The Talmud (*Shabbat* 21a) teaches that the mitzva of lighting the Ḥanukka candle is *"mishetishka haḥama,"* from the time that the sun sets. The Ḥanukka light has no function during the daytime. When the sun shines, there is no need for candles. When things are going well, faith does not represent a particularly great

---

1. December 6, 1975.
2. The author is referring to the fallout from the oil embargo that began in 1973, during which time Arab nations refused to sell oil to the United States due to its support of Israel during the Yom Kippur War.

achievement. The mitzva of lighting the Ḥanukka candle applies only when it's dark outside.

It is easy to answer *"Barukh Hashem"* ("thank God") when asked how you are, if you are basking in the sunshine of good fortune. But it is infinitely more difficult to say *"Barukh Hashem"* or recite the blessing *"Barukh Dayan Emet"* ("blessed is the true Judge"), when black clouds have darkened the light in your life and you are in deep gloom.

So, on these dark days, Judaism does not despair but rather lights candles. I am not offering nostrums or cheap consolations. I do not underestimate the gravity of the situation – although I believe it is not as terrible as most of us feel. But I believe that 3,500 years of experience in the course of history should have taught us something about how to act and react when it is dark outside.

The spiritual alternative – which is implied in the idea of the Ḥanukka candles – is not meant to be exclusive. I am not recommending that all Jews pull inwards and turn their backs on the whole world. Diplomacy, security, economics, politics, production – all must continue on the highest level possible. But the spiritual dimension of our lives must be enhanced. Jews have learned throughout history that when life is difficult on the outside, you must build up your inner resources and buttress the spiritual aspects of your existence. When the sun sets, there is one imperative: *nerot* Ḥanukka. When it is dark outside, light a candle.

How do you go about it? Where do you light the candles? The Talmud (*Shabbat* 21b) teaches: *"Mitzva lehaniho al petaḥ beito mibaḥutz… uvesha'at hasakana maniḥa al shulḥano vedayo."* Preferably, one should place the Ḥanukka menora at the entrance to his home, on the outside – so that the miracle of Ḥanukka can be proclaimed to all the world. However, during the Babylonian period, while the Talmud was being written, the Zoroastrian religion prevailed, and because they were fire-worshipers they forbade all non-believers to light torches or candles during this season, the winter equinox. Since this was prohibited under pain of death, the rabbis said that we may light the Ḥanukka menora indoors, placing it on the table, and that is sufficient.

It is our major mission as Jews to light candles for the entire world – "at the entrance to his home, on the outside." But if the whole *ḥutz*, the entire world seemingly, has turned anti-Semitic and has institutionalized its Jew-hatred in one organization and declared a *sakana*, a danger, for the Jew to hold aloft his Hanukka menora, then even if it is dark outside, we shall make it light and warm inside.

If the outside world makes a virtue of darkness and aggressively pursues a policy of forbidding light, so be it. We shall remove the *ner*, the candle, from the outdoors and place it on our *shulhan*, on our table which is the symbol of family and home and interiority. Let the table become the laboratory in which we fashion the life of our families; the *shtender* of the academy on which we study Torah; the foundry where young souls and personalities are formed; the source from which light will suffuse all our lives.

If on the outside we are plagued by enemies who bear us hatred, let us on the inside increase our love and concern for each other. Let husbands and wives, parents and children, brothers and sisters, friends and neighbors, draw closer together, forgive each other, act with more mutual respect and patience.

If on the outside we find that friends betray us, then on the inside let us do the reverse: let us act with greater loyalty to our own people. Whom then do we have if not each other?

If on the outside hypocrisy prevails in the world, then on the inside let us do the reverse: let us study Torah, the repository of truth and decency, and practice *ahavat Yisrael*, genuine love for our own people.

Two weeks ago Friday I woke up in my hotel room in Jerusalem, and turned on the radio. The news was traumatic. It informed us that during the night Palestinian terrorists had broken into a yeshiva in an isolated area, Ramat Magshimim, and there murdered three nineteen-year-old students. It was an especially devastating piece of news for me, because all three were classmates of one of my sons when we were in Israel several years ago. One young man, Shelomo Mocha, had been captured by the guerillas and wounded in his head, and the murderers intended to kidnap him and take him to Syria, but he escaped. It was he who told the story of what happened. That Saturday night, the television news informed us that the TV interviewer had gone to Ramat Magshimim to look for and interview Shelomo Mocha. He was not to be found in the office of the settlement. Where, the TV man inquired, could he find the young man? Was he perhaps in the hospital, recuperating from his wounds? No, Shelomo Mocha was not in the hospital. Had he possibly gone home, to reassure himself in the warmth of his friends and the bosom of his family? No, he was not at home. Had his parents possibly taken him on vacation to recover from this terrible trauma? No, he was not on vacation. Well, then, where was he? The TV interviewer found him: in the *beit midrash*, in the study hall, studying Torah! What was he doing there? The answer was simple: "I and my friends came here to study Torah. They were killed, but had they lived, they would be doing this. So now I am studying for them too." The interviewer looked at the camera and told his audience, with begrudging incredulity: *"Zehu koha shel Torah,"* "This is the power of Torah!"

Indeed, when it is dark outside, and it is dangerous to light candles *bahutz*, then *maniha al shulhano vedayo*, we shall light the candles on the table, we shall create and illuminate an enlightened world within.

Permit me to add one more item for your consideration concerning the gravity of our situation. This too deals with Hanukka, and it is a point that I take quite seriously.

We all know the classical controversy between the House of Hillel and the House of Shammai concerning the lighting of the candles (*Shabbat* 21a). The House of Shammai teaches that we begin with eight candles on the first day, and diminish it each day by one candle. The House of Hillel taught that we begin with one candle, and each day add another until we reach eight. What is the underlying theme of this controversy?

One of the greatest and most beloved of Hasidic teachers, the Apter Rav, Rabbi Abraham Joshua Heschel, known as the *Ohev Yisrael* (Lover of Israel), explained the controversy as follows: Consider that first menora in Maccabean times, the one in which the miracle was performed. With each successive day that the flame continued in the menora, although there was no oil to support it, the miracle seemed greater and greater. If on the second day the miracle seemed impressive, then on the third, fourth, fifth, and sixth day it seemed even more amazing. On the seventh day it was almost incredible the menora was still burning! On the eighth day, the miracle reached its overwhelming climax, for one day's oil had already lasted for eight days. Hence, insofar as our perception of the miracle is concerned, every day it grew greater.

However, the miracle itself took exactly the reverse course. Only a drop of oil was left after the first day, and that had to support eight days' worth of miracle. Thus, on the second day, for instance, the oil had to support six full days of light – truly a Herculean task. On the fourth day, it had to support only four more days of light – a miracle, of course, but not quite of the proportions of the first day or so. On the eighth day, the miracle was still there – a day's worth of light coming from but a drop of oil – but the miracle was quantitatively much smaller than the first day, when it had to stretch for eight days of light. Hence, the House of Shammai follows the reality of the miracle, which decreased with every day, whereas the House of Hillel follows the awareness of the miracle, which increased day by day.

So there is a discrepancy and a disjunctiveness between the facts of the miracle and the perception of them, between reality and appearance. The miracles of Jewish survival and redemption are paradoxically most obvious when they are least effective, and least apparent when they are most profound and far-reaching. When we are most conscious of the wonder of our salvation, that is when the miracles are all but spent, and we must beware of the future. And when we are in the depths of gloom, and seem to find no reason for light or confidence, then we may be sure that deep, deep someplace, God is preparing the greatest miracles for Israel.

I take this to be the deeper meaning of a key verse in this *sidra*. The most dramatic highlight of a highly dramatic *sidra* takes place when Joseph and the brothers meet, and Joseph recognizes the brothers but they do not recognize him. So the Torah tells us: "Joseph recognized his brothers, but they did not recognize him" (Genesis 42:8). That verse is somewhat difficult. Only a few verses earlier we were told that Joseph recognized his brothers, and the context itself informs us that they did not recognize him. Why, therefore, repeat it?

Perhaps what the Torah is referring to is not recognition of facial features, of mere physiognomy, but an existential recognition of a far deeper kind. Joseph was second only to Pharaoh, the ruler of all Egypt. But he had just come up from the most agonizing period of his life. He was in the pit, enslaved, abandoned, all alone, a stranger forgotten by his family and the world. From the depths of misery, he now sat on the throne of Egypt, at the pinnacle of his career. The brothers were in the reverse situation. While Joseph was suffering, they went about their business and their daily pursuits with a total neglect of and unconcern for him. But now they were suffering, now they were caught in a terrible vise, torn by their fidelity to their father, their search for food and survival, their guilt over what they had done to Joseph, their worry over Benjamin. Things indeed looked black for them. So, "Joseph recognized his brothers" – having come through the same experience, he understood what they were going through, and he understood too that their difficulties were the prelude to their salvation, for, as he later told them, "God has prepared this as a way of providing life-giving sustenance for you."

But while Joseph recognized their predicament, and understood that the miracle of their survival was at its height when they were most pessimistic, "they did not recognize him." Not having undergone this tremendous experience, as Joseph already did, they could not appreciate the situation, they could not know what he knew – and that is, the teaching we have been presenting in the name of the Apter Rav.

Take but one example from modern history. In 1947 or thereabouts, the British foreign secretary, Ernest Bevin, of unblessed memory, refused to allow a hundred thousand Jews who were DPs to enter Palestine. Just think of it: one hundred thousand straggling wrecks of humanity, emerging from the Holocaust which had consumed six million of their coreligionists – and the most civilized country on earth refused to allow them a haven in Palestine. It was not only scandalous and outrageous, but totally depressing. Jews felt sunken, abandoned, in the greatest despair ever. Yet from the perspective of years later, the greatest miracle was being wrought at that gloomy moment. Had Bevin permitted the hundred thousand Jews to come into Palestine, the pressure would have diminished for the founding of an independent Jewish state, and there would be no State of Israel today. Because he was stubborn, because he pressed us so much harder, from that oppression and that pressure and that pessimism there came forth the miracle of the State of Israel reborn.

So it is with the State of Israel in the course of its history. At the time of greatest elation – such as in 1948 and 1967 – we sometimes overestimated the good news, the miracle of survival. But in times such as these, when there are few signs of salvation, when it is unbearably dark outside, when miracles are as rare as they are necessary, at these times we Jews must be confident that the divine will spins its own plot in the fiber of history on a pattern far different from the trivial designs conceived by piddling mortal men and their pompous conceits. And it is mysterious. And it is deep. And it is miraculous. And it leads to redemption.

When it is at its darkest outside, the lights are beginning to stir on the inside, and sooner or later they will pierce the gloom of the outside world as well.

For the Ḥanukka candles are indeed the heralds of the light of redemption.

Vayigash

The Lunar Perspective[1]

his week's historic telecast of the moon's surface by the astronauts who orbited it, the telecast which concluded with the recitation of the first words of Genesis, no doubt brought great satisfaction to religious earth-dwellers. Most especially, religious Jews were delighted that the first verses of the Hebrew Bible were chosen for this memorable message transmitted across a quarter of a million miles of the great void.

But for those of us sensitive to history, this was more than just an occasion for understandable pride by religious folk. For the Jewish tradition teaches that Abraham emerged from a family and society of pagans and heathens who worshiped the stars and the planets. Modern archeology has not only corroborated this tradition, but has pinpointed more accurately the exact idols worshiped by the pagans of that time and place. We know today that the great metropolitan centers of Ur and Haran, cities well known to us from the biblical narratives about Abraham, were centers of moon-worship, a religion which left its imprints even on the names of early biblical personalities. Thus, the similarity of the name of Abraham's father, Teraḥ, to *yeraḥ* (month) and *yareiaḥ* (moon), and

---

1. December 28, 1968.

that of Laban, Lavan, which is the masculine form of *levana* (moon). It is from this background of the moon-cult that Abraham emerged to proclaim to the world the message of one God.

What a divine irony, therefore, what a singular historic vindication, that 3,500 years later, the first men to approach the vicinity of that celestial body once worshiped as a deity, should call out the words, *"Bereshit bara Elohim et hashamayim ve'et ha'aretz"*: one God – as Abraham taught – created both heaven and earth, this globe and its natural satellite. Girdling the lifeless carcass of that forlorn heavenly body, like some ancient gladiator with his foot on the neck of his enemy, mankind has thus proclaimed through those three American astronauts the final triumph of monotheism, of Judaism, over paganism, the victory of the religion of Abraham and Isaac and Jacob over that of Teraḥ and Laban.

The relevance of this latest feat of technology to religious thinking is more than that of just historical association. There is much more to be said, more than can be condensed into the confines of a brief talk. But it is important to mention what is one of the most significant items that emerges from a religious contemplation of this technological triumph, and that is what might be called the "Lunar Perspective" of life on earth.

An editorial writer for a large metropolitan daily mentioned that one of the interesting psychological insights that resulted from the orbiting of the moon was the feeling that earth is just another globe, and that the astronauts viewing the earth from the moon might have had occasion to ask themselves, "Is it inhabited?" In other words, seen from another heavenly body, the earth reduces in significance; it is just another small ball whirling about aimlessly in space. From this perspective, how puny man's ambitions suddenly become, how picayune his loves and his hates, how petty his triumphs and his failures, how trivial his endeavors and his aspirations! All that engages our attention on earth – the clash of world blocs, the problems of nations, the conflicts between communities and families, individual difficulties and dreams and disappointments – all this suddenly becomes meaningless when viewed from the lunar perspective.

This lunar perspective is therefore a good antidote for human superciliousness, when people take themselves altogether too seriously.

And yet, the lunar perspective can be very dangerous indeed. For when we view man and society against the larger cosmic backdrop, we are in danger of being overwhelmed into ignoring the infinite preciousness of every human being, the infinite sanctity of the individual personality. When dealing with the vastness of interstellar space, man reduces to insignificance as the earth itself is considered to be but a speck whirling aimlessly in the endless empty oceans of the cosmic abyss, and all of life appears meaningless and insignificant.

It is for this reason that great men throughout history were careful to go beyond drawing religious conclusions from a contemplation of nature. That is why the German philosopher Immanuel Kant, in the conclusion of his *The Critique of Pure Reason*, said, "Two things fill the mind with ever new and increasing wonder and awe: the starry heavens above me and the moral law within me." And of course, Kant was not the first to propound this idea. Centuries before, a Jewish king, David, wrote the Psalms, and he divided the nineteenth Psalm into two parts. The first half begins with, "The heavens declare the glory of God" – the firmament and the revolutions of the cosmos are the testimony of God's greatness. The second half of that Psalm begins with, "The Law of the Lord is perfect" – it speaks of man's ability to obey the will of God, of the moral law and the ethical instincts within man. The wise men of both religion and philosophy thus understood that a contemplation of the heavens and the glories of nature alone can lead us to an appreciation of the awesomeness of the Creator, but often this phenomenon brings with it an awareness of the nothingness of the creature – as Maimonides put it, "A dark and dismal creature" (*Hilkhot Yesodei haTorah* 2). Looking at life from the point of view of the heavens alone can make the distance between God and man so great, so infinite, that man's worth vanishes. It is therefore important to add, and to emphasize even more, the moral law, the ability of man to abide by "the Law of the Lord" which is "perfect."

The lunar perspective is therefore a healthy one – but only when taken in moderation. Indeed, it is new only quantitatively, not qualitatively. It is novel only in degree – never before have men been able to view their home planet from this distance and in this grand a manner. But it is not new in kind. For whenever men have dealt with large numbers, with great masses, they have tended to overlook and to derogate the individual human being. Single human beings are imperiled by statistics, by which they are often reduced to mere ciphers. Social thinkers from Marx to Fromm to Riesman have commented upon and analyzed the depersonalization of man in the mass-producing society. That is why many talented individuals today often refuse to work for large corporations, because they do not want to end up as but a file in someone else's cabinet. That is why students in the mass universities frequently revolt, because they do not want to become merely embodiments of an IBM card who have no relation with professor or administration.

In this sense, the problem of lunar perspective is taken up, even if only obliquely, in this *sidra*. We read of the historic reunion of Joseph and Jacob. When Jacob's children tell their old father that Joseph is still alive and the ruler of Egypt, his heart remains cold and he does not believe them. But when he sees the *agalot*, the wagons which Joseph sent to Canaan with which to bring Jacob and his family down to Egypt, "The spirit of their father Jacob was revived" (Genesis 45:27).

What did these wagons have to do with making the happy news of his beloved son more credible to the old patriarch? Rashi quotes the rabbis in an answer which, while it violates every rule of chronological sequence, affords us a profound moral and psychological insight. Their answer is based on the fact that the Hebrew word *"agala"* means both "wagon" and "heifer." These wagons, the sages said, were a symbol of the *egla arufa*, the ritual of the beheaded calf, which Joseph and Jacob had been studying just as Joseph left to seek out his brothers some seventeen years earlier. It was Joseph's way of signaling to his father that he still remembered the portion of Torah that they were studying when they last saw each other.

But what is the importance of the *egla arufa* which they were studying, even if we are willing to accept the anachronism? This ritual of the beheading of the heifer had to be performed by the elders of a town near which a man was found slain and his murderer was unknown. The elders, in a demonstration of mutual responsibility for all human beings, had to wash their hands after the beheading of the heifer, and declare, "Our hands did not spill this blood and our eyes did not see" (Deuteronomy 21:7). The Jewish tradition (*Sota* 38b) understood this last half of the sentence as a kind of self-indictment: it is true that we did not murder him, but perhaps we are partially guilty because our eyes did not see, because we allowed a stranger to come into our community unobserved, unwelcomed, unfed. We allowed him to leave without accompanying him and that is how he met his bitter end on the lonely road at night.

When Jacob heard of the survival of Joseph and his great success, he was not only blissfully happy but also worried. He was concerned not that Joseph had lost his faith in the one God of Abraham, or that he had failed in loyalty to the tradition of the House of Jacob. Jacob knew his son Joseph, he trusted his ability to resist all kinds of temptation. But he was afraid that Joseph might have lost contact with what is one of the greatest teachings of Abraham and Judaism: the value of an individual human being, the doctrine that each human is created in the image of God, and therefore every individual is infinitely sacred. Now, thought Jacob, that Joseph is running a whole empire, that he personally manipulates the entire grain market of Egypt and controls all its real estate, that at his will he shifts populations, perhaps he has forgotten what an individual human being is like; perhaps he has lost sight of the fact that individual people are as important as masses of people. In that case, he might believe in God, but he would no longer be a child of Abraham. Therefore, when Joseph sent him the wagons, symbol of the *egla arufa*, reminding Jacob symbolically that he still understood the principle of the beheaded heifer – namely, that the community and its elders must always be ready to assume responsibility for every hapless, unknown, anonymous stranger as long as he is human – "the spirit of their father Jacob was revived."

Few principles are more important for us today. We must diligently beware of the lunar perspective getting us deeper into depersonalization, into the diminution of the human worth. We must not allow the lunar perspective to justify a lack of care and compassion and concern for others, to become the apology for turning away any stranger without food or care or attention.

Our ancient forebears, it is said, were frightened by the eclipse of the moon. If we are to remain moral and sensitive human beings, we must become frightened by the eclipse *by* the moon – the eclipse of all human interests and social concern by overattention to the vast dimensions of space.

The United States is today suffering the agonies of revolution because for three hundred years we were too busy building up our country and did not care about the plight of the black man or the poor man. And so today we are paying with more than one "beheaded heifer" for having closed our eyes to the black man for all these years.

If there is anyone who appreciates the importance of care and concern for individuals in the face of "larger problems," it is the Jews. For during the last great war, the leaders of the "free world" were generally too busy and preoccupied with the great problems of the war to pay attention to the fate and the destiny of a few million Jews. The prime minister of one great democracy was too concerned with war tactics and maneuvers to care about the Jewish problem, and his foreign minister cried out in exasperation, "What in the world shall we do with a million Jews?" The secretary of state of another democracy protested that he could not waive technicalities of law in order to save a couple of million Jews, because he was involved in a great war against the Nazi war machine. And his president, in the anticipation a generation ago of what appears to be the new policy of the incoming administration, "even-handedly" maintained that he learned as much about the Jewish problem from one half hour with King Ibn Saud as he did from all the years with the New York Zionists. And so all these big people with their big problems overlooked six million people who were marched to their deaths. The Allied world did not spill this blood, but: their eyes did not see! And they are guilty, and no amount of washing of the hands will take away the stain of that blood. It is this week, on the fast of Asara beTevet, that in Israel there is commemorated the deaths of these millions of our fellow Jews, as a kind of "mass *yahrzeit*" for all those Jews whose precise date of death – or murder – is not known.

As we enter this new period of human history unfolding before us, let us therefore remember that the lunar perspective is all to the good if it brings man to his senses when he is over-obsessed with his own importance. But when it threatens to diminish our worth, to encourage us to indifference and apathy to our fellow-men, it is good to recall that this lunar perspective was obtained only because human beings conceived of this flight, because they paid for it, because they engineered it. It is good to remember that the lunar perspective was taken by human beings, for it is they who first gazed at the earth from the moon. And it was a human reaction to this lunar perspective that prompted the American

astronauts to recite to us, from literally another world, the divine proclamation, "In the beginning God created the heaven and the earth" – a
passage which ends, so appropriately, with the words: "And God saw
that it was good" – and indeed, it can yet be good.

History as His Story[1]

$\mathbf{T}$he change of the natural seasons often induces a retrospective mood in people. Therefore, at this time of the year, when we have just ushered autumn out and winter in, we tend to look back upon the past and contemplate our own lives. We survey where we are, what has happened to us, and how all this has come to be. And it happens that we wonder: could I have done things differently? And if I had, would it have made a difference?

Sometimes we see ourselves now as a product of all our past decisions. We recognize that both our failures and our successes are the results of specific actions that we have taken – or that we have failed to take. As a result, we feel satisfied or dissatisfied, as the case may be, because we recognize that we were ourselves responsible for what we have done and what we have become. At other times, we tend to feel that the facts of life are so insurmountable, the direction of events so ineluctable, the tide of life so irreversible, that we are what we are almost despite ourselves, and that we had and have very little to say about it. No

---

1. December 25, 1971.

matter what we did or did not do in the past, we would be in approximately the same position today.

In asking such questions, we confront one of life's great problems, which has been of concern to philosophers, theologians, and ordinary people in all walks of life, from the days of antiquity down to our own times.

Secular thinkers often view this question largely in the course of their interpretations of history. Many are determinists, such as Marx, who believe that we are propelled by massive, impersonal forces of history, and that individual men and women have little influence on the course of events. Others, however, believe that individual people play crucial roles at specific points in history. We know, for instance, of the theory of Carlyle who believed that "heroes" or outstanding men and women are those who by force of their personalities determine the direction of events. Several years ago, Professor Oscar Handlin wrote a book[2] in which he discussed eight turning points in American history: at each of these stations, a different decision could have sent all of American history into a different path. The American lawyer Benjamin Barondess, writing of Abraham Lincoln, maintains that different decisions by Lincoln at certain specific points in his career would have changed the face of American society, civilization, and politics. He writes, "There is no such thing as History. There is only His Story. An act is without significance unless we know the actor." In other words, history is your story and my story and his story; it is the unfolding of events initiated and changed by individual minds and personalities.

To which of these opinions do the Jewish sources subscribe? For one thing, mainstream Judaism does not consider blind fate, impersonal and uncontrolled forces, as dominating events. Judaism objected to Greek fatalism – and modern determinism as well. The question in Judaism is not between fate and choice, but between destiny, as the unfolding in history of God's will, and human initiative.

Generally, we may trace the two opinions in Judaism to two root-theories. One has been called "quietism," the belief that man attains his

---

2. *Chance or Destiny: Turning Points in American History* (Boston: Little, Brown and Company, 1955).

fullest spiritual development when he acknowledges that he is fundamentally a nothing in the presence of God, and when he suppresses his desire to impose his will and assert his ego. The highest act of man is to convert his "*ani*" to "*ayin*," his self or ego to nothing. Therefore, man must not make any attempt to interfere in the historical process, because that is an act of arrogance and presumptuousness against God. And, in effect, any such effort is doomed to failure. Taken to its extreme, this becomes the ideology of the Neturei Karta.

The second school is that of activism, the belief that man, created in the image of God, must exercise his freedom, his power, his initiative – and that this is the will of God.

Both schools can point to sources in the Jewish tradition. Quietism can cite support in the fact that Abraham was told in advance that his children would go into exile and that later they would be redeemed – apparently the divine will worked independently of what individual humans want or do not want to do. And the rabbis (*Tikkunei haZohar* 127a) were even known to make a statement as broad and comprehensive as, "Everything depends upon luck, even the very scroll of the Torah in the Ark."

Activism has an even broader range of support. The whole concept of reward and punishment symbolized and expressed in the "*Vehaya im shamo'a*" portion of the Shema is based on the idea that man can determine and that he is responsible for his actions. Some examples: Those who did not return to Zion with Ezra were blamed for their recalcitrance. Rabbi Akiba supported Bar Kokhba, the revolutionary, against Rome. Rabbi Ishmael interpreted the words of the Torah telling us to give healing, that one must not feel that interfering medically in the course of a disease is an act of presumption against the divine will, but that man is permitted to interfere in the natural process (*Bava Kamma* 85a). And Maimonides, himself a physician, maintains that this is not only "*reshut*," privilege, but a "mitzva," a commandment to interfere in the process and impose our desire for health upon a naturally deteriorating situation (*Peirush haMishnayot, Nedarim* 4:4). So too do the rabbis say that one who did not prepare before the Sabbath does not deserve to eat on the Sabbath (*Avoda Zara* 3a). Or, "Man works with his hands, and the Holy One blesses the work of his hands" (*Yalkut Shimoni* 11:483).

Thus, if we have two opposing views within the context of Judaism, how are we today to interpret the events of our history and, even more important, our own individual biographies?

If we turn to our *sidra*, we find, paradoxically, that both principles are contained within one narrative – that of the meeting of Joseph with his brothers. In the beginning of the *sidra*, Joseph has not yet revealed himself to Judah and the others. We find Judah making his great plea in his confrontation with Joseph, demanding that Benjamin be released. Often we wonder: why did Joseph make his brothers go through all this agony, this traveling back and forth, threatening to take away Simon and then Benjamin; can any sin by the brothers against Joseph justify this apparently calm and premeditated sadism? The answer, of course, is that there is no sadism whatsover intended by Joseph, whom tradition has called "*Yosef haTzaddik*," Joseph the Righteous. What Joseph is doing is, simply and logically enough, leading Judah and the brothers through the paces of that process called *teshuva*, or repentance. He wants to put them in the position once again where they will have the choice of accepting or abdicating responsibility for a younger brother, in this case Benjamin. When we find Judah and Joseph opposite each other at the opening of the *sidra*, that is precisely the position Judah is in – and he comes through with flying colors. The same Judah who seemed to be concerned only with the price he could get for Joseph earlier, now declares his life forfeit in favor of Benjamin; he is willing to give everything for a brother. It is therefore at this time that Joseph drops his disguise and reveals himself. But the very fact that Joseph wanted to make Judah atone for his sin means that he held Judah responsible for the original crime, that of selling Joseph. No matter what the subsequent developments were, Judah must be responsible for the original act, or else all of Joseph's actions cannot be explained except as a sadistic satisfaction of a desire for vengeance.

Yet immediately thereafter, when Joseph reveals himself and his brothers are aghast and overwhelmed, Joseph at once proceeds to lift from them the burden of responsibility and guilt (Genesis 45:5): "Do not be upset and angry with yourselves that you sold me here, because it is the Lord who sent me here in order to provide for you" and the entire family. What Joseph appears to be saying is that both opposite ideas are true – simultaneously! The brothers were responsible, and yet they were not the only actors in this great drama. Joseph over the course of his speech uses two key verbal roots – twice the root *m-kh-r,* "to sell," and three times the root *sh-l-ḥ,* "to send." It is as if he is saying to his brothers: From one point of view you are guilty because you perpetrated the act of selling your brother. You must be held responsible for this act, and you have every reason to feel guilty and contrite. Yet, at the same time, you and I are only pawns in the larger drama of the destiny of the people of Israel, for it is God who sent me here through you. You were merely performing an act determined by God who is ultimately responsible for our final felicity. So it is both human initiative and divine destiny that converge and act in parallel and simultaneous form.

We find a midrash (Midrash Tanḥuma, *Parashat Vayeshev* 11) giving us a similar insight, in ironical and charming manner, into how the two levels work out together, how history is a combination of *our* story and *His* story. The midrash comments on the verse from Isaiah, "For My thoughts are not your thoughts" (Isaiah 55:8). How so? And the midrash answers: The sons of Jacob were busy with the selling of Joseph; our father Jacob was mourning and grieving for his lost son; Judah was busy finding himself a wife (Tamar), and also the Holy One, as it were, was preoccupied; He was busy creating the light of the Messiah – the descendants of the match between Judah and Tamar. And the Messiah could never have come unless these individual acts took place separately and in an apparently self-contained manner. Each scene in the drama does indeed seem to be isolated. Each one acts responsibly; and yet, God stands behind all and weaves all the various strands together; and the resulting tapestry presents a picture of totally different dimensions.

We may then assume that Judaism teaches that both these elements are always present, and we never have the right to dismiss either the role of God or the role of man, either the element of destiny or the element of initiative. Of course, it then becomes a matter of emphasis. Some will emphasize reliance on God and faith in His destiny more than on human initiative. Thus, Rabbi Moshe Chaim Luzzatto, in his famous work, *Mesilat Yesharim,* pleads for a minimum of what he calls "*hishtadlut,*" human initiative, and a greater measure of "*bitaḥon,*" or faith in divine guidance. Others reverse the proportions, and ask for more human initiative and less passivity or quietism. But never do we abandon either role.

We find the same tendency to one extreme or another in talmudic literature, but never do we completely abandon either end. Thus, for instance, in a famous passage (*Mo'ed Katan* 28a), Rava says, in a brooding contemplation of the different fortunes that befell two great teachers, alike in sagacity and saintliness, that life and health; children and how they turn out, and whether or not they give us "*nahas*"; and sustenance and wealth – these are matters which depend upon "luck" rather than upon our own initiative or worthiness. And yet one of the great scholars of medieval days, the Meiri, refuses to accept this talmudic dictum as binding and authoritative. "Pay no attention to this opinion," he counsels us, "it is only a minority opinion, and cannot receive the sanction of religion under any circumstances." Rava places more emphasis on divine destiny than on human activity; Meiri declares the un-Jewishness of the "*bashert*" concept, and prefers to maximize the human role. But whichever opinion we feel more constrained to accept, both elements must be present.

Are there any practical conclusions to this dilemma, or is it a purely theoretical problem? Since we can never know the proportions of significance of our own and divine activity, since we can never know where they intersect and where they contradict, and since we can never know which element predominates – does all this make any practical difference?

I believe it does. Take the effort we put into our daily activities, our ambitions, our careers, or any branch of human life. The affirmation of the human role means that we can never absolve ourselves of responsibility and adopt a theologically sanctioned laziness or passivity, but we must always work and always try our very best. But the element of divine determination and foreordination means that we must never overestimate, we must never become obsessive or compulsive or overanxious about our efforts in any direction. We must at all times remember that our task is to try to succeed, but that success itself is something that God gives or withholds. Given the circumstances in which I can act, I must act to the best of my ability; but those circumstances are circumscribed, they are limited, and I can never know the ultimate divine plan.

So too, since human initiative does play a role, since there is always some element of *hishtadlut*, therefore I must retain my sense of responsibility. I am guilty if I have failed to try, and I deserve credit if I have fulfilled my tasks. But, since the divine will plays some role in human events, therefore never must I allow my guilt or my anxiety over my failures to crush me and become pathological. Recall the words we cited before, which Joseph used to comfort Judah and the brothers: "Do not be upset and angry with yourselves." Don't become overly anxious, do not allow your sense of responsibility to hurt you by crushing you, because unbeknownst to you, you are part of a larger divine scheme.

And so too, since the divine will does play such a key role in human affairs, there can be no arrogance if I succeed – because my success, even with all my efforts, does not come automatically with effort, but may be a divine gift, and for ends which I do not understand. And, because of the same reason, while I may hold those who offend me accountable for their actions, I must always respond, as did Joseph to the brothers, with forgiveness, forbearance, understanding, and tolerance – because the responsibility of man for his actions, good or bad, is limited, and who knows to what extent another human being had to do what he did because of forces of which he is totally unconscious.

Such are the moral and psychological conclusions to be drawn from this philosophical and theological dilemma. We must see man not as a competitor or displacer of God, and not even as a mere pawn of God. Rather, he is His *shaliah*, His ambassador.

Man must always use creative and original thought in determining his course of action. And yet he must always remember that verse the midrash cited, the words of the prophet Isaiah: "For My thoughts are not your thoughts." No matter how deep and profound and original and creative our thinking is, it is not the same as divine thought. We are responsible for what we do to ourselves and to others; and yet, we must always remain conscious of that mysterious, hidden, divine destiny that shapes our ends.

On Being Consistent to a Fault[1]

The drama of Joseph and his brothers, which draws to a climax in this *sidra*, is a source of endless fascination. One significant aspect of this strange narrative is that Joseph's actions toward his brothers are incomprehensible, both to the brothers who do not recognize him and to us who already know who he is. To the very end, both they – the brothers – and the readers are perplexed: they, by the Egyptian prince who seems irrationally bent upon tormenting them, and we by the anomalous and mysterious motives of Joseph in continuing to conceal his identity from them and carrying out this elaborate spiel. Then, suddenly, all becomes clear. Joseph's revelation of his identity is also the revelation of a master plan, conceived by a mastermind, a marvelous and beautifully consistent course of action. The purpose of this program is to help the brothers achieve *teshuva*, repentance or rehabilitation, to regain their sense of dignity, and to purge themselves of their shame. For this is the grand goal of Joseph, to which all his actions are inclined and aimed.

Their sin was that of hatred for their half-brother Joseph, the son of Rachel, a hatred which resulted in endangering his life. Now, Judah

---

1. January 6, 1968.

was willing to endanger his own life for the remaining half-brother, Benjamin, the other son of Rachel. The brothers thus fulfilled the requirements of *teshuva*. How beautifully everything falls into place and pattern! How symmetrical, how apropos! And how aptly does all this mesh with Joseph's earlier plan, which came to the fore in the two great dreams about their sheaves bowing to his sheaves and about the sun and the moon and the stars bowing to him, Joseph. No wonder that Pharaoh was so impressed by this young Hebrew lad. He is indeed wise beyond words, the *tzofnat paneiaḥ*, the one who has all the answers and solves all the problems. Moreover, Joseph's plan for his brothers' *teshuva* is right, it is moral. That is why the rabbis[2] were moved to declare that the expression, "merciful and gracious," refers to Joseph the Righteous.

And yet, the sages found cracks and chips in this picture of Joseph. Joseph was wise, and his heart was in the right place; but something was amiss. Perhaps one might say that he was just a bit too clever, the plan was too smooth, the operation too consistent.

For instance, when testing his brothers, he gave Benjamin a far greater portion. Did he not take too much of a chance in arousing those old and latent jealousies? Did he not realize that the brothers are, after all, but human? And then when he arrested Simon before their very eyes – was that not too cruel, though perhaps necessary? And when he demanded of them that they surrender Benjamin to him as a slave because of the "theft" of the cup, he caused them so much grief that they tore their garments as a sign of anguish. It is true that this act on his part was one aspect of a consistent plan; but it was pitiless and harsh. He might have yielded to human emotions, and he might have somehow softened the blow. In fact, the rabbis tell us that Joseph was repaid generations later for this act of agony that he caused his brothers: his descendant Joshua, who had otherwise experienced an unbroken string of successes in leading Israel in the conquest of Canaan, had one difficult setback in the war against the city of Ai, and so grief-stricken was Joshua that – he tore his clothes in anguish!

Finally, and most important, Joseph heard, no less than ten times, his brothers referring to their father Jacob as "your servant our father."

2. Cited in *Tzeror haMor* on Genesis 44:4.

Ten times he permitted them to refer to his own father as his servant! It is true that this was part of his consistent fulfillment of the dream whereby the sun too, symbolizing Jacob, will bow down to Joseph. But the rabbis (*Sota* 13a) were terribly upset with Joseph for allowing this piece of disrespect ten times over again. In punishment, they declare, Joseph lost ten years of his own life which he would have been permitted to live out had he not countenanced this discourtesy to his own father.

In a word, Joseph was consistent to a fault. He hewed too closely to his original plan. When a plan is overly consistent, when it leaves no room for contingencies, it becomes a machine – the kind of machine that grinds up human hearts and emotions, that leads brothers to grief, that makes servants of parents, and that ultimately diminishes the life of the mastermind himself. It is here that Joseph erred. He was too consistent and not sufficiently compassionate, too calculating and not sufficiently kindly.

Does this mean that we must make a virtue of inconsistency, that it is good to be illogical and self-contradictory? Of course not! One ought always to have a framework, a philosophy, some solid criteria by which to judge men and events and oneself. But never should the framework be so massive that you have to cut down the picture of life to fit it into the frame. Never should consistency be so rigid that you become callous to the cause of compassion. Never should a theory thwart the truth. In the general organization of one's *weltanschauung*, one ought always to strive for consistency, for otherwise life is haphazard and even hazardous. But, an overall consistent philosophy of life does *not* necessitate a stifling and petty consistency in every small segment of experience. For then, consistency becomes nothing more than the excuse for a closed mind.

What is it that is wrong with over-consistency?

First, it makes one inhuman. If I believe in the plan above all else, then I will follow it to the bitter end even if I must steamroller over people and feelings. This was the error of Joseph who had a marvelous and even generous plan, but followed it to its logical conclusion without adequate compassion.

Second, it is simply unscientific. It involves too much trust in reason, and therefore out of concern for a consistent, rational pattern I may fail to respect newly discovered facts and new situations. A theory that ignores facts, that twists logic instead of revising itself, that wards off unpleasant challenges by ignoring them – is simply wrong.

It is interesting that in the history of talmudic methodology the protest against extravagant dialectics, called *pilpul*, was largely a reaction against over-consistency. The protest against *pilpul*, from fifteenth-century Prague to sixteenth-century Poland to eighteenth-century Lithuania, was a reaction against consistency so strong and theory so powerful that they would not be altered by mere facts.

Indeed, there is a similar movement in contemporary American philosophy, which expresses itself in contempt for "ideology." The word "ideology" is taken as a synonym for the enthronement of the theory beyond any revision because of encounter with new facts.

An example of this disdain for facts in favor of a consistent theory is the matter of dialogues between Jews and Christians. One would have thought that after the Six Day War and the shameful betrayal of the Jewish community by those who had expressed such desires for dialogues with us, we would be done with the whole business. Indeed, some honorable and honest proponents of dialogue issued retractions soon after the Six Day War and announced that they were finished with these attempts.[3] Yet, too many Jews have preferred to go their old way and have refused to abandon the dialogue movement and all it implies. It is a pity that only a week or two ago an official of the Conservative movement authoritatively declared that his movement is in favor of more dialogue, not less. Apparently, a "line" once taken, must be continued to infinity even it if leads to no place. How wise Ralph Waldo Emerson was when he declared that "a foolish consistency is the hobgoblin of little minds."

Third, over-consistency is religiously sinful. It is a sign of a lack of humility before God. It assumes that humans have complete control over the future, that we can avoid surprise and novelty and contingency by exercising our own wisdom and shrewdness. It means that we have over-confidence in our own reason and ability, and therefore read God out of the world, that we substitute our plans for His, or, at best, we

---

3. Some Jews withdrew from efforts toward Jewish-Christian dialogue due to their belief that Christian leaders had remained silent during the Six Day War, when Israel's existence was at stake.

presume to know His plans to the last iota. Even religious folk, perhaps especially religious folk, ought never dare such presumptions. It is an act of arrogance against God: "There is no wisdom and no counsel and no understanding against the Lord" (Proverbs 21:30). The religious objection to over-consistency is in the form of a plea for humility, of an acknowledgment of our own limited visibility in the skies of history and our willingness to be guided by divine instructions.

But finally, perhaps the most serious objection to being consistent to a fault is that it is self-defeating and sometimes suicidal.

The best and most painful example of such over-consistency is the harsh and unwarranted criticism now being leveled against the forthcoming World Conference of Ashkenazi and Sephardi Synagogues in Jerusalem, which I hope to address later this week, and for which I leave tonight with rest of the Jewish Center delegation. This conference is to be the first international meeting of Orthodox synagogue leadership in our times, in order to consult with each other, to benefit from each other's experiences and help the less developed Orthodox communities, as well as to demonstrate our interest in worldwide problems and perhaps provide for the first time an address for Orthodox Judaism in the world. That is what we have in mind. It is rather modest, perhaps too modest.

Yet we have sustained relentless criticism and a barrage of charges against us by the extreme right wing of Orthodoxy. I do not intend to analyze here all that is involved in the World Conference, nor will I go into all the details of the opposition. I do think that we ought to ponder what our critics say, and that it ought to be a concern of ours. In doing so, let it be said to their credit that they are consistent; and to their discredit and our dismay, that they are consistent to a fault – suicidally so!

The issue, to put it clearly, is: the reconstitution of the Sanhedrin. The late Rabbi Maimon, Israel's first minister of religion, had long advocated the reconstitution of this supreme judicial body of Jewish law. Many other rabbis were opposed, fearing that this would be the opening for unwarranted reforms. In addition, they dislike the idea of Jewish legal decisions being proclaimed by a hierarchy, and preferred that such verdicts be issued by those recognized by the consensus of world Jewish opinion as qualified authorities. Furthermore, they had halakhic doubts as to whether a Sanhedrin could be legally reconvened in our day.

Now this is an issue about which men of good will can differ. Without any comments on the issue itself, let us for the sake of argument grant a point: it is wrong, for whatever reasons one may choose, to reconstitute the Sanhedrin today.

From this point on, however, reason is slowly abandoned, until nothing is left that makes much sense except in psychological terms of fear, retrenchment, and introversion.

After the movement for a Sanhedrin waned and was all but forgotten, the opposition to it kept on as a matter of general principle. When religious Zionists wanted to build a headquarters for the Chief Rabbinate in Israel, the "Heikhal Shelomo," the same right wing groups suspected that it was a cloak for a Sanhedrin – and banned entrance to the building. To this day, the ban stands, though it is largely ignored. Are they consistent? Certainly!

Then, every time we spoke of Orthodox leadership of different countries and communities meeting together, immediately the threat was raised of a ban against the Sanhedrin directed against such a meeting. Consistent? By all means.

And now that we have scheduled this worldwide meeting of synagogues, mostly of laymen, not one of whom, laymen or rabbis, particularly intends to convoke a Sanhedrin *sub rosa* and become the first member, the same extreme group here and in Israel accuses us of doing just that, and in a series of newspaper ads declares that Orthodox Jews may not attend this conference. Consistent? No doubt; but consistent to a fault – an irrational, wrongheaded, misplaced, extravagant and dangerous consistency that is destructive of the interests of all Orthodox Jews – those on the right as well as those in the center and on the left.

We live in a time of disintegration: of the home and the family, of religions and nations, of man himself. Assimilation is eating away at the fringes of the Jewish communities of the entire world. This is a time to seek out unity, not to snuff it out before it begins; a time to consolidate, not condemn; a time to ban futile issues, not to issue futile bans; a time for realistic construction, not unrealistic consistency.

As the Jewish Center delegation joins our fellow American Jews in meeting with fellow Orthodox Jews throughout the world, we do so in the knowledge and conviction that all of our intentions are for the sake of heaven. We are sad that others do not understand us and do not join us.

Our main prayer is that our modest goals be achieved and that they inspire us to yet greater goals; that those who are now suspicious be convinced of our integrity and join us, lending us their piety and their passion, their scholarship and their commitment, so that all together we may fulfill the great verse of the prophet Malachi, "Then will those who fear the Lord speak each man to his friend" (3:16). When will we prove the authenticity of our status as those who fear the Lord? When we will converse with each other, not condemn; when we will talk, not vituperate; in other words, when we will fear God and not the times in which we live; when we will revere heaven and not be frightened by lurking suspicions; and above all, when we will relate each of us to his fellow Jew as *ish el rei'eihu*, each man to his friend.

Vayeḥi

An Old Shirt for a Young Prince[1]

W hen our father Jacob was on his deathbed and just before he blessed all his children, he called over his favorite son, Joseph, and told him that he was giving him a special award, something the others would not get. "Son," he told his royal child who was now effectively the master of Egypt, "I have given you an extra portion over your brothers" (Genesis 48:22). The Torah does not say what that portion is. But our rabbis (*Targum Yerushalmi*, Genesis 48:21) suggested what that extra legacy was. Rabbi Yehuda maintains that it was the garment worn by Adam!

What a gift to give a king! That an inheritance for a man who controlled the greatest kingdom of antiquity, who had millions under his thumb, who regulated the commerce of the whole nation, who was an absolute potentate who had all that he wanted at his command: a shirt, and an old one at that! It was quite a buildup Jacob gave for what turns out to have been merely a family heirloom. A shirt twenty-three generations old may have some sentimental value, it may be of archeological value. You may give it to other children, or to a museum; but you don't give that to a fabulously wealthy viceroy as a "special" reward.

---

1. January 8, 1955.

But if that is what Jacob decided to give to Joseph, according to our sages, there must have been some very special reason for doing so. Our rabbis meant to tell us something of what Jacob wanted to teach Joseph, and the Josephs of all ages. There are three descriptions of that garment worn by Adam which indicate three major points that we must take to heart and remember. They are three lessons Jacob wanted to drive home to Joseph – because he was the wealthiest and most powerful of all his children – three correctives to the abuses that come so frequently with the acquisition of prosperity, power, and social recognition.

The first thing our rabbis said of this piece of clothing was that it was made of a special kind of leather. The Bible calls it *"katnot or"* (Genesis 3:21), a leather garment. And the rabbis add that it came from the skin that the serpent shed off. Joseph, he told him, I am afraid that your wealth or power is going to go to your head. You have every reason in the world to be proud of yourself. You started as a slave in a miserable prison, sold down the river by your brothers. Now you've achieved political eminence, economic domination of an empire, and social recognition, being heralded by all Egypt as its savior, and crowned by Pharaoh himself as second to him alone. You have money, you have real estate, you have power. You have, in other words, the greatest temptation any man can ever have – to lose his humility. You ride around in golden chariots; you are a titled prince; you are a shrewd businessman; the Egyptians may not want to break bread with you because you're a Jew, but still, you have made yourself your own palace. But don't forget, Joseph, don't forget that *it doesn't mean a thing.* Don't you ever pride yourself on being a self-made man. No man is self-made. His power is a dream. His wealth is illusory. His shrewdness is only in his imagination. His eminence is transitory. It's all a great spiel, nothing else. And just as a reminder, son, here, take this old, tattered snakeskin shirt and frame it and hang it on your living room wall for everyone to see. Every once in a while take a look at it. And let you and your descendants and all men forever remember that the original owner of that shirt once had a complete Paradise in which to disport himself. He had Trees of Knowledge and life, and had gold and silver. He must have thought it was all his – that he was self-sufficient – and he could live as proudly as he wanted to. But then remember that he was chased out of Eden, and he was left with nothing, not even a shirt on his back. And then, only through the goodness of God, was he given a garment to wear. And, Joseph, my princely and wealthy and powerful son: where do you think even that one shirt came from? Adam's own work? His handicraft? Nonsense. It came from the skin the snake sloughed off. Man, despite his delusions of grandeur, is ultimately only a parasite!

Remember, Josephs of all generations: you're not self-made, you're God-made. Forget your golden chariots or your Cadillacs; forget your empire-building or business sense; forget your social status, whether in ancient Egypt or modern America. Remember that whatever you have came from someone else, that even the shirt you wear came from the hair of a sheep or the skin of a snake or the back of an underpaid cotton picker down South. Use your power and wealth and all you now have, but use it with humility. Keep the snakeskin in front of you, Joseph. It's the greatest gift you can receive. It's the only thing that will help you keep your balance and keep you from submitting to that great abuse of prosperity: the belief that you are a god and that you are self-sufficient.

The second thing our rabbis said about that garment was regarding its design. It had, drawn upon it, pictures of birds flying. Here was the corrective to a second, and very unusual and unexpected kind of difficulty that power and prosperity bring in their wake. One writer, I think it was Max Lerner, has maintained that in the history books of the future, our age will not be called the Atomic Age or Hydrogen Age or any other such name. It will be called the Age of the Ulcer. With increasing prosperity and with the higher standard of living, we have inherited a whole line of diseases caused by the anxiety that grips us.

In ages gone by people hardly ever experienced or even knew of that whole array of illnesses we now call by that fancy name, "psychosomatic diseases" – something our ancestors would have preferred to call "*an aingerreter krenk.*" Why the plague of migraines, the necessity of visits to a psychiatrist, the ubiquitous ulcer? It is because we do not know quite what to do with our power and our money, and because we are always seeking to increase it – and this, because of another fear: that if we don't get more, we'll lose all we have. In the midst of all the luxurious blessing, we feel a curse – a sort of obsessive unhappiness, a neurotic anxiety and, of course, the ulcer. What good are all these things if the price we must pay is stewed prunes, sweet cream, and amphojel? We have better beds and mattresses, but can't sleep at night. Wonderful new reclining sofas, but we are no longer able to sit back and relax, so tense are we. We have television even in color, and can't even force a sincere laugh out of our systems; we're too worried to be able to be happy. We rack our brains devising timesaving devices – and then, when we do get home earlier, we take along the office in our minds and our phones, and leave no real time for our families. We're unhappy, busy, nervous, anxious, and – of course – ulcerous.

"Joseph," Jacob must have told his great son, "Joseph, don't fall victim to these plagues. Don't destroy the value of your greatness by submitting to the anxiety that goes with it. Here's Adam's garment. He had lost every penny, been driven out of a Paradise, forced to go to work – manual labor, no less – and had nothing to his name but this garment. And look: he managed to remain so happy and satisfied with his simple life that he drew the figures of birds in flight, the symbols of careless happiness, of unconcerned joy and a feeling of uninhibited and un-anxious well-being. Remember, son, after your day of business is done, be done with it. Don't worry about losing it. Just relax, trust in God who gave it to you to keep it for you, and don't get sick looking for amusement. Just determine always to be happy with what you have. Let your mind be as free as a bird, though all you may have after all is only a shirt." "When a king is at a celebration," said the Mezeritscher Rebbe, "he is approachable to many people who otherwise would be denied admittance to the palace. Likewise, when we serve God with joy, He is more approachable."

And finally, the third thing our sages had to say about this ancient garment worn by Adam was that it was no ordinary garment at all. It was, they maintained, *bigdei kehuna*, the robe of a high priest, worn while serving God, first used by Adam, then down the ages through Abraham and Isaac and Jacob and now being given to Joseph. That garment, in short, was the symbol of religious tradition. It was the service and worship of our one God, being transmitted from father to son, spanning all human history from its very beginnings. Oh how worried Jacob must have been when he took leave of his earthly existence and of his twelve sons. Joseph must have troubled him more than all the others. Such a wonderful son, such a clean-minded, upright young man of true integrity and fear of God. How would he fare when tested with wealth and might? Had he, perhaps, in all this luxury and regal splendor, forgotten his old father and his Eternal God? "What about these two young sons of Joseph I just blessed?" Jacob must have thought. "What is to become of them in this land of Egypt? Will they assimilate? Will they be Egyptian like all Egyptians, and angrily maintain that they are no different from other Egyptians who worshiped the sun as it rose on this Nile valley?" Joseph had to have a reminder with him at all times. And so Jacob gave him this high-priestly vestment, first worn by the first man. Religious responsibility, he meant to tell him, does not decrease with increased substance; it increases. Here, Joseph, is this yellow-greenish, ancient-looking, outmoded, outlandish, and, to Egyptian eyes, ridiculous-looking little robe. Wear it, Joseph. Maybe this garment of Adam, the robe of the high priest, doesn't go well with your royal purple. Maybe a brand new, shiny, and attractive Egyptian robe would look nicer and be more appealing to your young folks who never saw or understood the religious tradition of Adam and Abraham and Isaac. Maybe so, but this is yours, and now you're to wear it.

Even more than arrogance and unhappiness, the greatest victim of our American Jewish prosperity has been our religious tradition. It hasn't always looked good beside the shiny brassiness of our newfound wealth. Some of our non-Jewish neighbors might have snickered at it – or so we thought. The *tallis* hasn't always matched up to our tuxedos and riding habits and minks. And so we scrapped it. We disinherited ourselves from the ancient mantle which came down to us through the ages. We now wallow in the fat of the land – and the priestly garments lie somewhere unknown and un-mourned.

I have been stressing the outlandish and old-fashioned look of this garment of Adam, precisely because this is the test of the Jew. Any child will automatically grab for that which is new and shiny and colorful. The test of Jewish maturity is to hold to the heart the old mantle, perhaps to polish it up, but never to exchange it. The Jew who is ashamed of it because it is so ancient looking is not an authentic Jew. Ludwig Lewisohn has given us an excellent description of the authentic Jew when he said that it depends on your reaction when walking with gentile friends through New York's East Side and seeing bearded, kaftan-robed and *shtreimel*-decked Jews running to *Minḥa*. If you feel uneasy and embarrassed, you're not an authentic Jew, just like the Catholic ashamed of the robed nun is not an authentic Catholic. You can test it right here in Springfield. If you're ashamed of being identified with your religion on Main Street, then – sorry to say – you're not a full Jew. The true test of authenticity is to be as Americanized as Joseph was Egyptianized; as wealthy and mighty as Joseph – and still to proudly wear the mantle of your religious tradition.

"I have given you an extra portion over your brothers" – it is only one more trifle than the others received. But it is that one garment of Adam, with its triple message of humility, happiness, and holiness, which can spell the difference between successful, satisfying Jewish living, and abortive, unsatisfying, and un-Jewish living. The Torah offers it to us, even as Jacob offered it to Joseph. Let us not wait. Let us extend our hands, open our hearts, and take it – with humility, with happiness, and in holiness.

The Pit Revisited[1]

Following the marvelous story of fraternal strife and family reunion – a story of singular dramatic impact which addresses itself to each of us – our *sidra* relates something that almost becomes an anticlimax. After Jacob's death and his interment in Canaan, when the funeral procession has returned to Egypt from the Holy Land, we read, "Joseph's brothers saw that their father had died, and they said, 'Who knows but that now Joseph will hate us and avenge himself upon us for all the evil that we have caused him'" (Genesis 50:15). The peace and harmony of the House of Israel was threatened all over again.

Now, this is a disturbing report. Of lesser people, we expect that warring brothers live in an armed truce while their father is alive; but when he is dead, they resume their hostilities. We expect of an Esau that he should refrain from murdering his brother Jacob only as long as their father Isaac lived, but that once he is gone Esau should plan to destroy his antagonist brother. But of people of higher moral caliber, of *shivtei Yisrael*, we expect a continuation of brotherly feeling. For as long as a cherished and revered father is spiritually alive for his children, his very

---

1. December 19, 1964.

memory serves to keep them together in peace and friendship. It is only when the spiritual presence of Father has faded for some or all of them that fraternal strife breaks out unrestrained. But ought we expect this of the sons of Jacob, founders of the House of Israel?

The rabbis of the Midrash (Genesis Rabba 100:8) reveal a superb psychological insight not only into Joseph and his brothers, but into the universal dimensions of human relations. They tell us that on the way back from the burial of Jacob in Egypt, they passed the very pit into which the brothers had cast Joseph and whence began Joseph's long adventure. When they passed that pit, Joseph "went over to it, and stared and gazed into it."

The pit revisited! I can imagine what the brothers thought as their faces reddened with shame and chagrin. No doubt Joseph's long look at the pit where they had cast him made the brothers believe that surely this will recall for him the terror they had brought upon him, and that he will now take the revenge for which he had waited all along. It was this incident of revisiting the pit that aroused dread and struck paralyzing fear in the hearts of the brothers.

With the gift of hindsight, we know otherwise. We can reconstruct the thoughts that raced through Joseph's mind as he peered into the snake-infested, scorpion-populated pit where he was once cast and left to die. A *Yosef haTzaddik*, a righteous man such as Joseph, is not moved to revenge by such experiences. On the contrary, he was impressed by the contrast between his condition now and his condition then. He thought: now I wear the purple robes of royalty; then my coat of many colors was ripped off me, soaked in blood, and presented to my grieving father. Now I wear on my head the crown of Egypt; then I was sold as a slave, as a piece of human merchandise. Now I have majesty; then misery. Now honor; then horror. Now I sit in splendor; then I shuddered amidst serpents. Now I am rich; then wretched. I have come a long way in the world! I must remember my origins. I must never submit to delusions of grandeur, I must never let my good fortune go to my head. Remembering my miserable and impoverished beginning, I shall retain my humility and my humor, my sense of proportion and perspective. It is this kind of thinking which later informed the Torah's command to all

Israel, that when they are well established and independent in their own land, "*Vezakharta ki eved hayita be'eretz Mitzrayim*," they must always remember that they were a slave-nation in Egypt (Deuteronomy 24:22), and therefore must now treat with exemplary sympathy the outcast and the alien, the friendless and the forlorn.

This, then, is what the pit revisited did for Joseph: it kept him human, restrained his ego, controlled his self-importance. The pit reinforced his sympathy for the poor and the wretched, the anguished and the humiliated everywhere. That long, lingering look into the dark pit from which he began his tortuous climb up the ladder of success kept him from getting a dizzy head now that he stood at the very edge.

Is this not something that all of us can benefit from? Is it not of crucial importance for every man or woman who has achieved something of significance, who has attained a measure of fame or power or wealth, to revisit his own dark pit, his early period of privation and want?

I once visited, in another city, the home of a very wealthy industrialist. It was a house which was lavishly appointed. On the walls of his parlor there hung famous paintings, original masterpieces. Among them I noticed something quite unusual: surrounded by a very expensive frame was what looked like a discolored, frayed piece of cloth. At first I hesitated to inquire about it, fearing that I would thereby display my ignorance of avant-garde art. But after a while, I asked what this was. He said: "It is nothing but an ordinary rag. I had it framed so that I might look at it and remember that no matter how much I have now, I must always keep in mind that I began as a poor, hungry, barefoot lad whose few pennies were earned by being a menial ragpicker! It helps me keep my sense of balance and proportion. It is a reminder that I don't own the world. It does not let me forget what it is like to be hungry."

Pity our affluent society. I am sometimes sorry for our children who have no pit to return to, as did Joseph. How shall they ever learn to attain a true perspective on life? In the deeper sense, the children of our society of plenty are underprivileged, spiritually deprived. They have never known hunger or fear or poverty in the past, a lack of toys or gadgets in the present, or the inability to expect an abundance of cars and cruises and trips before they are ready for it in the near future.

Most parents, at least, remember their own humble beginnings. Some were refugees, and know what it is like to leave everything you have and go into flight for your life. But how can our children know how bitter the cup of life can be, how uncertain life is, and therefore to appreciate what they have and to use their affluence properly, without sacrificing character in the process?

American Jews are today assimilating at an unprecedented rate. I believe that one of the reasons is their false sense of security, for they know of the dreadful experiences of our people in Europe only in an abstract and theoretical sense. That is why I would urge parents and schools to teach our children, when they are ready for it, the complete story of the great holocaust of our people during World War II. The visit this past week of a German court to Auschwitz is deeply symbolic. Modern Jews too must make pilgrimages to the pits of horror which contain six million corpses of our people. I can understand the reluctance of parents who lived through this period who do not want to re-arouse the ghastliness of their experiences. But American-born Jewish children and parents *need* this experience. That is why I believe that any trip to Israel should have as its first and foremost feature a visit to the *Martef haShoah* in Jerusalem, the museum which contains the record of the destruction of one-third of our people. If we deny this pit revisited to ourselves and our children, we keep away not only the Jewish past, but the present, and a guarantee of the future as well.

Such thoughts, then, occurred to Joseph as he contemplated his lowly origin – his form of the rabbis' injunction, "Know whence you came" (*Avot* 3:1). Yet the brothers were terrorized. They were struck by fear. Why did they not ascribe such noble thoughts to Joseph as have been mentioned? Why did they not attribute to him these meditations, and why did they panic instead?

Perhaps because they too had an insight into human nature. They knew full well that reliving early misery, taking a long look at the pit of poverty, can have a humanizing effect. But they also appreciated that sometimes it can be counteractive; it has the reverse consequences. For some people, "He went over to it, and stared and gazed into it" results in a fanatic desire to cover up humble origins, to make up for lost time and benefits ignored and pleasures not enjoyed. Thus it sometimes happens that a man who was once hungry now overeats. A woman once poor, now overdresses and becomes over-acquisitive. A person once humiliated, now becomes arrogant and oppressive. An individual once ignored, now becomes insatiably publicity-hungry. Who knows, the brothers thought, but that Joseph staring into that black pit of despair may now destroy us who subjected him to this anguish and terror?

Indeed it was a very real possibility, and the brothers cannot be blamed for considering it.

But while they saw all that was to be seen, they did not hear all that was to be heard. For the rabbis (Midrash Tanḥuma) tell us that something else occurred at that time: When Joseph looked into the pit he also silently recited a blessing, which the halakha prescribes for any person who was miraculously delivered from danger upon revisiting the scene of his deliverance: Blessed is the Lord who performed for me a miracle in this place.

That is what they missed – the whisper of a blessing! The pit revisited can be equally divine or demonic; humanizing or dehumanizing. But if that visitation is accompanied by a blessing, then it invariably helps man restore his sense of balance and harmony. For by a blessing we mean: the acknowledgment that it is not by my own ability and skill that I rose to the top, but the will of God, "who performed for me a miracle in this place." It is not my wisdom but God's will, not my greatness but God's goodness, that have sustained me through my adventures.

The Jew at the Seder table eats *maror* as a token of his ancient servitude, but – he recites a blessing over it, and this blessing is what teaches him the path of righteousness rather than revenge. We recite *"Avadim Hayinu,"* but we conclude with the blessing of *"Go'el Yisrael"* – and so it leads us on to the way of honor and humility, not of oppression and retaliation toward our former taskmasters.

This is what Joseph did: he blessed God when revisiting the pit. Therefore, when the brothers became apprehensive, he said to them, *"Al tira'u ki hataḥat Elohim ani,"* which usually is translated, "Do not fear, for am I in place of God?" – or, preferably, as Onkelos translates it, "For behold, I am under God!" And one who is "under God" neither despairs when he lies forsaken in the pit nor turns pompous when he sits in splendor on the throne of Egypt.

The problem that confronted Joseph is one which none of us, in our society, can escape: how to attain affluence without forfeiting faith; honors without losing honor; prosperity without abdicating perspective.

Like Joseph, we must each revisit the pit, the symbol of our initial failures and lowliness. And like Joseph, we must each thank God and acknowledge Him as the one responsible for our triumphs.

The Jewish response to God's blessing is – to bless God.

The Jewish way is to recognize that our successes impose moral obligations upon us.

In the words of Joseph, "For God sent me before you to be a source of life and livelihood." Our function, then, must become: to enhance life, to restore peace, and to advance the cause of God in the world.

The Plot against Jacob[1]

T here is an important and apparently ancient theme in the *Aggada* concerning the episode of Jacob and his children that is both intriguing and disturbing.

The Scriptural tale is well known. The brothers decided to sell Joseph as a slave, removed his "coat of many colors" and dipped it in blood, and then showed it to their father Jacob. Jacob was convinced that the bloodstained coat indicated that Joseph had been devoured by a wild beast. He went into mourning for Joseph, and refused ever to be consoled.

For twenty-two years, Jacob did not find out that Joseph was still alive. So many people knew the truth, but the secret was never revealed to the old patriarch. Was this a plot against Jacob? Indeed so! It was a true conspiracy.

The *Aggada* (Midrash Tanḥuma, *Parashat Vayeshev* 2) tells us that the brothers, in order to protect themselves against the wrath of their father, pronounced a *ḥerem* or excommunication against anyone who would reveal the true story to Jacob. They even included God, as it were,

---

1. December 15, 1973.

in their ban! And the Almighty went along and agreed to be bound by the excommunication uttered by the brothers. Thus, the *Aggada* states, God withdrew His *Shekhina* or Presence from Jacob, and it did not return to him until he learned, over two decades later, that Joseph was indeed alive. (Thus, "And the spirit of their father Jacob lived again" [Genesis 45:27] is interpreted as referring to the "spirit of God" or the presence of the *Shekhina*.) Joseph himself did not contact his father during this time. Moreover, the rabbis (*Yalkut Shimoni* 1:143) interpret the words, "And his father wept over him" (Genesis 37:35), as referring not to Jacob weeping over Joseph, but to Isaac weeping over his son Jacob! At this point, Isaac was still alive, and he knew that Joseph had been sold by his brothers. He wept bitter tears over the anguish that his son Jacob was going through, but he did not reveal the secret to Jacob "out of respect for the Divine Presence," arguing that if God wanted to keep the secret from Jacob, he had no right to break the confidence.

So we have the makings of a true plot. The members of the cabal were Jacob's sons and his daughter, Joseph himself, Jacob's own father Isaac, and even God! Why this strange and apparently heartless plot against the old man?

Many answers have been offered in explanation. The brothers' action is unquestioned, because what they did was in their self-interest. But why did God, as it were, cooperate in this conspiracy? Some answer that it was a punishment in kind (*midda keneged midda*) for Jacob's neglect of the commandment to honor his father, when for the twenty-two years that he was in exile, fleeing from Esau, he made no effort to contact Isaac.

But there is one special answer which I would like to bring to your attention and which I consider both most troubling and most enlightening.

This response, offered by the author of the *Siftei Ḥakhamim*, is that the conspiracy was used by God in order to move all participants to a goal that none of them was able to discern at the time. God had promised Abraham (Genesis 15:13) that his descendants would be strangers, exiles in a foreign country, and only after this period of exile would they emerge to become not only a family or a tribe, but a great nation. First they would have to endure the pain of exile, and only then could they be redeemed to the dignity of nationhood.

Therefore, Joseph had to go down into Egypt and have enough time to become second to Pharaoh. Only thus would Jacob and his children later come into Egypt to begin the Israelite exile, and even later to leave and make their way to the Promised Land. But in order for this to be accomplished successfully, the secret had to be kept from Jacob, for had he known, he would most certainly have moved heaven and earth to get Joseph back. He simply loved Joseph too much, as a father, to sacrifice him for all that time in order for the promise to Abraham to be fulfilled.

Thus, the plot against Jacob was the entré into *galut* (exile) for the purpose of greater *ge'ula* (redemption); a descent for the sake of ascent;[2] pain for the sake of greater pleasure; suffering for the sake of more exquisite bliss. It was part of the growing pains of a chosen people.

This is what the conspiracy teaches us: that often it is necessary to endure a lesser evil for the sake of a greater good. And it reminds us that while we are suffering, we must have a measure of confidence that "All that the Merciful One does is for the good" – even if we do not realize or appreciate it at the time.

Who knows but that this same principle was operative in our own times! The Yom Kippur War has revealed the ghastly loneliness of our people. It seems as if there were a plot against Israel, when all her former friends have become her enemies, when we sometimes feel that, as it were, the Almighty Himself were against us!

If so, we must appreciate that this suffering we have to endure is defeat for the sake of triumph, loss for the sake of greater gain. Its purpose was to improve us, to make us worthier, better, nobler, and more deserving of the greater dignity that awaits us.

What exactly can we learn from the Yom Kippur War, other than the need for a better evaluation of military intelligence reports? What may we learn from it on a larger and more meaningful level?

I offer the followng analysis in fear and trepidation. I hope I will not be misunderstood, although I probably will.

Why this hesitation? Because who are we to criticize Israel? And is it not ungracious and presumptuous to sit here, in the comfort of the

2. See "Down the Up Staircase."

Diaspora, and pick out faults in the character of Israel when it has suffered so grievously?

Nevertheless, I shall proceed, and shall say what I genuinely believe, both here and in a week or so, God-willing, in Jerusalem, because we are one people, sharing one faith and one destiny. I shall say it, despite my own hesitation, because I have already said these things much before the Yom Kippur War, and have said them in Israel, to the people most directly concerned, those in the military academies. I shall say it because I love Israel, and to love means to refuse to be indifferent to flaws in the beloved, but always to seek to improve the beloved.

In the course of our long stay in the Diaspora, we have developed an unhealthy *galut* complex. Jewish character developed the traits of timidity and self-abnegation, self-blame and a sense of helplessness, a passion for invisibility and an aversion to "making waves." In order for the State of Israel to be born and to survive, Zionist leaders consciously had to change that image. Deliberate efforts were made to inculcate in Jews a sense of pride and self-determination, resolve and autonomy – a do-it-yourself attitude to life.

These efforts were successful – too successful! We disengaged ourselves from the *galut* complex so well that we went to the opposite extreme. From 1948 through 1956, through 1967 and up to the Yom Kippur War, we developed a national psychology that was unhealthy, unrealistic, and ultimately un-Jewish.

There is no question that Israelis developed some character traits that were noble, beautiful, and admirable. Israelis fought difficult wars, and yet never hated their enemy. They administered the occupied territories in manner that will forever be a model for other nations. They demonstrated an exemplary openness to immigrants that is unprecedented in human history.

Yet, certain mass attitudes that have developed in Israel are less than lovable or likable. Self-reliance was merged into self-confidence, with a remarkable lack of humility. Israeli leaders quite unself-consciously preached a doctrine against which Moses warned us in the Torah (Deuteronomy 8:17): the illusion that "*koḥi ve'otzem yadi asa li et haḥayil hazeh*" – that all my success is the result of my own power, strength, and wisdom. Israeli leaders do not tire of the old litany that "we can rely only upon our own strength, sometimes including the financial cooperation of American Jews." We have now learned that this is not enough! Israel's own strength was simply insufficient in this time of crisis. They had to rely not only on their own strength and the UJA, but on the good will of the United States government. And, perhaps, did God too have something to say about all this? Have we not yet learned that reliance on God is not a sign of weakness, that humility can be a sign of inner strength?

At bottom Israel is or was obsessed by an exaggerated and extravagant notion of independence. I have always faintly disliked that word, although it is a thousand times better than the obsequiousness that characterizes Diaspora Jewry. Modern Jews began to act as if national independence is not simply a desirable political state, but that it is all that counts, and that it is an absolute. We made a fetish of independence, and some of us declared our independence from God, too.

But is "independence" really an absolute value? Is Israel all that independent? Indeed, who is completely independent today? The Arabs – who need the USSR? The USSR – which needs American know-how and trade and most-favored-nation status? France, England, Japan, and the United States – who all need Arab oil? Let us face a fact of life: we are all of us dependent, beggars, even sycophants. There is no absolute independence. All of us are caught in a cycle of dependency.

Of course we must fight unto death to retain our political integrity and national independence. But we must never make a psychological, ideological, or theological absolute out of it.

For centuries, Jews were militarily impotent. In the past twenty-five years, we have demonstrated the exemplary qualities and bravery of the Israeli soldier. The Israeli Army deserve full honor and kudos. But does that warrant the attitude that *Tzahal* (the Israel Defense Forces) is the culmination of Jewish history, for which all the ages labored? Does it warrant the attitude of pity-cum-contempt by the Sabra for the victims of the Holocaust? Does it warrant the smugness and overblown self-esteem which too many Israeli military officers have evinced? Does it warrant the vague threat of militarism – as in the overproduction of generals who are going into government and industry in Israel?

Religious Jews have not fared much better. The dominant ideology of Religious Zionism in Israel by and large presses the idea that the

State of Israel represents a Messianic stage, the *atḥalta dege'ula* – the first stage of Messianic redemption. I have always been annoyed by the presumptuousness and arrogance in this dogmatic certainty that we know what God is doing in the great perspectives of history, that we can even dictate to Him the scenario of redemption. For with it comes the tendency to absolutize politics, to endow conquered territories with sanctity, to make popular ideas (and even policies of the state) immune to criticism.

And we Diaspora Jews? If anything, we have sinned more. The great majority of American Jews, from 75 to 80 percent, have given not one penny to the UJA or bought one bond! Does it mean that our majority does not sympathize with Israel? No, they certainly do! What, then? They are satisfied to sit on the side and talk glowingly about "tough, little Israel." So, it is tough and can fend for itself without our help; and it is little so it is too small for me to visit more than once or twice during my lifetime, certainly too small for me to want to live there. And so American Jews develop a vicarious thrill in the national machismo of Israel, a thrill which comes very, very cheap.

The Yom Kippur War has changed all that. It has smashed more than one myth which had victimized us. The war was a descent for the sake of ascent, a shock which will make us better. Following the pattern of the conspiracy against Jacob, it was the prelude to national greatness.

The Yom Kippur War has made us humble, without making us timid; made us more aware of the limitations of independence and the perils of self-confidence. We have learned that we can fight and fight brilliantly, but that we are not omnipotent; that our leaders are often wise, but never infallible; that we must be strong, but we cannot put all our faith in our strength; that we do need others, and we may even be in need of *siyata diShmaya*, the help of heaven.

Was it worth twenty-five hundred young lives, of the best of our youth and the flower of our people, to learn this bit of humility? Absolutely not. But we are not asked; it is not for us to negotiate the price in advance. Jacob suffered twenty-two years of agony, and more after that, so that his descendants would experience redemption and nationhood. Yet unquestionably Jacob would have given all that up in order to get back his beloved son Joseph – and it is for this reason that the conspiracy was necessary in the first place.

What I am saying, then, is that events are not always what they seem to be, and that it is uniquely Jewish to exploit adversity and find in it the spark of hope. The silver lining on the cloud indicates the sun shining above it. The *Aggada* on Jacob teaches that we must not give up hope or faith, that we must never despair!

Up to this past Yom Kippur, we (and especially the Israelis) were too self-confident, too smugly optimistic. Now we (and, again, especially the Israelis) are too fearful, too depressed, too pessimistic. A little more true *emuna*, proper Jewish trust in the Redeemer of Israel, would have counseled us against the illusion that our own power and wisdom caused us to succeed, and does now summon us to greater hope and confidence in the future.

We have suffered a setback, yes, but defeat – no!

Heaven forbid for anyone to assert that our present difficulties will lead to to the undoing of Israel's statehood. Jacob lived to proclaim "*Od Yosef ḥai*," "Joseph yet lives!" And his children reported to Joseph, "*Od avinu ḥai*, "Our old father still lives."

We shall do the same. "*Od Yisrael ḥai*" – Israel lives and will live, and not only will it live, but it will live on as a greater and stronger people, as a finer and nobler people, as a people worthy not only of political wisdom, military strength, economic well-being, and scientific progress, but also of exemplary character and moral discipline.

In a word, we shall yet become "*mamlekhet kohanim vegoy kadosh*" – a kingdom of priests and a holy nation.

About the Author

Rabbi Norman Lamm, chancellor of Yeshiva University and *Rosh haYeshiva* of its affiliated Rabbi Isaac Elchanan Theological Seminary, is one of the most gifted and profound Jewish thinkers today. He was the founding editor of *Tradition*, the journal of Orthodox thought published by the Rabbinical Council of America, and to this day convenes the Orthodox Forum – a think tank of rabbis, academicians, and community leaders that meets annually to discuss topics of concern in the Orthodox community. Before assuming the presidency of Yeshiva University, Rabbi Lamm served for many years as rabbi of the Jewish Center, one of New York City's most prominent and vibrant Orthodox synagogues.

A prolific author in the field of Jewish philosophy and law, a distinguished academician, and a charismatic pulpit rabbi, Rabbi Lamm has made – and continues to make – an extraordinary impact on the Jewish community. With a rare combination of penetrating scholarship and eloquence of expression, he presents a view of contemporary Jewish life that speaks movingly to all.

About the Editor

Stuart W. Halpern serves as assistant director of operations of the Zahava and Moshael Straus Center for Torah and Western Thought at Yeshiva University, assistant director of student programming and community outreach of the Bernard Revel Graduate School of Jewish Studies, and academic advisor on the Wilf Campus at Yeshiva University. He received his BA from the University of Pennsylvania, an MA in Psychology in Education from Teachers College at Columbia University, an MA in Bible from Revel, and is currently a doctoral candidate in the Azrieli Graduate School of Jewish Education and Administration. He is the co-editor of *Mitokh Ha-Ohel* and *Mitokh Ha-Ohel: the Haftarot*, and serves as a member of the Steering Committee of the Orthodox Forum.

The fonts used in this book are from the Arno family

Other works by Norman Lamm:

Rav Kook: Man of Faith and Vision (1965)

A Hedge of Roses: Jewish Insights into Marriage and Married Life (1966)

*The Royal Reach: Discourses on the Jewish Tradition
and the World Today* (1970)

Faith and Doubt: Studies in Traditional Jewish Thought
(1971:1986:2006)

*Torah Lishmah: Torah for Torah's Sake in the Works of Rabbi Ḥayyim of
Volozhin and his Contemporaries* (Hebrew 1972, English 1989)

The Good Society: Jewish Ethics in Action (1974)

*Torah Umadda: The Encounter of Religious Learning and Worldly
Knowledge in the Jewish Tradition* (1990:2010)

*Halakhot veHalikhot: Jewish Law and the Legacy of Judaism:
Essays and Inquiries in Jewish Law* (Hebrew) (1990)

The Shema: Spirituality and Law in Judaism (1998)

The Religious Thought of Hasidism: Text and Commentary (1999)

Seventy Faces: Articles of Faith (two volumes) (2001)

The Royal Table: A Passover Haggadah (2010)

Festivals of Faith: Reflections on the Jewish Holidays (2011)

The Megillah: Majesty and Mystery (2012)

Maggid Books
The best of contemporary Jewish thought from
Koren Publishers Jerusalem